THE
GOSPEL
—— OF ——
MARK

A REFLECTIVE
COMMENTARY

For my friends in the Philippines
whose joyful witness
amidst hardship
speaks its own Gospel.

DENIS McBRIDE, C.Ss.R.

THE
GOSPEL
—— OF ——
MARK

A REFLECTIVE
COMMENTARY

DOMINICAN PUBLICATIONS

First published (1996) by
Dominican Publications
42 Parnell Square
Dublin 1

ISBN 1-871552-55-9

British Library Cataloguing in Publications Data.
A cataloguing record for this book is available from the British Library.

Scripture quotations are from the
New Revised Standard Version of the Bible,
copyright 1989 by the Division of Christian Education
of the National Council of the Churches of Christ in the USA.
All rights reserved. Used by permission.

Cover design by
David Cooke
The crucifixion on the cover
is from the cross at Cruicetown, Co. Meath,
dating from 1688.
The symbol of Mark is based on a detail of
the holy shroud (*epitaphios*) of Mcxeta, Georgia,
an embroidery in silk and gild thread, 1646-1682.

Printed in the Republic of Ireland by
Colour Books Ltd, Baldoyle, Co. Dublin.

Contents

Introduction

How the Gospels developed backwards

When most Christians hear the word 'gospel', they normally think of a book, one of the four canonical Gospels, Matthew, Mark, Luke or John. Each of these writings is a narrative of the deeds and words of Jesus, recounting the main events of his public life and focusing on his death as the central act of his historical drama. But the early understanding of gospel was a spoken proclamation, what we would call a sermon, that was directed to different people in different situations. It was a new voice that celebrated the significance of Jesus as Lord, one that aimed to awaken or deepen faith in those who heard it.

The gospel as spoken proclamation reflected the personal, immediate form of communication Jesus used in his own ministry: human speech in face-to-face encounter. The spoken word, more than the written, is directed to an actual person at the present moment – consequently, the hearer of a living voice is confronted more immediately than the reader of sentences. Direct speech, more than sacred writing or places or times or rituals, has characterised the movement of Christianity from its beginning in Jesus. As Wilder observed:

> Jesus was a voice, not a penman, a herald not a scribe, a watchman with his call in the market-place and the Temple, and not a cry of alarm in the wilderness like John the Baptist. This deportment of Jesus is a sign ... Jesus' word was for the present, the last hour.[1]

The primitive preaching of the Church did not focus on the words Jesus spoke, but on the person his death and resurrection revealed him to be. The new voice in preaching celebrated a new understanding of who Jesus *is*: he is Messiah, Lord, and Son of God in the Father's presence, a status he received by being raised and exalted. An example of this early christology can be seen in Peter's

---

1. A.N. Wilder, *Early Christian Rhetoric: the Language of the Gospel* (Cambridge: Harvard University Press, 1976) pp. 13,14

sermon in Acts 2:32,36: 'This Jesus God raised up, and of that we are all witnesses ... God has made him both Lord and Christ, this Jesus whom you crucified.'

The earliest use in the New Testament of the terms *euangelion* (gospel) and *euangelizomai* (proclaim glad tidings) comes from Paul's letters, and both terms are used to designate the Christian message and the process of proclamation. Whether it is 'the gospel of God' (1 Thess 2:2; 2 Cor 11:7) or 'the gospel of Christ' (Rom 15:19; 1 Cor 9:12) Paul refers to *the* gospel, which creates faith and brings salvation. The content of the good news is the proclamation of the death and resurrection of Jesus (1 Cor 15:1-5), which Paul says he 'delivered' as he himself 'received'. Writing to the Church at Corinth, some twenty years after the death of Jesus, Paul was already referring to the tradition about Jesus, stating its two essential components: firstly, that Christ died (followed by an interpretation that this happened 'for our sins in accordance with the scriptures'); secondly, that he was raised on the third day (followed by an interpretation that this also happened 'in accordance with the scriptures'). This gospel tradition, which was intimately connected with apostolic experience, provided a common source of proclamation for the Christian mission.

In his writings Paul shows little interest in the history of Jesus of Nazareth, focusing rather on the theological significance of the crucified and risen Jesus who is to come again in glory. This primitive tradition raises the question: how did the spoken gospel, which at first concentrated on the death and resurrection of Jesus, come to us in writing as narratives about Jesus' public ministry?

A document from the Pontifical Biblical Commission, *Instruction on the Historical Truth of the Gospels*,[2] outlines a helpful way to understand the process of Gospel formation. In the view of the Commission, 'to judge properly concerning the reliability of what is transmitted in the Gospels, the interpreter should pay diligent attention to the three stages of tradition by which the doctrine and life of Jesus have come down to us.' (VI)

It might be helpful to note these three stages (the dates are approximate and not part of the document) and comment on them: stage 1: the public ministry of Jesus; stage 2: the preaching of the

2. English translation in *Catholic Biblical Quarterly* 26 (1964) pp.305-312

apostles; stage 3: the writing of the evangelists.

Stage 1 (ca. 30-33 AD): The public ministry of Jesus

The Commission limits the first stage of the tradition to the public ministry, excluding from consideration Jesus' infancy and early years. When the Commission refers to 'the beginning' it specifies the moment Jesus 'joined to himself chosen disciples' (VII). Even considering the public ministry, the Commission makes no claim that what we have in the Gospels is an exact record of that time. We have no resources available to us that were written at the time of Jesus' ministry: the only words written about Jesus during his lifetime were those ordered to be written by Pontius Pilate. The public ministry of Jesus lasted two or three years, and traditionally we have referred to the major part of his lifetime as the hidden years. That acknowledgement warns us how little we know about Jesus, which has led Meier to comment:

> The real Jesus is not available and never will be. This is true not because Jesus did not exist – he certainly did – but rather because the sources that have survived do not and never intended to record all or even most of the words and deeds of his public ministry – to say nothing of the rest of his life.[3]

Jesus lived as a Galilean Jew in the first third of the first century, a relatively peaceful period under the Roman occupation. He spent most of his life as a minor artisan, probably a woodworker, in the small country village of Nazareth. These years are not only unknown to us but unknowable. For the last three years of his life, however, much of what Jesus did and said was available to the public, especially to his disciples who travelled with him around Galilee, Judea and elsewhere. What Jesus really did and said, including the ways he chose to express himself, would help his followers to be witnesses of his public life and teaching.

Stage 2 (ca. 33-70 AD): The preaching of the apostles

The second stage of the tradition refers to what the apostles and disciples preached about Jesus after the first Easter. As the Com-

3. J.P. Meier, *A Marginal Jew: Rethinking the Historical Jesus* Vol. 1 (New York: Doubleday, 1991) p. 22.

mission says, the content of their proclamation was 'above all the death and resurrection of the Lord, as they bore witness to Jesus.' (VII) Examples of this can be seen 1 Corinthians 15:3-4; Acts 2:23-32; 3:14-15; 10:39-40. The earliest preached gospel began where our written Gospels finish – which is why we can say that the written Gospels developed backwards. As a result of their Easter experience and their enlightenment in the Spirit, the early preachers came to a fuller understanding of who Jesus was (cf Jn 2:22). Their new experiences enabled them to re-interpret the past and bring it up to date.

Given that the events surrounding Jesus' death were the central focus of the whole public ministry, the early preachers were bound to have first formed a standardised sequence of the last days of Jesus for their hearers. Their claims about the identity and mission of Jesus rested, above all, on an interpretation of what happened during his last days. Since their first listeners were all Jews, this interpretation also needed to show how these events corresponded with scriptural prophecy. This sequence can be seen in the formula Paul uses in 1 Corinthians 15:3-4: Jesus's identity was asserted by using the term 'Christ'; his mission was interpreted by saying that he 'died for our sins [and was] raised on the third day'; and the phrase 'in accordance with the scriptures' shows that all this was consistent with prophecy.

The early preachers then turned their attention to the deeds and words of Jesus, and thus collections of sayings, parables, and miracles grew. This attention to the ministry of Jesus would have been particularly useful for new converts who wanted to know about the earthly life and teaching of the One they professed as Lord. More importantly, attention to the ministry of Jesus would save the event of death and resurrection from evaporating into mythology. The death and resurrection are inseparably attached to Jesus, the one who came from Nazareth, called named disciples, preached the kingdom of God in Galilee and Judaea, healed the sick and disabled, told parables, challenged people to think and act differently. Rooting the significance of Jesus in the particular world of time and place was essential to a historical proclamation. The testimony of the preachers was suffused with faith in Jesus as Lord, as the Commission states: 'their faith rested on the things

Jesus did and taught.' (VIII) The apostolic preachers who followed Jesus during his public ministry were in a unique position to witness to the fundamental continuity between Jesus of Nazareth and Jesus the risen Lord.

The preachers did not just chronicle what Jesus did and said, but 'interpreted his words and deeds according to the needs of their listeners', using 'catecheses, stories, testimonia, hymns, doxologies, prayers, and other literary forms of this sort' (VIII). Already, in this pre-literary stage, oral tradition was recasting stories about Jesus according to various needs, for by this time the gospel was being preached in different languages, and in such different contexts as Antioch, Corinth, Ephesus, and Rome.

Stage 3 (ca. 70-100 AD): The writing of the evangelists

The stories and sayings about Jesus' passion and ministry that circulated in Stage 2, which were already modified in the light of an Easter faith, provided the evangelists' source material. Sections of that tradition, such as an outline passion narrative and brief collections of material relating to different subjects, were probably already in writing before the evangelists composed their own accounts. The Commission states that the evangelists wrote 'for the benefit of the Churches, with a method suited to the peculiar purpose which each one set for himself. From the many things handed down, they selected some things, reduced others to a synthesis, [still] others they explicated as they kept in mind the situation of the Churches.' (IX)

The Commission is silent about the identity of the evangelists and makes no claims that any of them was an apostle-eyewitness. Given the Commission's statement that the evangelists' source material was handed down from Stage 2, Fitzmyer comments on the text:

> This means, then, that none of the evangelists was an eyewitness of Jesus' ministry. They heard about Jesus and his ministry from others who were 'eyewitnesses' and who had become 'ministers of the word' (Lk 1:2).[4]

---

4. J. Fitzmyer, *A Christological Catechism: New Testament Answers* (New York: Paulist, 1991) p. 25.

What is important is the Commission's acknowledgement of the threefold process of Gospel formation. The Gospels are not Stage 1 documents: they are not a record of the deeds and words of Jesus from the first stage of the tradition. Neither are they Stage 2 documents: they are not examples of gospel preaching by those who had direct experience of Stage 1. The evangelists are *authors* of Stage 3 documents. While they were faithful to the tradition they received from the intervening generation, clearly the evangelists compiled their own narratives about Jesus. The recognition of the consequences of human authorship is repeated in the 1993 document from the Biblical Commission when it writes about all biblical authors as people 'who employed both their own capacities for expression and the means which their age and social context put at their disposal.'[5]

The task of the evangelists

There is a general consensus among biblical scholars that Mark was the first evangelist to shape oral tradition about Jesus into the narrative form we know as his Gospel, and this commentary will presuppose the priority of Mark. Of the 661 verses in Mark's Gospel, Matthew reproduces 606, and Luke 320. There are only 24 verses in Mark that do not occur in Matthew or Luke. Why was Mark so important unless his was the first writing to give shape to the words and deeds of Jesus? Scholars find it easier to understand how Matthew and Luke improved and supplemented Mark's narrative, than to understand why Mark, with Matthew and Luke as his source, would go to the trouble of rewriting his source stories, making them less clear and grammatical in the process, and eliminate important material found in the other two Gospels.

It is likely that Mark wrote his Gospel to be read aloud to the community, rather than to be read privately by individuals. The community which 'heard' his whole Gospel would already have been familiar with individual stories from oral tradition, presumably similar material to what Mark himself used.

Oral tradition continued alongside Mark's writing. The written word did not spell the death of traditional storytelling. Although

5. *The Interpretation of the Bible in the Church* (Rome: Libreria Editrice Vaticana, 1993) p. 85.

Matthew and Luke had Mark's Gospel available to them and largely followed his order of events, each called upon different forms of oral tradition alongside a common source (referred to as the 'Q' document). The 'Q' abbreviation (from the German *Quelle*, 'source') is the name scholars have given to the hypothetical source that would account for the Gospel material that is common to Matthew and Luke but not found in Mark. Clearly, both Matthew and Luke felt free to amplify Mark's finished account and omit some of his material, subject to their own interpretation of Jesus and their own theological purposes.

None of the evangelists was concerned with simply memorialising the message of Jesus, as if the power of that message was best preserved in literary storage. None of them was a detached observer who believed that Jesus' message was best communicated through a chronicle of names, places and dates. While all of them are concerned with the truth about Jesus, it is evident from their writings that none of them subscribed to the belief that that truth was best kept alive for later generations through historical reminiscence. Biography was not the chosen herald of salvation.

While the evangelists honoured the tradition, their focus was elsewhere: the One who was crucified and raised would come in glory to judge the world. Their principal pastoral purpose was, therefore, proclaiming and strengthening faith in Jesus as Lord. Each of them belonged to different communities of faith; each of them received and welcomed the message of salvation from an earlier generation of preachers and teachers; each of them passed on a living message about Jesus in such a way that it would meet the growing needs of his Church. As Crossan has observed: 'Jesus left behind him thinkers not memorizers, disciples not reciters, people not parrots.'[6]

The evangelists reflected on the identity and saving work of Jesus and re-interpreted stories from the tradition to answer the problems facing their communities. The most obvious example of this is Matthew 18, which confronts contemporary problems in Church life and order. For Matthew, the period of the Church was not separated from the period of Jesus: Jesus continued with his

6. J.D. Crossan, *The Historical Jesus: the Life of a Mediterranean Jewish Peasant* (Edinburgh: T&T Clark, 1993) p. xxxi.

followers until the end of time (Mt 28:20). Indeed, so successful was Matthew in adapting the message of Jesus to the needs of the later Church that, for the best part of two millennia, his Gospel was the primary source for Church teaching, liturgy and catechesis.

It is highly unlikely that any of the evangelists thought of his written document as a 'gospel'. That term was originally reserved for the spoken proclamation, just as the term 'scripture' was used to define what was later called the Old Testament. Early in the second century, Papias, Bishop of Hierapolis, says about Mark that he wrote down 'as much as he remembered of the Lord's words and deeds' and of Matthew that he composed 'the sayings'.[7] Even though Papias is concerned to show that apostolic names guarantee what is written, he does not refer to the writings of Mark and Matthew as 'gospels'. There is no evidence that anyone before Marcion (*ca* 140 AD) called a gospel writing *euangelion*. Marcion's innovative use of the term to apply to a written document may reflect that the written Gospels were 'heard' as liturgical readings by that time. If this is true, then Koester's point is well noted: 'In this case, Marcion would have elevated such popular understanding to a theologically conscious usage.'[8]

Authorship

The traditional headings of the four canonical Gospels according to Matthew, Mark, Luke, and John did not form part of the original manuscripts. All four Gospels are anonymous. We have no certain knowledge about their authorship, but we do know that they remained untitled until the last quarter of the second century, when ecclesiastical tradition ascribed names to them. The original anonymity may have been deliberate, as Sanders has argued:

The authors probably wanted to eliminate interest in who wrote the story and to focus the reader on the subject. More important, the claim of an anonymous history was higher than that of a named work. In the ancient world an anonymous book, rather like an encyclopaedia article today, implicitly claimed complete

7. Quoted in Eusebius, *Ecclesiastical History* 3.39.14-16.
8. H. Koester, 'From the Kerygma-Gospel to the Written Gospels,' *New Testament Studies* 35 (1989) p. 381.

knowledge and reliability. It would have reduced the impact of the Gospel of Matthew had the author written 'this is my version' instead of 'this is what Jesus said and did'.[9]

By the last quarter of the second century, however, there were a number of gospels claiming the attention of different Christian communities, including the Gospel of Truth, the Infancy Gospel of James, the Gospel of Peter, and the Gospel of Thomas. A decision had to made about which could be regarded as authoritative and normative for the faith and life of catholic Christianity. Marcion (*ca*140 AD) accepted only the Gospel of Luke, excising any references to Judaism and Jesus' family; Tatian (*ca*170 AD) composed a Gospel harmony in his *Diatesssaron*, which was used by the Churches in Upper Syria until the fifth century. In the Western Church Irenaeus (*ca*180 AD) argued for a compromise between a plurality of Gospels and the exclusive use of one Gospel, affirming the number to be fixed at four: those written by Matthew, Mark, Luke, and John.[10] Irenaeus' Gospel collection was considered entirely apostolic in origin.

The collective witness of the four writings acquired their scriptural standing as *the* Gospel, each writing being known as the Gospel *according to* its putative author. The Western Church used the order Matthew, John, Luke, Mark, giving precedence to Matthew and John, supposedly apostles, over Luke and Mark, supposedly disciples of apostles. The Eastern Church used the order Matthew, Mark, Luke, John, probably reflecting their belief in chronological order. When Jerome was commissioned in 383 by Pope Damasus to produce an authoritative Latin translation of the Bible, he adopted the Eastern order for the Gospels, which has remained the standard practice in the West.

The earliest evidence for ascribing the second Gospel to Mark dates from the early second century and is found in the Papias fragment, quoted by Eusebius two centuries later. In the fragment, Papias quotes someone identified as the Elder:

When Mark became Peter's interpreter, he wrote down carefully, but not in order, as much as he remembered of the Lord's

9. E.P. Sanders, *The Historical Figure of Jesus* (London: Allen Lane, 1993) p. 66.
10. Irenaeus, *Against Heresies* 3.11.8-9.

words and deeds; for he had not heard the Lord nor been one of his followers, but later, as I said, one of Peter's. Peter did not give a systematic exposition of the Lord's sayings, but adapted his teaching to the occasion, so that Mark was justified in writing down some things just as he remembered them. For he had but one purpose – to leave out nothing that he had heard, and to make no false statement about it.[11]

Some scholars are cautious about uncritically accepting the Papias tradition, arguing that it serves as an apologetic vindication of the Gospel's apostolic authority.[12] But it seems unlikely that Papias, or his source, would have invented the ascription to an author who had not been a follower of Jesus, for this would have lessened the work's apostolic authority. If apostolic weight had been the principal concern, surely Peter himself would have been a more likely candidate. Taylor's cautious comment still seems a fair one:

The Papias tradition has been widely accepted, and with good reason, but it ought not to be taken as covering everything contained in Mark, and not necessarily the greater part of the Gospel, for there are clear signs that the Evangelist used other traditions in narrative and sayings.[13]

Whatever differences are held about the Gospel's authorship, there is general agreement among critical scholars, especially in the light of form criticism, that much of Mark's material had a period of oral circulation in Greek before it was included in the Gospel, and that some of the material was written down before being incorporated into the Gospel text.

The popular assumption has been that Mark is the same person as the son of a woman in whose house the disciples often met (Acts 12:12) and was a travelling companion of Paul (Acts 12:25; 13:5-

11. Eusebius, *Ecclesiastical History* 3.39.15.

12. For example: W.G. Kümmel, *Introduction to the New Testament* (Nashville: Abington, 1966) p. 69, regards it as 'untrustworthy'; W. Marxsen, *Introduction to the New Testament* (Philadelphia: Fortress, 1974) p. 143, rejects it as 'historically worthless.' For a contrary view, M. Hengel, *Studies in the Gospel of Mark* (Philadelphia: Fortress, 1985) p. 47, argues that the Papias tradition has been 'mishandled in more recent scholarship'.

13. V. Taylor, *The Gospel according to St. Mark* (London: Macmillan, 1959) p. 3.

13; 15:37; Col 4:10; Phlm 24; 2 Tim 4:11) and a co-worker of Peter (1 Pet 5:13). The combination of disparate texts to build up a portrait of the evangelist in this way is an interesting speculative exercise, but nothing more. When one considers that Mark was one of the most common names among peoples who spoke Latin and Greek, it gives pause to such a ready association between 'Mark' the putative evangelist (associated with Peter) and 'John whose other name was Mark' (associated with Paul).

Although we cannot establish with certainty the identity of the evangelist, the internal evidence of the Gospel gives us a few hints about him. In spite of his focus on Galilee, it is unlikely that Mark was a native of Palestine, for he is clearly confused about Palestinian geography, even the whereabouts of the Sea of Galilee (see 7:31). Mark's origin outside Aramaic-speaking Palestine would seem to be confirmed by the readers for whom he wrote. Had the Gospel been written for Jewish Christians in Galilee, it would have been unnecessary to translate Aramaic words into Greek (5:41; 7:34; 15:34) or to explain Jewish customs (7:2-4; 14:12; 15:42).

Mark has clear sympathies towards the Gentiles: for example, only in his Gospel is Jesus followed by people from Idumea (3:8); in the story of the two feedings, emphasis is placed on twelve baskets in Jewish territory and seven in Gentile (8:19-21); and the elect are to be gathered from 'the ends of the earth' (13:27), a phrase absent from the other Gospels. Mark's Gentile interest, coupled with the mistakes he makes about Judaism, could indicate his own Gentile background. In reviewing the mistakes in Mark's Gospel, Parker states categorically: 'This Evangelist just cannot have been familiar with Palestine, its people or its religion.'[14]

However difficult it is to be categorical about anything touching on the identity of the evangelist, every commentary needs to build on a working hypothesis. The presupposition of this commentary is that Mark, a non-Palestinian Gentile convert, was the first to develop the Easter proclamation about Jesus into a single narrative form in his Gospel; and, further, in respect to the patristic tradition, that he was able to draw on a memory of Peter's witness for some of his work.

14. P. Parker, 'A Second Look at *The Gospel before Mark,*' *Journal of Biblical Literature* 100 (1981) p. 396.

Date and place of composition

Just as we cannot be certain about who precisely wrote the Gospel, neither can we be sure about the date or place of composition. The majority of scholars would fix the date somewhere between the years 65 and 75 AD. These outer limits roughly coincide with the Roman-Jewish War (66-74 AD), which saw the destruction of Jerusalem, the burning of the Temple, and the collapse of the political entity of Israel. Dating the Gospel from the internal evidence usually revolves around an interpretation of the apocalyptic discourse in Chapter 13. When Jesus leaves the Temple, he says to one of his disciples: 'Do you see these great buildings? Not one stone will be left here upon another; all will be thrown down.' (13:2) Did Mark write this verse before the destruction of the Temple, which happened in 70 AD, or after it?

There is nothing said in this verse or elsewhere in the discourse that presupposes the destruction of the Temple – which Josephus says was destroyed by fire.[15] Jesus' language in Mark is no more precise than that spoken by the Seleucid general Nicanor in 160 BC: 'I will level this shrine of God to the ground and tear down the altar' (2 Macc 14:33). Given that the Temple would be the most obvious Jewish symbol for any dominating power to destroy, the warning by the Sanhedrin that 'the Romans will come and destroy both our holy place and our nation' (Jn 11:48) hardly argues to prophetic percipience. That is merely an old likelihood repeating itself. The likelihood would look even sharper after the Jewish revolt in 66 AD, just as the Christian view from Rome in 69 AD would look even more forbidding with the rumours of Nero's return from a suicidal death and the news that Vespasian had moved against Jerusalem. Thus a date just before 70 AD would make sense for the writing of Mark's Gospel.

Early tradition favours Rome as the place of composition, although there is mention of Egypt by John Chrysostom. Antioch, the city in Syria where the gospel was first proclaimed to a large non-Jewish community (Acts 11:20-21), has a growing number of adherents. The region of Galilee is also advanced as a possibility. While the arguments favouring Antioch may hold some force, the

15. Josephus, *Jewish Wars* 6.4.3-7.

most likely place remains Rome, although the supporting arguments permit no certain conclusion.

The early tradition associating the Gospel with Peter in Rome would not only argue for the influence of the first apostle on the writing but also, by implication, the influence of other traditions. Before he was martyred under the Neronian persecution, Peter could only have spent a brief period in the imperial city. The Christian community existed in Rome for some twenty years before the arrival of Peter, and was probably founded by Christian immigrants from Palestine and Syria.[16] The Roman biographer Suetonius, in his life of the Emperor Claudius, tells of an expulsion of Jews from Rome 'for constant disturbance at the instigation of Chrestus'.[17] If it is right to interpret this as a confused reference to disputes between Jews and Christians over the messiahship of Jesus, then the Christian community was already established before 50 AD, at which time Peter was still in Jerusalem. The community in Rome did not, therefore, depend on Peter as their principal source for stories about Jesus. Neither did they depend on Paul. Paul, writing to the Roman Church about 56-58 AD, is clearly addressing a stable Christian community, which he has been wanting to visit 'for many years' (15:23).

Rome as the possible place of the Gospel's origin would still seem the best choice among the available options. It would honour the earliest tradition associating the Gospel with Peter's influence, however tenuously that influence is interpreted. It would account for an oral tradition which originated in Palestine and Syria, and an apostolic preaching wider than Peter's testimony. It would fit the profile of a Church consisting largely of Gentile members. It would be an obvious choice, though not a necessary one, as a place of suffering and persecution to give birth to such a Gospel as Mark's. It might account for Mark's pro-Roman point of view in the passion narrative (although it could be argued that this view was already in the pre-Markan material). As the major centre of influence in the world and the place where the two principal apostles were mar-

16. See S. Brown, *The Origins of Christianity* (Oxford: Oxford University Press, 1993) p. 130 ff; R.E. Brown and J.P. Meier, *Antioch and Rome* (London: Chapman, 1983) pp. 89-104; D. O'Connor, *Peter in Rome: The Literary, Liturgical, and Archaeological Evidence* (New York: Columbia University Press, 1969).

17. Suetonius, *Claudius* 25.4.

tyred, it would explain the early authoritative position accorded to the Gospel.

Mark's writing

Unlike Luke and John, Mark does not tell us why he wrote his Gospel. There is no statement of purpose to help us understand why he organised the tradition about Jesus into a coherent, narrative framework, but there is a growing library of scholarly works to supply the missing motive.[18] Something of his purpose may be detected from the framework of his Gospel and his own writing. Unlike the later Gospels, Mark retains the framework of early Christian instruction. In his speech to the centurion Cornelius in Acts 10:34-43, Peter begins the story of Jesus with John the Baptist's preaching and ends it with the resurrection. Mark follows that sequence in his Gospel, beginning with John the Baptist's proclamation in the wilderness and ending with the angelic proclamation at the empty tomb. Later, Matthew and Luke push back the beginning of the story to Jesus' conception and birth, while later still, John pushes back the beginning to the period before creation.

By staying within the outer limits of the Jesus tradition preached by the primitive Church (*John the Baptist* ➤ *resurrection*), Mark's Gospel is the closest to the apostolic preaching of Stage 2. There is one significant change. One of the things he makes clear in his writing is the messianic significance of Jesus' *whole* career, from the baptism onwards. This is a development from the earlier christology of Stage 2 which believed that Jesus was revealed as the Messiah only in the resurrection itself (Acts 2:32,36; Rom 1:3-4; Phil 2:8-9).

The whole style of Mark's writing, especially its immediacy in the use of the historical present and its narrative urge to move the story on, indicates that it was written to be heard as a complete story.

Mark did not write his Gospel in chapters and verses, ready-made for separation. It is a narrative unified by its purpose in

18. For a representative review of the debate, see L. Hurtado, 'The Gospel of Mark: Evolutionary or Revolutionary Document?' *Journal for the Study of the New Testament* 40 (1990) pp.15-32; E. Best, *Mark: the Gospel as Story* (Edinburgh: T&T Clark, 1983) pp. 21-54; 93-147.

reflecting on the identity and destiny of Jesus: even the tenuous links and connections between the stories, it can be argued, reflect the fractured nature of life. As Kermode has argued, the very inconsistencies in Mark's Gospel 'mime the fortuities of real life'.[19] Mark's urgent pace and the living quality of his style are enough to explain written untidiness; he wrote for his *whole* story to be taken into account, not for dissected units to be analysed in isolation or his Greek to be scrutinised for its style. Mark wrote as a pastor, not as an essayist; he wrote a story of action, not a series of discourses; he wrote for people facing persecution, not for literary critics facing a text.

Listening to Mark's Gospel read at one sitting or reading it in its entirety allows Mark's dramatic narrative to speak as a whole story; it exposes the listener/reader to what Rhoads and Michie call 'the unitary impact of the narrative itself.'[20] A picture emerges of a pastor building up the faith of his community by reflecting on the identity and destiny of Jesus, and inviting them to think of the consequences of their own discipleship in taking up their cross and following Jesus.

The identity and destiny of Jesus

Mark also shows continuity with the primitive preaching in his focus on the passion: a third of his narrative is devoted to the last week of Jesus' life. In this way, the death and resurrection of Jesus provide the necessary framework within which the identity and destiny of Jesus are interpreted. In Mark's view one can only understand the full identity of Jesus through suffering and the cross.

Mark uses the inability of the disciples to understand Jesus as dramatic proof of his point. Peter is the first person to publicly identify Jesus as the Christ, but Jesus responds with the command not to use the title publicly and then moves on to speak of the suffering Son of Man (8:27-33). Peter's reaction displays how poorly he has understood messiahship: the assumption that Jesus would be immune from suffering because he was the Christ is not

19. F. Kermode, *The Genesis of Secrecy: On the Interpretation of Narrative* (Cambridge: Harvard University Press, 1979) p. 64.

20. D. Rhoads and D. Michie, *Mark as Story: an Introduction to the Narrative of a Gospel* (Philadelphia: Fortress, 1982) p. 4.

only incorrect, it is satanic. In the story of the transfiguration, which reveals Jesus as God's beloved Son, Peter's confusion and the disciples' fear are emphasised (9:2-8). After the transfiguration, Jesus again emphasises to his disciples the certainty of his impending suffering and death, but the disciples remain steadfast in their incomprehension (9:31-32).

Each of the passion predictions is followed by the incomprehension of the disciples. This pattern of revelation followed by misunderstanding is not to deride the disciples as men who are stubbornly obtuse in the face of revelation; *it is to show that they have no control over insight into Jesus*. Mark underscores the point that understanding has been withheld from them: it is not within their capacity, for 'their hearts are hardened' (6:52). This means literally that God has hardened their hearts; their hearts have not been opened to understanding Jesus. Mark is consistent in noting the disciples' inability to understand Jesus fully: he tells the listener/reader that not even Jesus' closest followers *could* understand him until Jesus underwent suffering and the cross.

This does not mean, as Weeden has argued, that 'Mark is assiduously involved in a vendetta against the disciples. He is intent on totally discrediting them.'[21] Mark uses them in his narrative as a dramatic example of the truth that no one can understand Jesus until after his death. He arranges the traditions about the disciples in such a way that his own theology is more sharply focused. In spite of the revelations by Jesus, in spite of the disciples' close association with him, in spite of their determination not to run away before Jesus' arrest, they fail to understand him until after the death and resurrection.

In a sense it can be said that Jesus' identity cannot be understood until his destiny, which is in God's hands, is fulfilled on the cross.

The importance of Jesus' death for understanding his true identity is illustrated by the fact that no human being in Mark's Gospel recognises or understands Jesus as the Son of God until after his death – and then the acknowledgement is made not by one of Jesus' followers but by a Gentile, a centurion in the Roman army (15:39). Until Jesus fulfils his destiny on the cross, his true identity remains hidden.

21. T. Weeden, *Mark – Traditions in Conflict* (Philadelphia: Fortress, 1971) p. 50.

Jesus' true identity is most clearly revealed in the title that summarises his destiny, the Son of Man. In Mark this is the term Jesus applies to himself, and it is noteworthy that no one else calls Jesus by this title. Whenever Jesus' identity is the issue in Mark's Gospel, Jesus responds by referring to himself as Son of Man. *The question about who he is can only be answered when one understands what he must do, and it is the Son of Man title which tells that story.* Achtemeier observes:

> Can Jesus, as one who employs God's prerogative of forgiving sins, be recognised as Son of God (2:5,7)? No, he is Son of Man (2:10). Can he, when his actions reveal him to be Lord of the Sabbath, be recognised as son of David, who had acted in similar fashion (2:25)? No, he is Son of Man (2:28). Can he, as successor to John the Baptist and the prophets, be recognised as Christ (8:28-29)? No, he is Son of Man (8:31). Can he, in transfigured form, be recognised as Son of God (9:7)? No, he is Son of Man (9:9).[22]

Mark's focus on Jesus as Son of Man is further highlighted in the passion narrative. The high priest asks Jesus: 'Are you the Messiah, the Son of the Blessed One?' (14:61) In the high priest's question two titles are ascribed to Jesus, Messiah and Son of God. In his reply, Jesus focuses on a title the high priest does not use, to clarify his answer: 'I am; and you will see the Son of Man seated at the right hand of Power, and coming with the clouds of heaven.' (14:62) The Son of Man appears in Mark's writing, even when it refers to the second coming, as a necessary clarification to what is said about Jesus by others. Its main purpose, however, is to focus on the cross. No other title serves to capture the undivided unity between the person of Jesus and his destiny. Because of who he is, Jesus is destined to suffer. Is that also true of Mark's community? Because of who they are as followers of Jesus, does that mean that they are destined to endure the suffering of the cross?

Cross and discipleship
If Mark was addressing the Roman Church, he was writing for a

22. P. Achtemeier, 'The Gospel of Mark,' *The Anchor Bible Dictionary* Vol. 4 (New York: Doubleday, 1992) p. 556.

community that had already suffered persecution and probably lived in fear of more of the same. In the summer of 64 AD a fire broke out in Rome that raged unchecked for a week and destroyed half the imperial city. Popular rumour claimed that the fire had been officially ordered by Nero himself. To divert suspicion from himself, Nero chose a scapegoat in an already unpopular religious minority, the Christians, who were disliked for their exclusiveness and anti-social behaviour. Tacitus relates how Nero arrested known Christians and then, on information collected from them, condemned large numbers of others. Tacitus goes on to describe their execution:

> Their deaths were made farcical. Dressed in wild animals' skins, they were torn to pieces by dogs, or crucified, or made into torches to be ignited after dark as substitutes for daylight.[23]

For the last three years of Nero's reign (65-68, AD), being a Christian was a capital crime in Rome. During that time the Christian community had to face the reality of misrepresentation, betrayal, arrest, false accusation, persecution and violent death – including the loss of Peter and Paul. Clearly the Roman Church needed strengthening after its own time of suffering and passion. Although it seems unlikely that persecution was the precipitating cause for Mark's writing, his Gospel would have addressed such a community in its time of uncertainty. There is a warning that some who receive the word will 'endure only for awhile; then, when tribulation or persecution arises on account of the word, immediately they fall away.' (4:17) Those who have left home and families to follow Jesus will not only receive a hundredfold 'now in this age' but will have to live 'with persecutions' (10:30). In 13:9-13 the followers of Jesus are warned explicitly about persecution:

> they will deliver you up to councils
> you will be beaten in synagogues
> you will stand before governors and kings for my sake
> they will bring you to trial and deliver you up
> family members will betray one another
> you will be hated for my name's sake
> he who endures to the end will be saved.

23. Tacitus, *Annals* 15.44

That catalogue of suffering is originally told in the passion story of Jesus. For Mark, the pattern of Jesus' passion merges into the experience of his followers, just as his followers can see something of their own experience reflected in the suffering of Jesus. If the passion of Jesus becomes the interpretative key that opens up the mystery of his identity, so the passion of those who come after him will indicate their true identity as his followers. The three passion predictions of Jesus' impending suffering (8:31; 9:31; 10:32-34) are each followed by a statement about the nature of discipleship (8:34-38; 9:35-37; 10:38-45). Just as suffering characterises the way of the Son of Man, so taking up the cross will prove the principal challenge for all who would follow Jesus. This is the task of discipleship in Mark: to take up the cross freely and follow the way of Jesus in enduring what cannot be evaded. As Jesus 'had to suffer,' so the same destiny is outlined for his followers. This is the way that leads to salvation (8:34).

In hearing the Gospel, Mark's community is helped to see that the story of their own suffering, like the story of Jesus' suffering, is not some catastrophic mischance that is devoid of meaning, but a chronicle of salvation that was waiting to be told, one that rested within the prophecies of Jesus and the providence of God.

The structure of Mark's Gospel

Mark's writing can be divided into seven narrative blocks, which will form the main sections of the commentary. The longer ending, which was not written by Mark but forms part of the canonical Gospel, will be treated as an appendix.

Section 1: Prologue (1:1-13)
Section 2: Revelation in Galilee (1:14-3:6)
Section 3: Rejection in Galilee (3:7-6:6a)
Section 4: Revelation to disciples (6:6b-8:26)
Section 5: The suffering Son of Man (8:27-10:52)
Section 6: Ministry in Jerusalem (11:1-13:37)
Section 7: Death in Jerusalem (14:1-16:8)
Appendix: Longer ending (16:9-20).

1

The Prologue

1:1-13

Mark opens his work with a title sentence introducing his writing as the gospel of Jesus the Messiah, the Son of God. The opening of the story of Jesus is marked by the person and ministry of John the Baptist. Mark's beginning coincides with the starting-point of the earliest Christian preaching about Jesus, where the 'beginning' means the time John was baptising (Acts 1:22, 10:37). After his initial focus on the ministry of John, Mark tells the story of how Jesus is baptised by John and is then immediately driven into the wilderness where he is tempted by Satan.

The title   1:1

> The beginning of the good news of Jesus Christ, the Son of God.

Mark begins his story of glad tidings by announcing his belief in the identity and authority of Jesus who is Messiah and Son of God.[1] The secret of Jesus' identity, unknown to most of the characters in the ensuing drama, is opened up to the readers in the first sentence. That initial claim will shape the way the readers approach the story of Jesus. Mark's opening affirmation is strikingly similar to the fourth evangelist's concluding statement of purpose: 'these are written so that you may come to believe that Jesus is the Messiah, the Son of God, and that through believing you may have life in his name.' (Jn 20:31)

Mark announces at the beginning of the story what becomes evident only at the end of it: only after the death of Jesus does a human being come to acknowledge that Jesus is Son of God (15:39). Mark's writing, however, is a post-Easter proclamation of the community's belief in Jesus as Christ and Son of God. What before was confessed but misunderstood by Peter (8:29) can now be asserted in the light of Jesus' whole story: Jesus is the Christ.

---

1. For a study on how each evangelist chooses to begin his Gospel, see F.J. Moloney, *Beginning the Good News: A Narrative Approach* (Homebush: St Paul, 1992); D.E. Smith (ed), *How Gospels Began* (Semeia 52; Atlanta: Scholars Press, 1990).

What before was known only by God and the demons during the ministry can now be proclaimed after the death and resurrection: Jesus is the Son of God.

Mark is now going to re-tell the story of Jesus in such a way that his readers can understand what the disciples of Jesus could not understand when they followed him. He can do this because he is not a historian recording what *actually happened*, but a pastor opening up the significance of *what was going on* in the events he recounts. He will interpret those events so that the meaning will be revealed in the way the story is told. Past misunderstandings will be noted but not shared; the blindness of the first disciples will look like stubborn obtuseness in the new light of faith in Jesus as Lord.

Mark brings an Easter faith to his pastoral task of proclaiming the story of Jesus, and he is writing for a community that shares his faith. In that way the readers will be wiser than the participants in the story, because the readers can interpret everything that has happened in the light of their living faith in the identity of Jesus, who is Christ and Son of God.

The ministry of John   1:2-8

> 2. As it is written in the prophet Isaiah,
> 'See, I am sending my messenger ahead of you,
> who will prepare your way;
> 3the voice of one crying out in the wilderness:
> 'Prepare the way of the Lord,
> Make his paths straight,'
> 4John the baptizer appeared in the wilderness, proclaiming a baptism of repentance for the forgiveness of sins. 5And people from the whole Judean countryside and all the people of Jerusalem were going out to him, and were baptized by him in the river Jordan, confessing their sins. 6Now John was clothed with camel's hair, with a leather belt around his waist, and he ate locusts and wild honey. 7He proclaimed, 'The one who is more powerful than I is coming after me; I am not worthy to stoop down and untie the thong of his sandals. 8I have baptized you with water; but he will baptize you with the Holy Spirit'.

All four Gospels agree that before one can understand the ministry of Jesus, one must first look at the ministry of John the Baptist. John is the major, independent religious figure who stands between Jesus' hidden life and his public ministry. The teaching and baptism of John, which Jesus accepted, are offered to the reader as the occasion for Jesus' new beginning and his emergence into public life.

Each evangelist draws his own portrait of John and his ministry. Compared to the other Gospels, Mark seems the least interested in John for his own sake: all his material about John is subordinated to his primary interest in Jesus.

In his Gospel Matthew tells us how John believed that all Israel was threatened by God with an imminent fiery judgement, one that could only be avoided by repentance and acceptance of his baptism (Mt 3:7-11 par.); how John harshly attacked the Pharisees and Sadducees (Mt 3:7-10); how Jesus preached the same message as John (Mt 3:2, 4:17); how Jesus regarded John very highly (Mt 11:9-14 par.); how John had doubts about whether Jesus was the Messiah (Mt 11:2-6 par.); how John was accepted by the marginalised, such as the tax-collectors and prostitutes, but was rejected by the Jewish leaders in Jerusalem (Mt 21:31-32).

Luke uses his infancy narrative to interweave the stories of the births of John and Jesus; John preached through the whole Jordan district (Lk 3:3); people sought John's help to find a new direction for their lives (Lk 3:10); his authority was so great that people began to think he might be the Messiah (Lk 3:15); he opposed Herod Antipas for all the evil things he did (Lk 3:19); the Pharisees and lawyers opposed him (Lk 7:30).

The fourth evangelist never refers to John as the Baptist, but is anxious to portray him as someone who is not the light, only a witness to speak for the light (Jn 1:8); he is not the Messiah or Elijah or the Prophet (Jn 1:19-25); Jesus, while he was among the Baptist's circle, recruited his first disciples from the ranks of John's followers (1:35-42); Jesus and John baptised in parallel missions (Jn 3:22-23).

A picture emerges of John as a charismatic leader whose great popularity among the people is exercised apart from Jesus. His ministry begins before Jesus, and when John dies he leaves behind him a religious following that exists independently of Christianity. John's ministry dominates the beginning of the Gospel, and Jesus submits to John's baptism of repentance for the forgiveness of sins. As an independent nomadic prophet, John displays no discernible respect for religious hierarchy and he appears alienated from institutional religion. His natural sanctuary is the wilderness, not the Temple; his ritual act centres around the waters of the river, not around the priestly altar of sacrifice. John's alienation from normal society is underscored by his ascetic lifestyle in an uninhabited place, his Bedouin dress of animal skin and his peasant diet of locusts and wild honey.

The composite picture of John and his ministry that emerges from the Gospels seems to set a stage of conflict, one that Jesus will enter on the side of John:

Jerusalem and the Temple	*versus*	the wilderness
the institutional	*versus*	the charismatic
the priestly	*versus*	the prophetic
the temporal power	*versus*	the religious critic
the aristocracy	*versus*	the marginalised
the settled	*versus*	the nomadic.

Mark's stage is deliberately smaller since he has only one function for John the Baptist in his Gospel: he is the fulfilment of ancient prophecy in being the forerunner of the Lord (vv. 2-3). Although Mark admits that John's independent prophetic career was immensely popular with all the country of Judea and all the people of Jerusalem submitting to John's baptism and confessing their sins to him (v. 5), he effectively limits John's role by making it wholly dependant on the unidentified figure: 'The one who is more powerful than I is coming after me; I am not worthy to stoop down and untie the thong of his sandals.' (v. 8)

John does not identify who this mightier one is. The only clue is that he, like John, will be a baptiser. He is named as stronger because he will baptise with the Holy Spirit, whereas John baptises with water. John's baptism by water is a symbol of past sins washed away, but the superior baptism with the Holy Spirit would bring eternal life rather than destruction on the last day.

From his opening verse, Mark clearly imposes a Christian interpretation on the John the Baptist material by domesticating this wild man and securing him within the story of Jesus. But John's independent ministry among the people, the moral authority he exercised and the respect he commanded, all still linger in the Gospel tradition. John's place is assured at the beginning of the

Gospel as the nomadic prophet who attracted Jesus from his settled life in Nazareth. Jesus' beginning was not a solitary event in a landscape empty of people. Like many others, Jesus was attracted by John's reputation and was moved to journey to see this man who spoke the word of God with authority. And after he saw John, Jesus' life was to take a new direction.

The baptism of Jesus   1:9-11

⁹ In those days Jesus came from Nazareth of Galilee and was baptized by John in the Jordan. ¹⁰And just as he was coming up out of the water, he saw the heavens torn apart and the Spirit descending like a dove on him. ¹¹And a voice came from heaven, 'You are my Son, the Beloved; with you I am well pleased.'

The story of Jesus submitting himself to John's 'baptism of repentance for the forgiveness of sins' is clearly an embarrassing memory for the early Church, and each evangelist deals with it in his own way. How does a Stage 3 proclamation, written in the belief that Jesus is the Christ and Son of God, handle a fixed memory from Stage 1 that Jesus pursued his ministry as a convert of John the Baptist?

Mark briefly mentions Jesus' baptism by John and goes on to concentrate on Jesus' vision of the heavens opening, the Spirit descending, and the heavenly voice addressing him as beloved Son. In Matthew's account John recognises Jesus as the giver of the greater baptism, and Jesus gives John permission to baptise him (Mt 3:14-15). Before telling the story of Jesus' baptism, Luke has John conveniently locked up in prison; Luke then passes over the baptism of Jesus to concentrate on the wonderful elements that now happen during Jesus' prayer experience (Lk 3:19-22). The fourth evangelist suppresses the story of Jesus' baptism – it would hardly be fitting for the eternal Word that was God to submit to John's baptism – although the theophany is retained but is now addressed to John, not Jesus (Jn 1:32-33).

The structure of Mark's story has two basic elements, the simple and the wonderful. The simple element is made up of two events: Jesus leaves home in Nazareth travelling south to see John the Baptist; with many others Jesus is baptised by John in the river Jordan. There are three components in the wonderful element: the heavens open; the Spirit descends; a heavenly voice speaks Jesus' identity.

In the simple element of the baptism story, the historical figure of Jesus is introduced for the first time as a man from Nazareth in Galilee who comes south to the wilderness of Judea and is baptised in the Jordan by John. In this part of the story the Baptist is the principal actor and Jesus is the recipient. What does this baptism mean? How is it to be interpreted for the readers of the Gospel? The wonderful element, the vision and the voice, interprets the significance of the baptism for the reader.

The focus now dramatically shifts away from John the Baptist: God and his Spirit are now the main actors; Jesus is still the recipient. Mark uses a selection of Old Testament texts to bring out the meaning of the baptism of Jesus:

Ps 2:7

> I will tell of the decree of the Lord:.
> He said to me, 'You are my son,
> today I have begotten you.'

Is 42:1

> Here is my servant, whom I uphold,
> my chosen, in whom my soul delights;
> I have put my spirit upon him,
> he will bring forth justice to the nations.

Is 63:7-64:12 – The Prayer of Israel

> Where is the one who brought them up out of the sea
> with the shepherds of his flock?
> Where is the one who put within them his holy spirit? ...
> Look down from heaven and see,
> from your holy and glorious habitation ...
> For you are our father ...
> our Redeemer from of old is your name ...
> O that you would tear open the heavens and come down ...
> to make your name known to your adversaries ...
> Zion has become a wilderness,
> Jerusalem a desolation ...
> Will you keep silent, and punish us so severely?

The wonderful element successfully removes the embarrassment of the simple element, diverting attention away from John the Baptist's role and focusing on Jesus as the anointed Son of God.

Writing earlier than Mark, Paul speaks of the *resurrection* as the moment Jesus is designated Son of God (Rom 1:4). Likewise in Acts 13:33, Luke has Paul's *resurrection* kerygma use the quotation from the Davidic enthronement psalm: 'You are my son, today I have begotten you.'(Ps 2:7) Mark now applies this verse, together with Isaiah 42:1, to the baptism of Jesus.

Further, the prayer of Israel can be considered answered in the baptism scene: the heavens are now torn open, the holy Spirit of God is now in the midst of the people; God's silence is overcome as he makes his name known anew. Thus interpreted, the baptism of Jesus is not an individual event, but is read as the answer to the longings of Israel.

There is no suggestion by Mark that John the Baptist or anyone else is a witness to the wonderful element – the revelation is addressed to Jesus alone. The only witnesses are the readers of Mark's Gospel. As readers we can see that all prophecy is being fulfilled: Jesus, the Davidic Messiah and Son of God, is anointed with God's Spirit to be a servant of the Lord sent to a sinful people. What Mark declared in the opening verse of his Gospel is now seen to be confirmed by God himself.

The wonderful element fulfils the function of clarifying the identity and mission of Jesus, at the same time asserting the importance of Jesus over John the Baptist. The wonderful element is not a videotape description of a Stage 1 experience of Jesus. As J.P. Meier argues in his extensive reflection on Jesus and John the Baptist:

> The theophany does not mirror some inner experience Jesus had at the time; it mirrors the desire of the first-generation Christian church to define Jesus as soon as the primitive Gospel story begins – all the more so because this definition was needed to counter the impression of Jesus' subordination to John, implicit in the tradition of the former being baptized by the latter ... I think the basic point is clear: a psychological interpretation of the baptismal story as a path to Jesus' inner experience ignores the basic insights of close to a century of tradition, form, and

redaction criticism.[2]

What we are left with, therefore, is the simple element that prefaces the public ministry of Jesus: the memory that Jesus left his home in Nazareth; he travelled south to the wilderness where John ministered; he was baptised by John. The fact that Jesus was baptised by John presupposes that the newcomer from Nazareth first heard John's message of judgement on a sinful Israel and accepted John's authority as a prophet. Whether Jesus first began as a disciple of John is not a question that can be answered from Mark's Gospel alone.[3]

What Mark finds worthy of noting, however, is that when Jesus returns to his relatives in Nazareth, they want to restrain him because they think he is out of his mind (3:21). Similarly, when Jesus preaches in the Nazareth synagogue, his hearers wonder 'Where did this man get all this?' and they fasten on to the identity of the Jesus they know, rejecting his new identity as a prophetic preacher (6:1-6). The voice from Nazareth says of Jesus: 'Is not this the carpenter, the son of Mary ... ?' – in dramatic contrast to what the voice of God says of Jesus at his baptism. This is the voice of the people who knew Jesus before he went south to see John the Baptist, people whose everyday familiarity with Jesus did not prepare them for believing there was anything exceptional about him. That voice from Nazareth is a measure of how much Jesus had changed in the eyes of those who knew him. To account for that change in Jesus' life, the Gospels point us to John the Baptist and his ministry. It is the rugged person of John, not just a ritual of washing, that stands at the turning-point of Jesus' life.

Jesus is tempted by Satan   1:12-13

[12] And the Spirit immediately drove him out into the wilderness. [13]He was in the wilderness forty days, tempted by Satan; and he was with the wild beasts; and the angels waited on him.

Mark moves his story of Jesus from the waters of the Jordan to the

2. J.P. Meier, *A Marginal Jew: Rethinking the Historical Jesus* Vol 2 (New York: Doubleday, 1994) pp. 107,108.
3. For a discussion of this question, see W.B. Tatum, *John the Baptist and Jesus* (Sonoma: Poleridge, 1994); J. Murphy-O'Connor, 'John the Baptist and Jesus: History and Hypotheses,' *New Testament Studies* 36 (1990) pp. 359-374.

wilderness, the hilly, arid area that lies between the Judean hills and the Jordan valley. John the Baptist prophesied that a stronger one would come who would baptise with the Holy Spirit; the heavens have opened and the Spirit has descended on Jesus; now that same Spirit appears as an overpowering force that impels Jesus into the wilderness. The Spirit is the principal actor – Jesus himself is not named in Mark's account of the temptation. It is worth noting that after Jesus' baptism by John, the ground shifts dramatically: we the readers are suddenly standing on a cosmic stage with the heavens opening, the voice of God speaking, and the Spirit descending. That cosmic stage is still set as the Spirit drives Jesus into the wilderness to be confronted by Satan. There is no human actor on this stage apart from Jesus himself.

The ultimate significance of Jesus is measured by a larger stage than regional geography can provide: this is not a local debate between two human combatants, but a cosmic struggle between good and evil, between the Son of God and Satan. Thus Mark ends his Gospel prologue with an eschatological struggle between Jesus as God's agent and Satan, with wild beasts and ministering angels in attendance.

Mark tells the story of Jesus being tempted by Satan in one verse, a brief account that J. Jeremias calls 'astonishingly obscure. It consists of statements which bear the stamp of symbolic biblical language.'[4] Both Matthew (Mt 4:1-11) and Luke (Lk 4:1-13) narrate a series of three temptations against a background of texts from Deuteronomy that explore Israel's ordeal in the wilderness. Mark has no mention of fasting or hunger; no mention of the nature of the struggles; no mention of the outcome. All we know is that the Spirit does not protect Jesus from trial, but projects him to the place of ambiguity where he must reckon with Satan.

Mark uses the Hebrew term, 'satan', rather than the Greek equivalent, 'devil'. In the Old Testament a satan was an accuser or an adversary, either human or celestial. The first human being to be called a satan is David (1 Sam 29:4). In the first two chapters of the Book of Job, Satan is a son of God whose task is to wander the earth testing and accusing the upright. In the New Testament Satan reflects current Jewish ideas and is represented as a ruler of the

4. J. Jeremias, *New Testament Theology* Vol 1 (London: SCM, 1972) p. 69

kingdom of evil whose function is to attract people to do evil; he is assisted by his own subjects and servants, known as demons. In Mark's prologue the ruler of the kingdom of evil tests the one who will preach the kingdom of God.

Before the ministry begins, Mark establishes a dramatic inaugural confrontation that is open-ended, one which sets the stage for later confrontations in the exorcism stories. As J. Robinson notes:

> In this initial encounter between the eschatological Spirit and the ruler of the present evil aeon, the kingdom of God draws near ... The basis has been provided for the ministry of Jesus, which consists in proclamation of a new situation (1:15), and in carrying through the struggle against Satan in the power of the Spirit.[5]

Thus the prologue ends with a trial of strength that is unresolved. The stage is set for conflict. When the ministry begins, we the readers will be able to interpret the ensuing drama in the light of what we have learned in the prologue, *theological* insights that are not given to the participants in the Gospel story. We have learned God's understanding of Jesus' identity; that Jesus moves in the power of the Spirit; that he will have to struggle and endure Satan's opposition. This insight makes us companions in faith with Mark as we move to interpret the story of Jesus' public ministry and death.

5. J.M. Robinson, *The Problem of History in Mark and other Marcan Studies* (Philadelphia: Fortress, 1982) p. 80.

Tear this off and keep it as your record until you get your statement.

Amount £ 157—14 _____ Date _____ 16 / 05 / 16

Receipt Number: 207528976

BARCLAYS

2

Revelation in Galilee

1:14-3:6

Having established the identity of Jesus in the prologue, an identity confirmed by God and his Spirit, Mark describes the beginning of Jesus' ministry in Galilee.

Jesus proclaims the good news of God, calls the first disciples, reveals himself in Capernaum as a healer and teacher, and faces those who enter into open conflict with him. Although Jesus' ministry is first welcomed with enthusiasm, by the end of this section the Pharisees and the Herodians are already plotting to destroy him.

Jesus begins in Galilee   1:14-15

[14]Now after John was arrested, Jesus came to Galilee, proclaiming the good news of God, [15]and saying, 'The time is fulfilled and the kingdom of God has come near; repent, and believe in the good news.'

These two verses form a programmatic statement that sums up the basic meaning of the public ministry; they also act as a transition from the prologue in the wilderness to Jesus' ministry in Galilee. Mark opened his Gospel by introducing us to John the Baptist and honouring the unique role John played in the story of Jesus' beginning. Now Mark tells us that Jesus' beginning to preach in Galilee is directly related to the arrest of John: after John is handed over, Jesus' ministry begins. Both Matthew and Luke follow Mark, consciously excluding John from the time of Jesus' ministry. This avoids anything that looks like rivalry between the two major actors; instead, Jesus is presented as John's successor.

In direct contrast, the fourth evangelist tells us that Jesus chose his first disciples from the followers of John, that Jesus and his disciples baptised in Judea, while John baptised in Samaria – 'John, of course, had not yet been thrown into prison.' (Jn 3:24) Eusebius (*ca* 260-340 AD), bishop of Caesarea, argues that the fourth evangelist wrote his Gospel to record the period that the earlier evangelists passed over in silence – all that happened *before* the

Baptist's imprisonment.[1] While this theory of composition can hardly be accepted uncritically, at least it witnesses to a memory held without embarrassment: that Jesus did not begin his ministry alone, but that he and John preached and baptised in a co-ordinated ministry in Judea and Samaria before the arrest of John.

Mark, followed by Matthew and Luke, is clearly intent on giving the stage to Jesus alone – even the story of John's arrest and execution is postponed. The two summary verses, however, indicate that Jesus will follow John in three important ways. Like John, Jesus preaches God's word: both men are messengers of God, official heralds, who move out of the prophetic compulsion to proclaim a word they are caught by themselves. Both men call people to repentance and challenge them to use the present moment to fit them for the future. And as John was 'handed over' (*para-dothenai*), this same verb will be used twenty times by Mark, usually to indicate the violent fate that will befall Jesus in his passion and death, and to summarise a similar fate facing Jesus' own disciples (e.g. 9:31; 10:37; 13:11; 14:10; 15:10).

Whereas John proclaimed the one who was to come after him, Jesus proclaims 'the good news of God'. The phrase 'the Gospel of God' is a standard Christian designation for the post-Easter proclamation about Jesus, beginning with John the Baptist and concluding with the death and resurrection of Jesus (see Introduction). Using the term here, Mark clearly wants to root the whole Gospel in the preaching of Jesus himself. Thus Mark assimilates 'the good news of Jesus Christ' (1:1) that he is proclaiming in writing with the living word that Jesus announces in his ministry.

Jesus announces that the time is fulfilled and the kingdom of God has come near. The beginning of Jesus' ministry marks the end of waiting; his time is *kairos*, God's appointed moment of opportunity. God keeps his appointment with his people in the person and preaching of Jesus; the time is ripe, for now the kingdom of God has come close.

Although the kingdom of God forms the centre of Jesus' teaching, he never defines it and he is never asked to explain it to his hearers. The assumption is that his hearers knew what he meant, that it was a common term in their thinking vocabulary. Geza

1.See Eusebius, *Ecclesiastical History*, 3.24.5-15.

Vermes notes: 'By the time Jesus first meditated on it, the idea of the Kingdom of God had already a lengthy history in the Hebrew Bible and in early post-biblical or inter-testamental literature.'[2] Although the *idea* has a lengthy history, the phrase 'kingdom of God' appears only once in the Old Testament (Wis 10:10). As an expression, it is basically a New Testament one, yet Jesus took it for granted that his listeners could catch its meaning.

The term 'kingdom of God' yields a variety of interpretations which scholars have attempted to harmonise – not least whether it is 'present' or 'future' or both. The ambiguity is rooted in the Synoptic Gospels themselves where Jesus speaks of the kingdom as both future and present. When Jesus is referring to the final vindication of God's purposes, clearly this kingdom is in the future. When Jesus is referring to the sovereign rule of God in the world, this reality is not only in the future but present in Jesus' ministry of forgiveness and healing and exorcism. Norman Perrin refers to the kingdom of God as a 'tensive symbol'[3] – one that does not have a single defined meaning but a whole range of meanings that defy neat definition. In this understanding, it is storytelling, metaphors, sayings and parables that will illustrate the different meanings of the kingdom of God as the Gospel proceeds.

In Mark 1:15 the kingdom of God lies in the immediate future: God's kingly rule has drawn near, but it will not be long before people experience its power in the deeds and words of Jesus. Before that happens, Jesus makes the imperative appeal that is clearly addressed to all the hearers/readers of the Gospel: 'Repent, and believe in the good news.'

If the kingdom is what God does, if the good news is what Jesus proclaims, repenting and believing are the appropriate human responses we make. As hearers of the Gospel we are not passive notetakers of an abstruse lecture, but people challenged to do something about our own lives and become engaged in an adventure of radical change.

The verb 'to repent' (*metanoeo*) literally means to think beyond the way we think now, to change our minds. That change involves taking to heart the good news of God in Jesus, believing the

2. G. Vermes, *The Religion of Jesus the Jew* (London: SCM, 1990) p. 121.
3. N. Perrin, *Jesus and the Language of the Kingdom* (Philadelphia: Fortress, 1976) p. 29ff.

message of the Gospel. The hope is that if our minds are schooled in the Gospel, if our hearts are formed by the message and values of Jesus, God's rule will quicken in our damaged world.

The call of the first disciples   1:16-20

[16] As Jesus passed along the Sea of Galilee, he saw Simon and his brother Andrew casting a net into the sea – for they were fishermen. [17]And Jesus said to them, 'Follow me and I will make you fish for people.' [18]And immediately they left their nets and followed him. [19]As he went a little farther, he saw James son of Zebedee and his brother John, who were in their boat mending the nets. [20]Immediately he called them; and they left their father Zebedee in the boat with the hired men, and followed him.

When Jesus first speaks in Mark's Gospel, he makes an announcement about the arrival of the kingdom of God and a general call to repent and believe the good news (1:14-15). Jesus' general call now leads to the particular call of four individuals, two sets of brothers, Simon and Andrew, James and John, who are called into the service of the kingdom. The Galilean rural setting of the story is noteworthy, reflecting as it does the preference of the itinerant Jesus to conduct his ministry in the open air. This is in dramatic contrast to the final conflict that will take place in the city of Jerusalem, where Jesus will be condemned by the principal religious and political institutions.

As Jesus found John the Baptist not in the Temple but in the wilderness by the river Jordan, so he finds his first disciples not in a religious sanctuary but in the open country by the sea of Galilee. They are Galilean fishermen, actively engaged in their normal round of daily work, fishing and mending nets, when they are interrupted by a stranger's imperative.

Once Jesus is introduced to the reader at the baptism and the master theme of the ministry is announced, Mark as narrator wastes no time in moving the story forward. Unlike Luke's measured style, he does not explain why Jesus of Nazareth chooses his followers by the lakeside rather than in the hills of lower Galilee; nor does he give the prospective disciples time to see for themselves the power of Jesus at work in their own neighbourhood. Unlike John, Mark makes no previous connection between those first called and the Baptist's circle of followers, preferring to focus on the compelling call of Jesus himself. Mark's account displays no interest in biographical or psychological details, concentrating instead on Jesus' ability to summon ready and absolute allegiance. Nevertheless, as Donald Senior observes:

> The process that drew the disciples to Jesus was probably more extensive and built on a developing relationship to him ... It is obvious that, as always, the gospel accounts have one eye on Christian life and commitment. The reaction of the disciples models what the response of each Christian is to be to the gospel.[4]

In Mark's scene Jesus is the only one who speaks. In the first encounter he calls Simon and Andrew to follow him, at the same time making them a promise – literally, 'I will make you become fishers of men.' They are called not to an insular community whose principal devotion is self-improvement, but to an apostolic community founded in personal attachment to Jesus. Their new identity as disciples entails a new direction in life, which will, in time, involve a share in the mission of Jesus. Appropriately, their first response is summarised by what they do: immediately, they leave behind their nets, the secure means of their livelihood, to invest their unknown future in Jesus.

In the second interaction, when Jesus sees James and John he calls them immediately – that is, without any preparation. Mark notes the people they leave behind, their father and the hired men, as if to emphasise how the cost of discipleship is told in renunciation of family and working relationships. Not just things have to be left behind. This is reminiscent of the call of Elisha, who leaves his plough, kills the oxen he has been following, and takes leave of his family: after cutting these ties, he sets out to follow Elijah (1 Kgs 19:19-21) and remains with him until his ascension. The story of new attachment inevitably involves other stories of separation and loss.

Jesus takes the initiative in choosing his own, a move that runs counter to the normal pattern of rabbi/disciple or philosopher/ student association. In Judaism the prospective disciple would seek out the rabbi, attach himself to him for the purpose of studying the

4. D. Senior, *Jesus: a Gospel Portrait* (New York: Paulist, 1992) p. 52.

Torah, and prepare himself for the day when he would become a rabbi himself. Jesus summons his disciples not to study the Torah but to follow him and become part of his mission. Seán Freyne writes:

> In addition, abandonment of home – one of the traditional places for learning torah – was also part of Jesus' life-style for himself and his close retinue. Thus, to the extent that an explicit teaching role must be ascribed to Jesus, a new centre for learning had to be provided that was neither the home nor the synagogue, and this is the function that the permanent band of disciple-companions actually fulfils around him.[5]

The new community that Jesus calls to follow him will, therefore, be the school for learning the message of the kingdom of God.

In writing the story of the beginnings of discipleship in such a spare way, Mark highlights the important points that hold for all time: the authority of Jesus' word and the response of discipleship in attachment to him and his mission. More particular issues, such as biography or personal differences or individual feelings, however interesting, are excluded from the narrative, not least because they might limit *our* imagination as readers in associating ourselves with such a venture. Discipleship is clearly not limited to Galileans and fishermen: it is open to all who hear the challenge of Jesus to come after him, be formed in his outlook and values, and, from that basis of personal affinity, reach out to others in his name.

The authority of Jesus   1:21-28

[21] They went to Capernaum; and when the sabbath came, he entered the synagogue and taught. [22]They were astounded at his teaching, for he taught them as one having authority, and not as the scribes. [23]Just then there was in their synagogue a man with an unclean spirit, [24]and he cried out, 'What have you to do with us, Jesus of Nazareth? Have you come to destroy us? I know who you are, the Holy One of God.'' [25]But Jesus rebuked him, saying, 'Be silent and come out of him!' [26]And the unclean spirit, convulsing him and crying with a loud voice, came out of him. [27]They were all amazed, and they kept on asking one another, 'What is this? A new teaching – with authority! He commands even the unclean spirits, and they obey him.' [28]At once his fame began to spread

5. S. Freyne, *Galilee, Jesus and the Gospels* (Dublin: Gill and Macmillan, 1988) p. 250.

throughout the surrounding region of Galilee.

Jesus and his newly chosen followers come into Capernaum, which Matthew calls 'his own town' (Mt 9:1). Capernaum as Jesus' chosen base for his Galilean ministry enjoys multiple attestation among the Gospels. The original Semitic name of the settlement was *Kepar Nahum* (the village of Nahum), which is located on the north-west shore of the lake of Galilee, about three miles from the upper Jordan river. It was a border town along the main imperial highway leading to Damascus, a customs-post between the tetrachy of Herod Antipas and the Golan across the river, a territory assigned to Philip. Whereas Nazareth was an isolated hamlet in the hills of lower Galilee, Capernaum was a commercial centre beside the lake, a cross-road for many travellers, a home to fishermen, farmers, merchants, tax-collectors and soldiers. By all accounts, Capernaum was a promising place for Jesus to make a beginning.

Jesus begins his teaching ministry in the local synagogue, which Luke says was built by a Roman centurion sympathetic to the Jewish people (Lk 7:5). From 1968 until 1985 the Franciscan archaeologists Virgilio Corbo and Stanislao Loffreda worked on the excavations of Capernaum. During the restoration of the late fourth century synagogue, built from white limestone, they exposed the areas surrounding the white synagogue and cut several trenches inside the building. Their excavations revealed a magnificent find as Loffreda explains:

> Both Fr. Corbo and the writer agree that the very large stone pavement of the first century A.D. uncovered beneath the central nave of the white synagogue does belong to the long-looked for synagogue built by the Roman centurion and visited by Jesus.[6]

The synagogue visited by Jesus, like others of its kind, functioned as a meeting place for the neighbourhood, not unlike a small town hall. It also served as the local school. Its principal use, however, was as a prayer hall where people assembled on the sabbath to hear the scriptures and pray. Unlike the Temple, it was

---

6. S. Loffreda, *Recovering Capharnaum* (Jerusalem: Edizioni Custodia Terra Santa, 1985) p.45; see also V. Corbo, 'Capernaum,' *The Anchor Bible Dictionary* Vol 1 pp. 866-869.

not a place of solemn ritual or sacrificial worship presided over by priests. The synagogue was managed by a small committee of laymen, a group of elders, who elected a leader to oversee the smooth running of the community, a task that included appointing local judges and teachers. Anyone judged fit by the synagogue leader could officiate at the services, which began with prayers, moved into a reading from the scriptures and an exposition, and ended with final prayers and a blessing.

The story of Jesus' visit to the synagogue begins Mark's account of the first full day of ministry in Capernaum (1:21-34). Although Mark tells us that Jesus teaches, he says nothing of the content of the teaching: he is clearly more interested in noting the impression Jesus makes and the excitement he generates among the people. The effect of Jesus' instruction is that his listeners are astounded because, unlike the scribes, Jesus teaches with authority. The scribes, who were the acknowledged experts in Jewish Law and guardians of the tradition, are used as a foil to show Jesus to advantage. Mark invites us to look at Jesus through the reaction of his first congregation: Jesus is the one who exercises a unique authority.

As readers, however, we know more than the participants in the story. We know that Jesus' authority emerges from his unique identity as the Son of God. That authority is now illustrated in his command over the unclean spirit, a charge that makes no use of magical incantations. Apart from ourselves as readers, the demons are the only ones who know right from the start of the ministry the true identity of Jesus as the Holy One of God (1:24) and as the Son of God (3:11). In both cases the disclosure of the demons echoes what is said by the voice from heaven at the baptism and the transfiguration. Curiously, it is the demons who acknowledge the supremacy of Jesus, but, as Räisänen points outs, 'the focus of attention is the content of the confession, not those who are making the confession.'[7] In Mark's account Jesus silences the demons because he does not want his true identity to be revealed, although there is no indication in this passage why it should remain a secret.

Interestingly, the participants in the story are no wiser about

7. H. Räisänen, *The 'Messianic Secret' in Mark's Gospel* (Edinburgh: T&T Clark, 1990) p. 172.

Jesus' identity after the exorcism: there is no suggestion that they hear the demon's confession, even though it is exclaimed in the synagogue before Jesus' command to silence. Mark focuses on the people's amazement that Jesus teaches not just with wisdom but with power: 'A new teaching – with authority!' The amazement is not that Jesus performs an exorcism – that form of ministry was neither uncommon nor particularly remarkable at the time – but that *Jesus' own word carries its own authority*. Thus, Mark says, Jesus' fame begins to spread throughout the surrounding region. The gathering renown is not because of who Jesus is but because of the singular command of his word.

Jesus heals many people and moves on   1:29-39

[29] As soon as they left the synagogue, they entered the house of Simon and Andrew, with James and John. [30]Now Simon's mother-in-law was in bed with a fever, and they told him about her at once. [31]He came and took her by the hand and lifted her up. Then the fever left her, and she began to serve them.

[32]That evening, at sundown, they brought to him all who were sick or possessed with demons. [33]And the whole city was gathered around the door. [34]And he cured many who were sick with various diseases, and cast out many demons: and he would not permit the demons to speak, because they knew him.

[35] In the morning, while it was still very dark, he got up and went out to a deserted place, and there he prayed. [36]And Simon and his companions hunted for him. [37]When they found him, they said to him, 'Everyone is searching for you.' [38]He answered, 'Let us go on to the neighboring towns, so that I may proclaim the message there also; for that is what I came out to do.' [39]And he went throughout Galilee, proclaiming the message in their synagogues and casting out demons.

Mark's story now moves from the drama of a public meeting place to the intimacy of a domestic scene. After Jesus' authority is revealed in the synagogue at Capernaum, he goes with his four chosen disciples to the house of Simon and Andrew. This is the house where Jesus will be at home in Capernaum (Mk 2:1; 3:20; 9:33), his chosen base during the course of his Galilean ministry.

During the excavations in Capernaum in 1968 the house of Simon Peter was rediscovered, situated some thirty metres south of the synagogue. The living quarters of the house, like the others excavated in the town, consisted of small roofed rooms clustered around an inner courtyard. The common courtyard, which was entered from the street through a single doorway, was normally shared by two or more kindred families living together. Loffreda, one of the archaeologists working on the excavations, writes that the identification of the house is based on the combination of archaeological data and literary sources, and he summarises the former in this way:

> (1) the house was built in the Late Hellenistic period; (2) in the late first century A.D. it was changed into a 'domus-ecclesia', i.e. became a house for religious gatherings; (3) in the fourth century A.D. the same 'domus-ecclesia' was enlarged and was set apart from the rest of the town through an imposing enclosure wall; (4) in the second half of the fifth century A.D. an octagonal church was built on the house of St. Peter and remained in use until the seventh century.[8]

The clan dwelling uncovered at Capernaum would have been home for the extended family of Simon and Andrew, and also served as a temporary home for the itinerant Jesus. Inside the house the mother-in-law of Simon is confined to bed with a fever, and when Jesus is told of her personal suffering he goes to her.

In the previous scene Jesus liberated the demoniac by the power of his command; now he cures the sick woman by the power of his touch. No spoken word is reported, no special technique is employed, no dramatic reaction is recorded. There is only the simple gesture of human touch as Jesus lifts her by the hand. That contact with him makes her well again. The silence in the scene is palpable; the spareness of the writing provides its own scenery. For a moment it is as if the world is suddenly reduced to a tableau of two people, a man and a woman, the willing healer and the fevered sufferer. And as Jesus put his power at her service, she promptly repays the compliment by putting her renewed self at the service of Jesus and his disciples.

As this memorable day closes, the whole town of Capernaum flocks to Simon's house. The Jewish day was measured from sunset to sunset, so sundown on the sabbath is a signal for the pious Jews of the town to bring their sick to Jesus. They have no patience

8. S. Loffreda, *Recovering Capharnaum* p. 51.

to wait until dawn. The earlier exorcism of the demoniac in the synagogue has established Jesus as a man of authority who can command even the evil spirits. Now sickness and possession and hope make a strange night-time procession through the streets of the town to the house and there they press around the door. The expectant crowds meet a willing Jesus who ministers to their various needs.

For Mark, the whole ministry of exorcism is a dramatic illustration of how Jesus attacks the power structure of evil. Jesus' announcement of the kingdom involves opposition to the forces that threaten and destroy human life. Mark notes that Jesus prevents the demons from speaking because they knew him. Their recognition, however accurate, can be understood only by the reader. As for the participants in the story, they can come to recognise the identity of Jesus only when his *destiny* is fulfilled. Only after Jesus dies on the cross will a human being make the one and only true confession of Jesus in Mark's Gospel (15:39).

It is still dark, even though it is now morning, when Jesus leaves the house and goes to a lonely place, to be by himself and pray. After the previous scene of intense ministry, Jesus finds his temporary wilderness away from the pressing needs of the crowds. This is one of the few occasions in the Gospel where we see Jesus alone. He is rarely to be found far from people, and he is now tracked down by Simon and his companions. Simon is already prominent among the disciples, although Mark does not call them disciples in this scene, perhaps because they have come not to follow Jesus but to persuade him to return to the town. The people's need is not wholly satisfied, and the disciples voice their reproach on behalf of the people: 'Everyone is searching for you.'

Jesus, however, has other places to go, other promises to keep. The crowds in Capernaum are attracted to Jesus as a miracle-worker, but Jesus refuses to be distracted from his principal goal of proclaiming the message. For that purpose he has already left Capernaum, and he now calls the disciples to do likewise and follow him. Jesus moves on. He will neither be held by success nor kept by kindness; his mission takes him on a preaching tour throughout the region of Galilee.

Jesus cleanses a leper   1:40-45

[40] A leper came to him begging him, and kneeling he said to him, 'If you choose, you can make me clean.' [41] Moved with pity, Jesus stretched out his hand and touched him, and said to him, 'I do choose. Be made clean!' [42] Immediately the leprosy left him, and he was made clean. [43] After sternly warning him he sent him away at once, [44] saying to him, 'See that you say nothing to anyone; but go, show yourself to the priest, and offer for your cleansing what Moses commanded, as a testimony to them.' [45] But he went out and began to proclaim it freely, and to spread the word, so that Jesus could no longer go into a town openly, but stayed out in the country; and people came to him from every quarter.

After mentioning Jesus' preaching tour of Galilee, Mark now tells the story of Jesus cleansing a leper. There are no personal or place-names in the terse account, and there is no obvious connection with the surrounding context of the first two chapters. It was probably an isolated unit of oral tradition which Mark has chosen to insert here. Since the story begins with an interruption, and since interruptions by definition break in on what is planned, the story is as well placed here as anywhere else.

Leprosy was a comprehensive term that covered a wide variety of skin diseases, including eczema and psoriasis, and was not used with much medical precision. In chapters thirteen and fourteen of Leviticus, which include the priestly decrees on the subject, the Hebrew word also refers to fungal growth or mould on personal clothing, on fabric, and on the walls of houses.[9] The legislation is clear about protecting the community from unwanted contact with lepers: 'The person who has the leprous disease shall wear torn clothes and let the hair of his head be dishevelled; and he shall cover his upper lip and cry out "Unclean, unclean." ... He shall live alone; his dwelling shall be outside the camp.'(Lev 13:45-46)

In Mark's account a leper comes to Jesus. Rather than shouting 'Unclean, unclean,' he begs Jesus to make him clean. He does not address Jesus by any title, although he believes that Jesus has the power to cleanse him. The language of his kneeling posture indicates a mixture of reverence, desperation and hope. 'If you choose, you can make me clean,' he says. The leper has no doubt that Jesus has the power to cure him; but he wonders if Jesus has the

9. See J. Wilkinson, 'Leprosy and Leviticus: A Problem of Semantics and Translation,' *Scottish Journal of Theology* 31 (1987) pp. 153-166.

will to do it. In our translation it says Jesus was 'moved with pity', whereas some ancient manuscripts read 'moved with anger'. Most modern scholars opt for the more difficult version – that Jesus was moved with anger – on the grounds that it fits well with the harshness of verse 43 and, further, it seems more likely that Christian copyists would have changed anger to pity rather than vice-versa. It would also explain why Matthew and Luke, reading 'anger' in the Marcan text, dropped any mention of Jesus' emotions from their accounts (Mt 8:3; Lk 5:13). The New English Bible tries to compromise, reading Jesus' reaction as 'warm indignation'; but while this phrase might unite conflicting textual sources, it is difficult to see what warm indignation would look like even on a clear day.

Whatever Jesus is angry about, it does not distract him from his willingness to cure the leper. He stretches out his hand and touches the afflicted man, making direct contact with uncleanness. Jesus declares his choice to heal the man and then speaks him better with the power of his word. The language becomes stronger again as Mark writes about what Jesus does next: *embrimsamenas*, which the NRSV translates as 'sternly warning him'. This translation lacks the emotional agitation of Mark's choice of language. As Taylor writes: 'Strong feeling which "boils over" and finds expression appears to be indicated.'[10] Thus Jesus is angry again as he sends the cured man on his way with a command to be silent and to go and show himself to the priest.

Although Jesus' word of cure cleanses the leper immediately, his word of command makes no difference to the cured man, for he broadcasts what has happened freely. We are not told if he goes to the priest to offer his cure as testimony. Jesus' command to silence is not automatically effective; in fact it is instantly ignored. Mark explains that Jesus pays a price for the cured man's disobedience, for the fame of Jesus as a miracle-worker now becomes his handicap. Ironically, the leper is now free to go anywhere he pleases and say anything he likes; Jesus is the one who now stays out in the country, away from the community. It is as if, in some curious way, their roles are reversed.

We can only guess at why Jesus was angry. It seems reasonable

10. V. Taylor, *The Gospel according to St. Mark* p. 188.

to suppose that if he believed his principal message of the kingdom was carried through preaching, people's stubborn focus on his miracle-working outside that context would make him angry. No amount of Jesus' healing is going to exempt people from experiencing pain or enduring suffering: to believe otherwise is dangerous foolishness, not least for Mark's readers. Mark will soon show how the Son of Man will illustrate that in his own experience when he endures unavoidable suffering for the sake of the kingdom.

Conflict about forgiveness   2:1-12

2:1 When he returned to Capernaum after some days, it was reported that he was at home. [2]So many gathered around that there was no longer room for them not even in front of the door; and he was speaking the word to them. [3]Then some people came, bringing to him a paralyzed man, carried by four of them. [4]And when they could not bring him to Jesus because of the crowd, they removed the roof above him; and after having dug through it, they let down the mat on which the paralytic lay. [5]When Jesus saw their faith, he said to the paralytic, 'Son, your sins are forgiven.' [6]Now some of the scribes were sitting there, questioning in their hearts, [7]'Why does this fellow speak in this way? It is blasphemy! Who can forgive sins but God alone?' [8]At once Jesus perceived in his spirit that they were discussing these questions among themselves; and he said to them, 'Why do you raise such questions in your hearts? [9]Which is easier, to say to the paralytic. 'Your sins are forgiven,' or to say, 'Stand up and take your mat and walk'? [10]But so that you may know that the Son of Man has authority on earth to forgive sins' – he said to the paralytic – [11]'I say to you, stand up, take your mat and go to your home.' [12]And he stood up, and immediately took the mat and went out before all of them; so that they were all amazed and glorified God, saying, 'We have never seen anything like this!'

In the preceding chapter Mark established Jesus' identity for the reader and his authority as a teacher and healer. Neither Jesus' authority as a teacher nor his effectiveness as a healer leads the participants in the story to insight about who he is; if anything, his fame as a miracle-worker becomes a hindrance to his preaching ministry, so that he ends up in hiding (1:45). Mark now moves his story from the suspect enthusiasm of the crowds to the gathering opposition of their leaders. This he does through five stories of conflict (2:1-3:6). It seems probable that the conflict stories were originally compiled according to their subject matter; and while they don't reflect historical sequence, they do move the Gospel story on to a new level, that of opposition to Jesus. By the end of the section, the Pharisees will be scheming with the Herodians to destroy Jesus (3:6).

The first conflict story involves the healing of the paralytic and a debate with the scribes on the subject of forgiveness. When Jesus returns to Capernaum after his preaching tour of Galilee, the report quickly spreads that he is 'at home' – presumably at Peter's house. What follows is a vivid and colourful account, its very strangeness recommending it as a story fixed in the community's memory of Jesus' ministry. As Jesus preaches the word, so many people gather in a crush that the entrance to the house is obstructed. A small procession of hopefuls arrives on the scene, bringing a paralytic who is carried by four of their number. There is no access to Jesus. The four stretcher-bearers seem to be blessed with lateral thinking as well as faith: since they cannot bring the paralytic through to Jesus, they decide to bring him down to Jesus. Thus they assault the roof.

While working on the excavations of the houses in Capernaum, the archaeologist Loffreda wrote:

> The private houses so far excavated are rather unpretentious but by no means poor, at least according to the living standard of an ancient village ... Local volcanic basalt stones in their natural state were used to build walls and pavements. Walls were built without true foundations, and the one storey rooms could hardly reach more than 3 m in height, judging from the several staircases leading to the roof ... Light roofs made of wooden beams and of beaten earth mixed with straw covered the squat rooms, and they were reached from open courtyards through a flight of stone steps.[11]

This description helps us to visualise Mark's scene.

The determined supporters of the paralytic start digging through the roof for access, no doubt showering everyone underneath with dry mud and straw; they then lower the mat on which their afflicted friend is lying. Mission completed. The first thing Jesus sees is the faith of the determined foursome, which he rewards by saying to the paralytic, 'Son, your sins are forgiven.'

11. S. Loffreda, *Recovering Capharnaum* p. 20.

That word of forgiveness provides the setting for the ensuing conflict. Mark's story now changes key and shifts into a controversy about who can forgive sins. Denis Nineham observes:

> In its present form the story clearly contains artificial elements. The scribes do not voice their feelings; Jesus is represented as discerning them by supernatural insight, but how was St Mark able to formulate them so precisely? Clearly, they are in fact *representative* Jewish reactions to the Christian claim that sins could be forgiven by, and in the name of, Jesus.[12]

The basic argument of the scribes, whose teaching authority has already been compared unfavourably to that of Jesus (1:22), is that no one can forgive sins but God alone. Curiously, the majority of commentators on this passage agree with the scribes, presented here as the *opponents* of Jesus, although Jesus is seen to be rejecting their teaching that forgiveness of sins is exclusively limited to God. The scribes in Mark are hardly making a point about the divinity of Jesus despite themselves. If forgiveness of sins is proof of divinity, why does Jesus extend the power to forgive sins to his followers? From the earliest times in the church, not only the apostles but the whole Christian community were involved in disciplining and forgiving sins (Mt 18:17; Jn 20:23; 1 Cor 5:1-13; 2 Cor 2:5-11; Jas 5:16; 1 Jn 5:16). Doubtless they did not consider they were committing blasphemy.

Jesus poses a question to his opponents: 'Which is easier, to say to the paralytic, "Your sins are forgiven," or to say, "Stand up and take your mat and walk?" ' The argument is set in terms of easy-difficult, thereby rejecting the scribes' claim that the forgiveness of sins is impossible for a human being. Jesus then does the more difficult task (healing the paralytic) in order to show that the easier task (forgiveness of sins) can indeed be done by him and, by implication, those who are willing to forgive. As G. McCauley comments: 'What Jesus refuses to collude in is the pretence that God's forgiving is so closely guarded that we can never imitate it or embody it in ourselves.'[13]

Jesus has already pronounced a word of forgiveness over the

---

12. D.E. Nineham, *Saint Mark* (London: Penguin, 1969) p. 91.
13. G. McCauley, *The Unfinished Image* (New York: Sadlier, 1983) p. 254.

paralytic but he wants to prove that his word is real. He speaks a new word, commanding the paralytic to stand up, lift up his mat and go home. When Jesus' word is seen to take immediate effect, everyone is amazed because they have never witnessed anything like this before. Because they can see that the man has been restored to health, they believe that he has also been restored to God by the forgiving word of Jesus. Jesus as Son of Man is seen to exercise the power to heal and the power to forgive.

And as Mark's community and readers know, neither of those powers disappeared from the face of the earth after Jesus; both are exercised in the name of Jesus by his followers.

Conflict about associating with sinners   2:13-17

[13] Jesus went out again beside the sea; the whole crowd gathered around him, and he taught them. [14] As he was walking along, he saw Levi son of Alphaeus sitting at the tax booth, and he said to him, 'Follow me.' And he got up and followed him.

[15] And as he sat at dinner in Levi's house, many tax collectors and sinners were also sitting with Jesus and his disciples – for there were many who followed him. [16] When the scribes of the Pharisees saw that he was eating with sinners and tax collectors, they said to his disciples, 'Why does he eat with tax collectors and sinners?' [17] When Jesus heard this, he said to them, 'Those who are well have no need of a physician, but those who are sick; I have come to call not the righteous but sinners.'

The scene now changes from Peter's house to a location outdoors by the sea of Galilee. In this summary statement Mark emphasises again that wherever Jesus goes – a deserted place, Peter's house, the seashore – the expectant crowds soon gather around him. Jesus' authority as a teacher of the common people, not his fame as a miracle-worker, is Mark's editorial link to the second conflict story.

The story of the call of Levi is reminiscent of the call of the first disciples by the lake (1:16-20). Again Jesus is seen to take the initiative in choosing and calling: there is no instance in the Synoptic tradition of an individual successfully volunteering to become a disciple. Like the first disciples, Levi is already engaged in his regular work, and, like them, his response is immediate and unconditional.

Since Galilee was not directly under the Roman prefect during the ministry of Jesus, Levi would have been a customs official in the service of Herod Antipas, the Jewish client king. In addition to the principal taxes, there were a number of indirect taxes, particularly on the transport of goods. Collection of the indirect taxes was subcontracted to officials like Zacchaeus, the chief tax collector (Lk 19:2), who would have employed others to collect the duties at toll booths or tax offices. These toll booths were situated at commercial centres, such as Jericho, or transport centres at border crossings, such as Capernaum. Presumably Levi's workplace would have been in Capernaum, which was a border town on the great road that ran south from Damascus through Capernaum to Caesarea on the Mediterranean.

Interestingly, when John the Baptist preaches to tax collectors (Lk 3:12-13) he tells them to collect no more than is appointed – which suggests they were well known for their lucrative arithmetic. When Jesus calls Levi, whose occupation meant that he was a professional sinner and excluded from the synagogue, there is not a word about repentance, making restitution, or conforming his life to the Law. The tax collector leaves whatever he is doing and attaches himself to Jesus. Whoever Levi is, his identification with Matthew (Mt 9:9) is supported neither by Mark nor Luke. He is absent from Mark's list of the twelve (3:16-19), and his name is never mentioned in the Gospel again.

The scene shifts to dinner at Levi's house. The new disciple's guest list makes for a strange concoction: Jesus, his disciples, tax collectors and sinners. That irreligious mix, all eating together, leads the Pharisees to ask Jesus' disciples: 'Why does he eat with tax collectors and sinners?'

The name 'Pharisees' comes from the Hebrew word *Perushim*, which means 'the separated ones' – those who separated themselves from sinners and ritual impurity. Many Pharisees were *soferim*, scholars or scribes not only of the Law but also of the oral traditions, which detailed the requirements of the sabbath, the dietary laws, the ritual laws of purity, and the regulations for tithing. Mark's phrase 'the scribes of the Pharisees' refers to the scholars of the Pharisaic party. The Pharisees' dedication to being separate also expressed itself in *haveroth*, in a table fellowship of friends. Both Jesus and the Pharisees believed that sharing a meal meant fellowship with God and with those who share the blessings of God. But whereas the Pharisees' table fellowship was limited to those whose lives were morally upright, Jesus' table fellowship was extended to all as a messianic symbol of God who cherishes all and graces all equally.

The Pharisees object that Jesus eats with tax collectors and sinners. The term 'sinners' refers to those who have flagrantly and persistently disobeyed the Law and have not repented; it is not, as some commentators argue, a synonym for the common people. The idea that the Pharisees regarded the common people as sinners because they were uneducated, therefore unable even to know the minutiae of the Law, is a Christian caricature unsupported by rabbinical evidence. Ritual impurity was not a sin. E.P. Sanders comments:

> Jesus saw his mission as being to the 'the lost' and the 'sinners': that is, to the wicked. He was doubtless also concerned with the poor, the meek and the downtrodden, and in all probability he had a following among them. But the charge against him was not that he loved the *'amme ha-arets*, the common people. If there was a conflict, it was about the status of the *wicked*. It is a mistake to think that the Pharisees were upset because he ministered to the ordinary pious common people and the economically impoverished.[14]

As Mark outlines in this story, it is Jesus' ready association with the tax collectors and sinners, in particular his table fellowship with them, that the Pharisees find offensive.

Jesus' defence of his behaviour is the proverbial saying that just as the sick, not the healthy, need the attendance of a doctor, so sinners, not the righteous, are going to receive his attention. Rather than wait for sinners to approach him, Jesus the physician reaches out to them by holding a mobile surgery in different towns and villages, on the open road, by the lakeside, in people's houses, wherever he sees the need.

The difference between Jesus and the Pharisees is not their pastoral attitude to sinners but their pastoral strategy in dealing with them. His practice is association, not separation; closeness,

14. E.P. Sanders, *Jesus and Judaism* (London: SCM, 1985) p. 179.

not distance. In his study of Pharisaism, Abrahams writes: 'There was in the Pharisaism of all ages a real anxiety to make the return of the sinner easy, though it was inclined to leave the initiative to the sinner, except that it always maintained God's readiness to take the first step.'[15] Jesus shares the concern of the Pharisees for sinners, but, unlike them, he decides to take the first step himself.

The offence that Jesus gives in eating with sinners is reflected elsewhere in the Gospels (Mt 11:19 par; Lk 15:3; 19:7). Jesus causes offence by reversing the accepted sequence that repentance must precede forgiveness, that forgiveness and restitution must precede table fellowship. For Jesus, table fellowship is not *a reward* for conversion but *a way* to associate with him. It is a gift that is first offered, with no conditions attached.

From the tradition there is a strong memory that Jesus had a truly catholic taste for table companions, making him the most indiscriminate host/guest in the biblical tradition. Behind his pastoral practice is the radical belief that unrestricted table fellowship is the best way of associating with people who might otherwise remain aloof not only from organised religion but from God's offer of salvation. Table fellowship breaks through moral and religious barriers; it opens up new possibilities; it provides a human context for revelation and forgiveness; it creates a natural sanctuary where people can experience the reign of God in their lives. It is little wonder that table fellowship becomes an activity forever associated with Jesus. It is his way of calling sinners.

Conflict about fasting
2:18-22

[18]Now John's disciples and the Pharisees were fasting; and people came and said to him, 'Why does John's disciples and the disciples of the Pharisees fast but your disciples do not fast?' [19]Jesus said to them, 'The wedding guests cannot fast while the bridegroom is with them, can they? As long as they have the bridegroom with them they cannot fast. [20] The days will come when the bridegroom is taken away from them, and then they will fast on that day.

[21] 'No one sews a piece of unshrunk cloth on an old cloak; otherwise the patch pulls away from it, the new from the old and a worse tear is made. [22]And no one puts new wine into old wineskins; otherwise, the

15. I. Abrahams, *Studies in Pharisaism and the Gospels* (New York: KTAV, 1967) p. 58.

wine will burst the skins, and the wine is lost, and so are the skins; but one puts new wine into fresh wineskins.'

In the previous passage Jesus was feasting at the house of Levi with tax collectors and sinners and was criticised by the Pharisees. Now, in this third conflict story, there is further ground for complaint, this time on the subject of fasting. Jesus is asked by an unidentified group of people to explain why his disciples do not fast like the disciples of John and the Pharisees. Fasting on the Day of Atonement (*Yom Kippur*) was required by the Law (Lev 16:29), and while other commemorative fasts were observed by pious Jews, these were not a matter of obligation. In all likelihood, the fasting mentioned here refers to voluntary ascetic practice.

Most commentators agree that the reference to the Pharisees was added to the story before Mark wrote the Gospel, when the incident was included in a collection of conflict stories illustrating the rupture between Jesus and the religious authorities. Probably the original comparison was between the disciples of John and the disciples of Jesus, just as elsewhere in the Gospels the different lifestyles of the two leaders are summarised as penitential fasting for John and feasting with sinners for Jesus: John is criticised for being too abstemious to be sane while Jesus is criticised for being too unrestrained to be upright (Mt 11:16-19 par). In Mark's passage the questioners' presumption is that the disciples of Jesus will follow the ascetic style set by John the Baptist – further testimony, it would appear, of the perceived influence of John as the mentor of Jesus.

In Stage 3 of the tradition (see Introduction) Mark is writing at a time when the Christian community does fast: he has to explain why their practice of fasting is the opposite of what Jesus' disciples practised in Stage 1 of the tradition. In Mark's story Jesus replies to the questioners with a brief parable. Since weddings are occasions for rejoicing, it would be wholly inappropriate for the guests to fast during the celebrations, when the bridegroom is still with them. According to Mark, the presence of Jesus marks the time of the joyful marriage feast of the Messiah with Israel; therefore it would be unthinkable that Jesus' disciples, the friends of the bridegroom, should show signs of sorrow or mourning in the presence of the bridegroom.

The bridegroom will not always be with his friends. If the presence of the bridegroom means freedom from fasting, his physical absence cancels that freedom. Verse 20 is a veiled reference to the violent death of Jesus, 'when the bridegroom is taken away from them'. This is probably a Christian composition, justifying the different practice of Mark's community who fast in the physical absence of Jesus. It is improbable that the historical Jesus made this prophecy – not because it was impossible for him, but because he could not have expected his listeners to make any sense of a future change of fasting based on his death. It does make sense, however, to believe that the historical Jesus distinguished his disciples from all other groups by supporting their freedom from voluntary fasting, a freedom based on sharing his joyful presence. This special freedom is discontinuous both with Jewish tradition and Christian practice.

In Mark's passage there is a memory of the first disciples' freedom and the necessary recognition that Christians now live in a different time. As E. Schillebeeckx comments:

> The tone of the passage is heart-rending: when Jesus was still there – it is saying – they could not fast, they were in no position to do that: because of Jesus' living presence. The non-fasting of the disciples at that time was in no way a juridical dispensation from fasting, but a question of being existentially unable to do otherwise. In these words are revealed something of the enchantment and the power exercised upon them by the living Jesus of Nazareth. The Christian tradition has preserved this memory with the utmost care; for apart from that spell-binding quality Christianity would never have become a fact of history.[16]

Mark's message is that Jesus has introduced in his person and ministry a radically new change. The double parable of the patch and the wineskins, which has no connection to the tradition about fasting, serves to illustrate the incompatible differences between the old ways and the new (2:21-22). To follow Jesus is to do something new and unprecedented. It is not simply a matter of patching up the old, however new the patch; nor is it about

16. E. Schillebeeckx, *Jesus: an Experiment in Christology* (London: Collins, 1979) pp. 204-205.

squandering a new spirit in old containers, however well they have served in the past. The values of Jesus cannot simply be used to repair the old institution or their ways. In this case, bringing the old and the new together does not work. The old must give way to the new.

Conflict about working on the sabbath   2:23-28

²³One sabbath he was going through the grainfields; and as they made their way his disciples began to pluck heads of grain. ²⁴The Pharisees said to him, 'Look, why are they doing what is not lawful on the sabbath?' ²⁵And he said to them, 'Have you never read what David did when he and his companions were hungry and in need of food? ²⁶He entered the house of God, when Abiathar was high priest, and ate the bread of the Presence, which it is not lawful for any but the priests to eat, and he gave some to his companions.' ²⁷Then he said to them, 'The sabbath was made for humankind, and not humankind for the sabbath; ²⁸so the Son of Man is lord even of the sabbath.'

The fourth conflict story in this series focuses on a dispute between Jesus and the Pharisees about the disciples' behaviour on the sabbath. Elsewhere the Gospels tell us of Jesus' established custom of going to the synagogue each sabbath (Mk 1:21; 3:1; Lk 4:16 etc), honouring his people's tradition to keep the day holy. The fourth commandment of the Decalogue (Ex 20:8-11; Deut 5:12-15) enjoins rest on the people. In Exodus the original motivation is because the creator God rested on the seventh day, thus making the sabbath sacred for *human beings*; in Deuteronomy it is because God redeemed *his people* from slavery and the sabbath is thus observed as a sacred memory of that liberation.

The understanding of the sabbath in the Book of the Covenant (Ex 20:22-23:33) develops the idea of a sacred covenant between God and his people. Later instructions declare, 'Six days shall work be done, but the seventh day is a sabbath of solemn rest, holy to the Lord; whoever does any work on the sabbath day shall be put to death.' (Ex 31:14). Interestingly, in Mark's narrative, it is after the second contravention of the sabbath law that the Pharisees join forces with the Herodians to plot the death of Jesus (3:6).

As Jesus and the disciples pass through cornfields on the sabbath, the disciples start plucking the ripe grains and eating them. Hungry travellers were allowed to do this by the Law, but doing it on the sabbath could be regarded as reaping, which was numbered among the thirty-nine types of work forbidden on the day of rest. The Pharisees, who happen to be there, lodge their complaint because they interpret the disciples' action to be contravening the sabbath. Their interpretation, however, does not necessarily mean a sabbath violation. As P.M. Casey has pointed out: 'the Pharisaic life-stance should not be confused with the whole of post-exilic Judaism. Most Jews did not belong to it: hence the action of Jesus' disciples in the first place.'[17]

The setting for the debate seems somewhat unreal: it hardly seems credible that the Pharisees organised themselves into groups to spend their sabbath in Galilean cornfields in the hope of catching people transgressing the sabbath laws. R. Bultmann observed that the disciples (representing the church) are criticised, not Jesus, and argued that the passage represents a Christian response to Jewish criticism.[18] Although there is no suggestion in the Gospels that the first day of the week should replace the sabbath, by the time the Gospels are written the Christian community has changed its holy day to the first day of the week, 'the Lord's day' (Rev 1:10), in celebration of the resurrection.

In Mark's story Jesus moves to defend his disciples by appealing to a scriptural precedent for the priority of human need over observance of the Law (1 Sam 21:1-6). When David and his friends were hungry, they ate the twelve loaves of bread that were laid out in the holy place in the tabernacle. Normally this holy bread would have been eaten by the priests after it had been replaced on the sabbath. Although the incident has nothing to do with the sabbath, the humanitarian need of such a respected person as David, and that of his companions, was acknowledged by the authorities as more pressing than honouring the niceties of ritual law.

Within the context of a *Jewish* dispute about sabbath observance, the claim that Jesus as Son of Man is lord of the sabbath is hardly an argument calculated to persuade the Pharisees. It does make sense as an argument to Mark's community and all who already believe that Jesus is Lord (*Kyrios*) of all. This supports the

17. P.M. Casey, 'Culture and Historicity: the Plucking of the Grain,' *New Testament Studies* 34 (1988) p. 19.
18. R. Bultmann, *The History of the Synoptic Tradition* (Oxford: Blackwell, 1963) p. 16.

earlier point that this passage originally came from the Jewish-Christian disputes in the early church. Mark outlines the *Christian* argument that if the sabbath was made for humankind (v.27), and Jesus is Lord of all that belongs to humankind, then Jesus is Lord of the sabbath.

Conflict about healing on the sabbath   3:1-6

Again he entered the synagogue, and a man was there who had a withered hand. [2]They watched him to see whether he would cure him on the sabbath so that they might accuse him. [3]And he said to the man who had the withered hand, 'Come forward.' [4]Then he said to them, 'Is it lawful to do good or to do harm on the sabbath, to save life or to kill?' But they were silent.[5]He looked around at them with anger; he was grieved at their hardness of heart and said to the man, 'Stretch out your hand.' He stretched it out, and his hand was restored. [6]The Pharisees went out and immediately conspired with the Herodians against him, how to destroy him.

In the previous passage Mark established Jesus' unique authority as lord of the sabbath. Now, in this final conflict story of the series, he illustrates that authority in recounting how Jesus deliberately provokes his opponents by healing in the synagogue on the sabbath day.

The Pharisees, again presented as the antagonists of Jesus, are in the synagogue, but they seem be there on their own surveillance mission, rather than for community prayer. They say nothing throughout the story, but play the part of silent watchers, on the lookout to see if Jesus will cure on the sabbath. They are primed for accusation. The rabbinical principle held that healing could be offered to sufferers on the sabbath only when they were in danger of death. The man with the withered hand is clearly not in danger of his life, so he can perfectly well wait a day until the sabbath is over. In this story he seems prepared to do that, since he makes no request of Jesus to heal him. It is Jesus' initiative, not a sufferer's request, which sparks the open conflict.

Jesus' response to the unspoken conflict is not to ignore it but to confront it boldly, to bring it to the centre of attention. He commands the afflicted man to come forward. Before healing him, Jesus addresses the point of healing on the sabbath by framing his question in such a way that it supposes doing good cannot contradict the purpose of the law: 'Is it lawful to do good or to do harm on the sabbath, to save life or to kill?' The supposition is that the sabbath was instituted not only for resting the body and reverencing God, but to do good and to save life. Contrariwise, to refuse to do good when it can be done is to do harm; to refuse to make life whole when it can be made whole is to kill. Jesus' accusers are silent, refusing to enter into a debate set on Jesus' chosen ground.

In the silence of the synagogue Jesus looks around with anger at his opponents. His anger at their stubborn silence is tempered by grief at their hardness of heart. He commands the man to stretch out his hand, and it is restored. The response to the healing is neither astonishment nor praise, but unrelieved hostility. The Pharisees leave the synagogue and make common cause with the supporters of Herod Antipas to destroy Jesus. Unlike Jesus, their sabbath agenda is to do evil.

Part of the function of this final conflict story is the foreshadowing of the passion. Mark's readers can interpret the last verse in the light of Jesus' whole story. In his study of the role of Jesus' opponents in Mark's Gospel, S.H. Smith notes about this passage:

> The passion-foreshadowing tendency becomes even more pronounced in 3:1-6 ... The intention to 'accuse' in 3:2 anticipates the actual accusation in 15:3; likewise, although the Pharisees and the Herodians may seem unlikely bedfellows, their resolution to 'take counsel' together under what Mark may understand as a political/religious alliance foreshadows the scene in 15:1 in which the result of 'taking counsel' there leads to the transfer of Jesus from the control of the religious to that of the political authorities.[19]

The five conflict stories (2:1-3:6) illustrate the hostility of the religious authorities to Jesus, a hostility that will culminate in his execution. These stories also mirror the hostile attitude of official Judaism to Mark's community. Informing all the stories is Mark's faith in the identity of Jesus and his unique authority, an authority Jesus exercises in favour of doing good. One thing Mark makes clear: Jesus' doing good is not an activity of such transparent

19. S.H. Smith, 'The Role of Jesus' Opponents in the Markan Drama,' *New Testament Studies* 35 (1989) p.168

probity that it receives ready recognition and approval from the religious authorities. Doing good is proving to be a dangerous affair, one that will have its inevitable end on the cross.

3

Rejection in Galilee

3:7-6:6a

In the previous section Mark described the beginning of Jesus' ministry in Galilee, how Jesus summoned his disciples and revealed himself as a teacher and healer, and how his unique authority met with growing opposition from the religious leaders. The note of hostility on which the section ended in now developed further. Mark begins this section with a summary statement of Jesus' popularity with the crowds and the story of the appointment of the twelve. These are followed by the negative response of Jesus' family and the scribes. A series of parables comes next, including Jesus' private teaching to his disciples, followed by a series of miracles that shows Jesus' power over nature, possession, disease and death. The section concludes with the rejection of Jesus by his own people of Nazareth.

Jesus and the crowds   3:7-12

[7]Jesus departed with his disciples to the sea and a great multitude from Galilee followed him; [8]hearing all that he was doing, they came to him in great numbers from Judea, Jerusalem, Idumea, beyond the Jordan, and the region around Tyre and Sidon. [9]He told his disciples to have a boat ready for him because of the crowd, so that they would not crush him; [10]for he had cured many, so that all who had diseases pressed upon him to touch him. [11]Whenever the unclean spirits saw him they fell down before him and shouted, 'You are the Son of God!' [12]But he sternly ordered them not to make him known.

In this summary statement, which comes after five conflict stories, Mark returns to the earlier themes of Jesus' popularity with the crowds and the recognition of his identity by the demons. Again Jesus is in the open air by the sea, but if he withdraws from houses and synagogues, he is not free from the press of the expectant crowds. The regional diversity of the great multitude who come to Jesus is an indication of his wide popularity. Referring to the renown of the Baptist, Mark wrote that 'people from the whole Judean countryside and all the people of Jerusalem were going out to him' (1:5). Clearly Mark now wishes to note that Jesus commands a wider geographical appeal.

Judea and Jerusalem are mentioned for the first time in relation to Jesus' ministry. To the south of Judea lay Idumea, which John Hyracanus 1 had captured in 169 B.C., forcing all the non-Jewish inhabitants to be circumcised: it was at this time that the ancestors of Herod the Great converted to Judaism. The region 'beyond the Jordan' refers to Perea, ruled by Herod Antipas; it was here that John the Baptist had his base for ministry. To the north of Galilee was Syro-Phoenicia, and although the coastal cities of Tyre and Sidon numbered Jews among the population, the territory was largely Gentile. Jesus' reputation has clearly spread beyond the confines of Galilee, and great crowds now gather by the lake.

Jesus cures many of them, and the throng of the diseased press forward to touch him. The crush is so hazardous that Jesus alerts his disciples to prepare a ready sanctuary in one of the boats. Amidst all this surge of need the only voice we hear as readers is that of the demons, who fall down before Jesus and shout, 'You are the Son of God!' Again we are reminded of the true identity of Jesus, even if our unconventional tutors are the demons. The paradox is repeated: the demons, the supernatural enemies of Jesus, readily recognise his true identity, while the religious authorities, his natural opponents, do not. The secrecy charge is imposed on the demons, but not on the sick people. Jesus sternly warns the demons not to reveal his true identity: this is not the right time for such a proclamation, neither are they the right heralds to make it.

At the beginning of this new section, Mark succeeds in keeping us focused as readers on the true identity of Jesus; he also reminds us that in spite of the opposition of official Judaism, the ministry of Jesus is welcomed by a growing multitude of ordinary people. Perhaps the great multitude who follow Jesus, who come from far and near, represent for Mark the new Israel, out of whom Jesus will choose the foundation members of his new community.

Jesus appoints the twelve 3:13-19a

[13] He went up the mountain and called to him those whom he wanted, and they came to him. [14] And he appointed twelve, whom he also named apostles, to be with him, and to be sent out to proclaim the message,

¹⁵and to have authority to cast out demons. ¹⁶So he appointed the twelve: Simon (to whom he gave the name Peter); ¹⁷James son of Zebedee and John the brother of James (to whom he gave the name Boanerges, that is, Sons of Thunder); ¹⁸and Andrew, and Philip, and Bartholomew, and Matthew, and Thomas and James son of Alphaeus, and Thaddaeus, and Simon the Cananaean, ¹⁹and Judas Iscariot, who betrayed him.

The scene now shifts from the lakeside to the mountain, from a great multitude following Jesus for their own needs to Jesus choosing the twelve to serve the needs of the kingdom. Out of his would-be followers, Jesus calls those he wants; then, from these chosen ones, he selects twelve.

The gradual movement of choosing the twelve is simply told: Jesus calls ... they come to him ... and he appoints twelve. Our translation includes the variant reading 'whom he called apostles', but since the word 'apostle' is never used by Mark in this technical sense, it is probably a scribal inclusion to harmonise with Luke 6:13 and Matthew 10:2. The reason for the number twelve is probably a symbolic one, representing the twelve patriarchs of the new Israel. If Jesus believed in the restoration of Israel (Mt 10:6; 19:28), the principal function of the twelve would be to judge the twelve tribes of Israel. In that understanding their role is unique – which would explain why they were not replaced as the *twelve* when they died.

In calling the twelve, Jesus has a twofold purpose: firstly, he calls them to be with him; secondly, he calls them to share in his mission. That personal and community attachment to Jesus, which will grow into doing the things Jesus does, begins a living chain of witness through the generations. As Kelber observes: 'What lies at the root of the Markan Gospel is therefore the desire to remain in living attachment to Jesus and to preserve continuity between Jesus and the Markan community of followers.'[1]

The twelve are all laymen; there are no priests or religious officials among those listed. There are three other lists of the twelve in the New Testament (Mt 10:2-4; Lk 6:14-16; Acts 1:13) and the lists of names are not identical. The slight variations, all of which appear at the end of the lists, point to the fact that Jesus' choice of *twelve* was more firmly rooted in the tradition than the memory of

1. W.H. Kelber, *The Kingdom in Mark: a New Place and a New Time* (Philadelphia: Fortress, 1974) p. 5.

who exactly they were. Apart from Peter, we know remarkably little about the individual lives of the twelve, but early tradition points to their fixed number as a group (1 Cor 15:5). Luke's story of the election of a new twelfth member of the group, to replace Judas Iscariot, is an indication of the importance of the fixed number (Acts 1:21-26): even though we learn that Matthias is elected, we never hear of him again. For Luke, the person of Matthias is not important for the story of the early church, but the reconstitution of 'the twelve' is essential before the event of Pentecost.

Among the four lists the name of Peter always stands first and that of Judas at the end – even in Acts the name of Judas comes at the end, though it is now 'Judas son of James' – a name that does not appear in the lists of Mark and Matthew. After Peter's name, Mark gives the two brothers James and John priority over Andrew – thus preserving the inner circle of three, who are with Jesus in the house of Jairus, on the mountain of transfiguration, and closest to him in Gethsemane. These three have nicknames, which refer to personality rather than function. Simon is called Peter, and as R.E. Brown comments:

> The play on 'Peter' and 'rock' is not good in Greek where the former is *Petros* and the latter is *petra*; it is perfect in Aramaic where both are *kepha*. Neither *Petros* in Greek nor *Kepha* in Aramaic is a normal proper name; rather it is a nickname (like American 'Rocky') which would have to be explained by something in Simon's character or career.'[2]

Mark does not explain why Jesus gives the first disciple this nickname. The two sons of Zebedee are called 'Sons of Thunder', possibly reflecting their fiery temperament (Mk 9:38; Lk 9:54).

A second Simon appears in Mark's list, designated 'the Cananaean'. The adjective does not refer to the village of Cana in Galilee, but probably to the nationalistic sect that later became known as the Zealots, and this is how Luke translates the meaning (Lk 6:18). Judas Iscariot is given special mention as the one who 'betrayed' Jesus – the only verb associated with any of the twelve

2. R.E. Brown, *The Gospel according to John I-XII* (New York: Doubleday, 1966) p. 76.

on the list. That Mark sounds such a negative note in this solemn account of appointment is a measure of his forthright realism. The name 'Iscariot' is variously interpreted as a man (*ish*) of Kerioth, a village in Judea (Josh 15:25); a literal translation of *(i)skariot*, 'the one handing over'; a member of the *sicarii*, dagger-wielding assassins.[3] None of the evangelists explains the obscure name, and it is possible that none of them knew what it meant.

An argument has been made that the appointment of the twelve is a later Christian invention to give substance to the understanding of the church as a new Israel. But why should the church invent the group of twelve and then produce lists of names that disagree? The variation of names within the lists would not count against the fact that Jesus had a *group of twelve* around him during the ministry, since each list has the fixed number. It is more likely that the Gospels honour a fixed memory that Jesus appointed twelve; whatever precise reason twelve were appointed, they formed his inner circle of companions, men whose close association with Jesus would later equip them to be his witnesses.

Opposition from the family and scribes   3:19b-35

Then he went home; [20]and the crowd came together again, so that they could not even eat. [21]When his family heard it, they went out to restrain him, for people were saying, 'He was gone out of his mind.' [22]And the scribes who came down from Jerusalem said, 'He has Beelzebul, and by the ruler of the demons he casts out demons.' [23]And he called them to him, and spoke to them in parables, 'How can Satan cast out Satan? [24]If a kingdom is divided against itself, that kingdom cannot stand. [25]And if a house is divided against itself, that house will not be able to stand. [26]And if Satan has risen up against himself and is divided, he cannot stand, but his end has come. [27]But no one can enter a strong man's house and plunder his property without first tying up the strong man; then indeed the house can be plundered.

[28] 'Truly I tell you, people will be forgiven for their sins and whatever blasphemies they utter; [29]but whoever blasphemes against the Holy Spirit can never have forgiveness, but is guilty of an eternal sin' – [30]for they had said, 'He has an unclean spirit.'

[31]Then his mother and his brothers came; and standing outside, they sent to him and called him. [32]A crowd was sitting around him; and they said to him 'Your mother and your brothers and your sisters are outside,

3. See Y. Arbeitman, 'The Suffix of Iscariot,' *Journal of Biblical Literature* 99 (1980) pp. 122-124.

asking for you.' [33]And he replied, 'Who are my mother and my brothers?' [34]And looking at those who sat around him, he said, 'Here are my mother and my brothers! [35]Whoever does the will of God is my brother and sister and mother.'

This unit includes three passages: the attempt by Jesus' family to restrain him (vv. 20-21); the charge made by the scribes that Jesus colludes with Beelzebul (vv.22-30); Jesus' teaching on his true family (vv.31-35). The whole episode is framed by the family of Jesus in the first and third passages, and the debate with the scribes is inserted in the middle. Mark's framing technique is also evident in 5:21-43: we are told that Jairus' daughter is near death, but we have to wait through the event of the woman being healed to see how the story of the little girl is resolved. Similarly in this episode: when the family of Jesus come to restrain him, we have to wait for the resolution of the story until after the debate with the scribes. The following table, based on W. Harrington's outline,[4] illustrates the unity and chiastic structure of the whole passage:

A The family of Jesus seek to restrain him: 3:20-21
   B First accusation: Jesus possessed by Beelzebul: 3:22a
      C Second accusation: Jesus empowered by prince of demons: 3:22b
      D Jesus'statement about Satan: 3:23-26
      C' Response to the second accusation: 3:27
   B' Response to the first accusation: 3:28-29
A' The true family of Jesus: 3:31-35

The family and the scribes oppose Jesus in their different ways, just as Jesus responds to them differently. Since the episode is a long and complex one, it will be easier to take each passage separately.

The family come to restrain Jesus 3:19b-21

After the scene on the mountain, where Jesus appointed the twelve to be with him and share in his mission, we are back inside the house again, where Jesus will face opposition from his family and the scribes. Presumably the house is Peter's home in Capernaum, which serves as Jesus' temporary base. The crowd converge on the

4. W. Harrington, *Mark* (Dublin: Veritas, 1984) p. 43.

house again, making it impossible for Jesus and his companions to eat. The crowd's coming to benefit from Jesus' power stands in striking contrast to the reason why the family of Jesus and the scribes approach him.

Jesus' family appears for the first time in Mark's narrative, in a passage that is omitted by Matthew and Luke. The family come with their own agenda, intending to restrain their difficult relative. The use of the verb (*kratesai*) suggests the strength of their opposition; it has the meaning to lay hold of him, to take possession of him, and is used in the passion narrative as 'arresting' (14:1,44,46 etc.). Long before the religious authorities successfully arrest Jesus, his family try to do the same. The reason the family want to take hold of Jesus is because they believe he is beside himself, that he is not in charge of himself. In the next passage the scribes express their belief that Jesus is possessed, that demonic forces are in charge of him. From the way Mark has set these two charges side by side, it seems that he sees a logical relationship between them.

Our translation makes the family into reporters of what other people are saying, but this translation/interpretation is not warranted by the Greek text.[5] Even if it were, the fact that the family represent the charge against Jesus so forcefully means that they subscribe to it themselves. This embarrassing truth, which Mark is bold to tell and which the early Christian community would never have invented, gives an unusual insight into how the ministry of Jesus aroused such hostility even in those close to him. The fourth Gospel notes the point in milder fashion: 'For not even his brothers believed in him.' (Jn 7:4)

The misunderstanding and opposition of Jesus' family are a measure of how much Jesus has changed since he left his own village of Nazareth to go and see John the Baptist. Since that encounter, Jesus' direction in life has undergone a radical change, one that has taken him away from Nazareth and the family, and that change is not greeted with enthusiasm by those who knew Jesus as one of their own. Mark will return to this point when he tells how Jesus is received by his own people in the Nazareth synagogue (6:1-6). More immediately, Mark will return to the theme in verses 31-35, where the family will find themselves outside the house,

---

5. See V. Taylor, *The Gospel according to St. Mark* p. 236.

recipients of the hard message that the elected family of Jesus are inside, gathered around their new relative.

The scribes come to accuse Jesus 3:22-30
The family of Jesus have unlikely allies in the scribes who arrive from Jerusalem to accuse Jesus of expelling demons by the power of Beelzebul. The name *ba'al zebul* literally means 'Lord of the House' – a meaning that Jesus will exploit in his response to the accusation. Behind the scribes' charge there is a recognition that what Jesus is doing has to be ascribed to some supernatural power: is the power of Jesus of God or of Satan? Official Judaism makes its voice heard in the allegation that Jesus is not only possessed by the prince of demons but is empowered by the evil one in his work of exorcism.

The extremity of the scribes' hostility and rejection is underlined by the illogical nature of their second claim, which Jesus answers first. As Jesus asks: 'How can Satan cast out Satan?' Their proposed picture of what Jesus is doing defies even common sense: Satan organising the fall of his own house by employing Jesus to initiate and prolong a civil war. Any being that fights itself will destroy itself, and Jesus credits Satan with more sense than an obsession with his own destruction. Ironically, if the scribes are correct in their reading, they have no need to worry, since Satan's power is at an end. But Jesus and Satan are declared enemies in a cosmic and historical struggle. What Jesus is doing in his ministry is announced in parabolic form: Jesus first overpowers the strong one and then plunders his house. That activity is a clear signal that Jesus is Satan's antagonist, not that he is Satan's employee.

Jesus turns then to the scribes' first accusation, that he is possessed by an unclean spirit. This is regarded as blasphemy against the Holy Spirit and, as such, cannot be forgiven. This attitude is unforgivable because it is elected blindness, a cold decision to ignore the evidence of the real. When someone sees an action that is obviously good and perversely interprets it as the work of Satan rather than God, this deliberate misreading of reality puts him beyond the reach of forgiveness because it rejects the very agent of God's forgiveness and healing.

Jesus' act of liberating someone from bondage is called diabolic; kindness is called satanic; pastoral care is dismissed as the work of the devil. Language becomes meaningless in the service of such professional jealousy; words are used as vandals to lay waste what is manifestly good. To sustain the big lie, language itself is deformed. The ordinary people who go to Jesus can see what the scribes refuse to see: Jesus works through the power of the Spirit of God, a power for good that is stubbornly opposed to the destructive power of Satan. In choosing to ignore the transparent beneficence of Jesus' ministry, the scribes ultimate irreverence is towards the Spirit of God. That is the sin against the Holy Spirit.

The true family of Jesus 3:31-35

This passage serves as a sequel to the earlier story in this complex, where Jesus' family came to restrain him because they were convinced he was out of his mind (vv.19b-21). That attitude shows how distant they are from recognising Jesus' ministry as the work of God. In contrast to the family and the scribes who fail to accept Jesus, there is a group gathered around him, inside the house, listening to his teaching. Jesus' mother and brothers stand *outside* this group; they send in a message asking for Jesus. The message reiterates the stance of the family: 'Your mother and your brothers and sisters are outside asking for you.' The physical division between the two groups, Jesus' family and his hearers, prepares for the theological division Jesus will recognise in his reply. (For comment on the brothers of Jesus, see commentary on 6:1-6.)

Jesus refuses to respond to the call of his family. Instead, he elects to remain within the inner circle of his listeners. The occasion is turned into a teaching with the question: 'Who are my mother and my brothers?' The question is not left unanswered: 'And looking around at those who sat around him, he said, "Here are my mother and my brothers. Whoever does the will of God is my brother and sister and mother." ' The bond of kinship that counts for Jesus is not blood but fidelity to the will of God. He reinvents his family and opens membership of it to anyone committed to doing the will of God.

This teaching will be heard as good news by all Mark's readers who cannot claim blood kinship with Jesus or his nation. If natural kinship by itself proves nothing, then gathering around Jesus in faith and discipleship proves itself to be the relationship that matters in the kingdom. That relationship might involve a rupture of family ties (10:28-30), but the fellowship with those who struggle to do the will of God makes for a new family gathered around Jesus.

The parable of the sower   4:1-9

Again he began to teach beside the sea. Such a very large crowd gathered around him that he got into a boat on the sea and sat there, while the whole crowd was beside the sea on the land. ²He began to teach them many things in parables, and in his teaching he said to them: ³'Listen! A sower went out to sow. ⁴And as he sowed, some seed fell on the path, and the birds came and ate it up. ⁵Other seed fell on rocky ground, where it did not have much soil, and it sprang up quickly, since it had no depth of soil. ⁶And when the sun rose, it was scorched; and since it had not root, it withered away. ⁷Other seed fell among thorns, and the thorns grew up and choked it and it yielded no grain. ⁸Other seed fell into good soil and brought forth grain, growing up and increasing and yielding thirty and sixty and a hundredfold.' ⁹And he said, 'Let anyone with ears to hear listen!'

After two chapters busy with controversy, and following Jesus' conflict with his family and the scribes, Mark now presents us with one of the few sections in his Gospel devoted to the teaching of Jesus (4:1-34). The selection is not varied but is made up of parables or teaching about parables. The word parable comes from the Greek root *para/ballein,* which literally means 'beside/to throw'. It expresses the act of throwing something beside something else, comparing, showing how different things are like one another. For example, the words of the song 'You are my sunshine' take the *dissimilar* ('you' and 'sunshine') and throws them side by side in a sentence. This strange alliance celebrates the joy someone experiences, a joy that goes beyond the limits of ordinary language.

When Jesus speaks about the kingdom, he never says what the kingdom actually is, only what it is like: 'The kingdom is like a ...' Speaking about the kingdom, Jesus throws a story beside the unseen reality that is the focus of his preaching. He has to face the limits of language to express what he thinks and believes and feels. We all face this problem when we try to find words to express our deepest beliefs. As the poet T.S. Eliot noted:

It's strange that words are so inadequate.
Yet, like an asthmatic struggling for breath,
So the lover must struggle for words.

To explain the unknown, we have to begin with what people know; we have to move from the familiar to the unfamiliar. Our own experience can become the ground for new possibility. Jesus borrows images and drama from the people and countryside around him and uses that concrete language-world in a new way to catch something of the unseen reality of the kingdom of God.

The sower goes out to sow and does so in throwaway style, broadcasting the seed over the most unlikely territory. Jeremias has defended the farmer's throwing the seed on the path as reflecting the normal Palestinian custom of sowing preceding ploughing.[6] This has been contested by White, who quotes extensive evidence that the normal practice was to plough first.[7] Reviewing the evidence, Payne has argued that with *autumn* planting there was no first ploughing since the ground was already broken and the autumn rains would weaken the soil.[8] The debate seems somewhat irrelevant, however, since the focus of the parable is not on the practice of the sower but on the fate of the seeds.

The first planting is a total failure: some seed falls on the path, and the birds devour the seed before it can germinate. Other seed falls on rocky ground, probably thinly covered soil that has limestone underneath, and the seed germinates. Its early promise, however, remains unfulfilled; it is rootless and soon withers under the scorching sun. The third failure happens when other seeds fall among thorns. It germinates and grows, doing better than the previous seed, but its fate is inevitable as it is choked by the surrounding thorns.

After elaborating a story of triple failure, the parable moves to a climax of threefold success. Other seeds fall into good soil and make it to harvest, yielding thirty and sixty and a hundredfold. The plot of the parable moves gradually from absolute failure through to generous success. The failure is not unimportant, but forms an

6. J. Jeremias, *The Parables of Jesus* (London: SCM, 1972) pp. 11-12.

7. K.D. White 'The Parable of the Sower,' *Journal of Theological Studies* 15 (1964) pp. 301-302.

8. P. Payne, 'The Order of Sowing and Ploughing in the Parable of the Sower,' *New Testament Studies* 25 (1978-79) pp. 123-129.

essential part of the gradual movement of the story. As Amos Wilder noted:

> At the core of the vision and at the heart of the parable is the motif of miscarriage or waste. This note three times invoked is not only a foil to the extravagant outcome, as it might be in a romantic analogue; it is part of the mystery of the total transaction, a transaction which has its dead ends and blind alleys. God finds his way through miscarriage and impasse to incommensurable fruition.[9]

The parable makes failure and success essential ingredients in God's enterprise, a truth that reflects not only the historical progress of Jesus' ministry but the eventual growth of the Gospel, an achievement that lies beyond the confines of Mark's book. In recognising the mixed fate of waste and abundance assigned the seed, Mark warns us against any magical or automatic expectation of instant growth. The seed needs more than itself to flourish; it depends on factors outside itself for its eventual fruition. That throws the issue back to the listener/reader: 'Let anyone with ears to hear listen!'

The purpose of the parables   4:10-12

[10]When he was alone, those who were around him along with the twelve asked him about the parables. [11]And he said to them, 'To you has been given the secret of the kingdom of God, but for those outside, everything comes in parables; [12]in order that
they may indeed look, but not perceive,
and may indeed listen, but not understand;
So that they may not turn again and be forgiven.'

These three verses enshrine Mark's view of the purpose of parables. The absence of a specific setting serves to emphasise the note of privacy: when Jesus comes to be alone, he uses the occasion to speak about the mystery of the kingdom of God that has been entrusted to his followers. The secret is going to be revealed only to the initiated, not to those outside for whom everything is obscure. This decree of limitation will serve to explain to Mark's

---

9. A. Wilder, *Jesus' Parables and the War of Myths: Essays on Imagination in the Scriptures* (London: SPCK, 1982) pp. 97, 98.

readers the partial success of Jesus' teaching and why so many who heard him did not come to believe in him. This places the rejection of Jesus under the governing rubric of God's plan; it meets the hard truth that Jesus was rejected by Judaism with the consoling belief that 'it was meant to be'.

As it stands, the explanation for speaking in parables makes little sense, suggesting that Jesus was deliberately formulating parables as enigmatic, impenetrable teachings, to confuse ordinary people and withhold from them the good news of the kingdom. This makes him out to be a theological sadist, which is hardly consistent with the one who reaches out to a whole variety of people and rejoices that his message is understood even by the little ones.

If Jesus did not want people to learn things, it would have been easier not to teach them. There seems little point in Jesus appealing to the crowds, 'Let anyone with ears to hear listen!' immediately after telling a parable contrived to bewilder them. Neither does it make sense to argue that Jesus tells parables to hide the truth from people and then have him say a few verses later: 'For there is nothing hidden, except to be disclosed, nor is anything secret, except to come to light.' (4:22) And even if the 'insiders' are granted full access to Jesus and his message, Mark's ensuing drama will highlight how inadequately the disciples understand both subjects.

We have to look elsewhere for an answer. The text reflects the popular semitic tendency to attribute all inexplicable things to the will of God – thus if people fail to understand Jesus, it must be that God has hardened their hearts. Everything that God knows in advance is understood as directly willed, as if he had arranged it. Nothing is simply permitted; everything that happens appears necessarily so by divine decree. This comes close to determinism; its value, however, is to interpret everything that happens in the light of the ultimate purpose of God.

Mark's quotation is from Isaiah 6:9-10, which he takes from the Targum – the Aramaic free translation of the Hebrew text. Mark's text has two purpose clauses: 'in order that "they may indeed look, but not understand ... so that they may not turn again and be forgiven".' Jeremias points to the underlying ambiguity of the Greek and Aramaic purpose clauses and translates Mark thus: 'in order that they (as it is written) may "see and yet not see, may hear and yet not understand, unless they turn and God will forgive them".'[10] Jeremias argues that the secret is given to the disciples, but the words of Jesus remain obscure to outsiders *because* they do not recognise his mission and repent. This translation retains the everlasting hope that things can change in the human story. Thus hope, which imagines the real, leaves open the possibility that people will attend to this message and will indeed repent.

The parable of the sower explained   4:13-20

> [13] And he said to them, 'Do you not understand this parable? Then how will you understand all the parables? [14] The sower sows the word. [15] These are the ones on the path where the word is sown: when they hear, Satan immediately comes and takes away the word that is sown in them. [16] And these are the ones sown on rocky ground: when they hear the word, they immediately receive it with joy. [17] But they have no root, and endure only for a while; then, when trouble or persecution arises on account of the word, immediately they fall away. [18] And others are those sown among the thorns: these are the ones who hear the word, [19] but the cares of the world, and the lure of wealth, and the desire for other things come in and choke the word, and it yields nothing. [20] And these are the ones sown on the good soil: they hear the word and accept it and bear fruit, thirty and sixty and a hundredfold.'

The secret of the kingdom has been given to the disciples, but they fail to understand the parable of the sower. Jesus rebukes the insiders: 'Do you not understand this parable? Then how will you understand all the parables?' Jesus then proceeds to interpret the parable, identifying the seed as the word (*ton logon*). The word *logos* was a technical term for the gospel, devised and regularly used by the early church (e.g. Acts 4:4, 6:4, 8:4; Gal 6:6; 1 Thess 1:6; Col 1:5; 1 Pet 2:8; Jas 1:21). In the synoptics the absolute use of *ho logos* by Jesus occurs only in the explanation for the parable of the sower, and it is used eight times by Mark in his version.

Most scholars argue to the conclusion that the allegorical interpretation of the parable is a product of the early church. A length of time is assumed in which the genuineness of the Christian response would be tested, and religious persecutions would have arisen (v.17) to test people's faith. The early church applies the

---

10. J. Jeremias, *The Parables of Jesus* p.17.

parable of the sower to her own experience in preaching and hearing the gospel ('the word'). It reflects conditions in the primitive church when difficulties of converting others and establishing them in the faith were all too evident.

The sower is not identified in the interpretation, but probably refers to any preacher of the gospel. The seed stands for the word that is offered, the birds represent Satan, and the soil refers either to the hearers or the difficulties they face. The story explores four kinds of responses to the word. There are those who hear but who have no ground for the word to take, making them an easy target for Satan. There are those who hear gladly but have no capacity for persistence, so when the first signs of trouble arise they immediately fall away. There are others who hear the word but cannot honour it because they are confused by many other calls and their desire for many other things, and their hearing yields nothing. Finally, there are those who hear the word, accept it, and bear fruit appropriately.

The parable acts as a warning and an encouragement to all Christians. Its characteristic note of unrelieved realism remains dateless. The seed is subject to a variety of fates, adversity and rejection, delay and loss. Much is wasted. Most Christian proclamation is wasted because the majority of people are not receptive, persistent, single-minded, and responsive. That sense of realism is not a reason to retire from the struggle of proclaiming the word of God; it is, however, a warning against banal optimism and a magical view of the work of proclamation. Waste and failure are always going to be part of the Christian enterprise, not least because it depends for its effectiveness on the free responses of other people. When that is accepted, losses are registered and successes are celebrated. And the sowing continues.

Wisdom sayings   4:21-25

²¹ He said to them, 'Is a lamp brought in to be put under the bushel basket, or under the bed, and not on the lampstand? ²²For there is nothing hidden, except to be disclosed, nor is anything secret, except to come to light. ²³Let anyone with ears to hear listen!' ²⁴And he said to them, 'Pay attention to what you hear; the meausre you give will be the measure you get, and still more will be given you. ²⁵For those who have, more will be given; and from those who have nothing, even what they

have will be taken away.'

In choosing to insert this cluster of five sayings here, Mark sets them in the context of Jesus' teaching on parables. Both Matthew and Luke provide different settings for the sayings, scattered throughout their accounts, thus interpreting their meaning differently from Mark and from one another. The presumption is that the sayings originally circulated without a context, which had to be provided by each evangelist. The sayings are undeniably obscure, and we have to guess at their meaning.

In Greek, verse 21 reads: 'Does the lamp come to be placed under a bushel or under a bed, not to be placed on the lampstand?' The awkward construction might suggest a reference to Jesus himself 'who came to Galilee, proclaiming the good news of God' (1:14). For Matthew, the light refers to the good works of the disciples (Mt 5:14-16); for Luke, the light refers to the disciples' inner illumination (Lk 11: 33-36). In each case, the obvious function of the lamp is to give light to others. Mark's parable setting, however, suggests that it refers to the mystery of the kingdom of God. Taken in concert with verse 22, 'nothing hidden, except to be disclosed ... ', one can interpret the meaning in terms of enlightenment. As the lamp is meant to give light, so the parables are meant to enlighten those who hear them. Concealment is not their ultimate purpose. Revelation is not only about what is hidden but about what can be told. This softens the note of ordained secrecy in verses 11-12: what appears as riddle now will eventually be revealed; what is impenetrable now will become clear in the light of Jesus' death and resurrection.

In telling people to take heed to what they hear, it appears as if Mark is counselling people to weigh carefully the meaning of the parables – unlike Luke, who focuses on *how* people hear (Lk 8:18). Mark applies the sayings about the measure one gives and receives to the act of hearing. Whatever measure we use ourselves – whether small or large – will be the one in which truth is measured out to us. The increase in understanding will be in proportion to the original measure we use; so whether our original measure is small or great, the increase will be likewise.

The final saying, probably a popular proverb, tells us that the increase of nothing is nothing; the increase to those who have will

obviously be greater than what they already possess. Matthew and
Luke have the saying after the parable of the talents/pounds (Mt
25:9; Lk 19:26). Mark's understanding seems to be that fruitful
hearers of the parables are given to understand even more; fruitless
hearers will go on hearing nothing. It is a promise, in the language
of the parable of the sower, that those who hear, accept and respond
will know increase in their understanding and bear fruit in various
yields.

Parables of growth   4:26-34

[26] He also said, 'The kingdom of God is as if someone would scatter seed
on the ground, [27]and would sleep and rise night and day, and the seed
would sprout and grow, he does not know how. [28]The earth produces of
itself, first the stalk, then the head, then the full grain in the head. [29]But
when the grain is ripe, at once he goes in with this sickle, because the
harvest has come.'

[30] He also said, 'With what can we compare the kingdom of God, or
what parable will we use for it? [31]It is like a mustard seed, which when
sown upon the ground, is the smallest of all the seeds on earth; [32]yet
when it is sown it grows up and becomes the greatest of all shrubs, and
puts forth large branches, so that the birds of the air can make nests in
its shade.'

[33] With many such parables he spoke the word to them, as they were
able to hear it; [34]he did not speak to them except in parables, but he
explained everything in private to his disciples.

Mark concludes this section on parables with two parables of
growth and a final editorial remark on Jesus' parabolic teaching to
the disciples. The parable of the seed growing by itself, verses 26-
29, is unique to Mark and is offered as an insight into the gradual
and independent growth of the kingdom of God. After the farmer
scatters the seed on the ground, the dynamic connection between
seed and earth will make its own story. The farmer's effort is not
needed for the process of growth itself; neither does he need to
know how growth happens. His own cycle of sleeping and rising is
irrelevant to what is happening between the seed and the soil. That
irresistible growth is independent of human effort, for 'the earth
produces of itself'. The seed becomes stalk, then the head, then the
full grain. The farmer's intervention is needed only when the
process is complete, and he gathers the fruit of the earth's labour.
What the earth produces is given back to him as gift.

At the heart of the parable there is warning and assurance. The kingdom of God grows in its own mysterious way, not because we can force its coming by our own intervention or effort. Paul's teaching makes the best commentary: 'I planted, Apollos watered, but God gave the growth. So neither the one who plants nor the one who waters is anything, but only God who gives the growth.' (1 Cor 3:6-7) The parable also assures us that God's purposes are being worked out in the endless round of ordinary life. To trust in God's providence, knowing that we do not understand his mysterious ways, is to live a profoundly carefree life. It is to allow God to be God, as the farmer allows the earth to be its own mysterious agent of growth for the scattered seed. Sometimes the most constructive thing we can do is to leave well alone.

In the parable of the mustard seed, verses 30-32, the kingdom of God is compared to the minuscule mustard seed that grows into a shrub so large that the birds of the air can make nests in its shade. The mustard plant normally grew to four feet, although it could grow higher, and was used as a seasoning for food and for medicinal purposes. As we learn from Pliny, 'It grows entirely wild, though it is improved by being transplanted: but on the other hand when it has once been sown it is scarcely possible to get the place free of it, as the seed when it falls germinates at once.'[11]

The apparent insignificance of the mustard seed belies its possibility; we could be easily fooled into believing the seed's size told the whole story. It is only a matter of time before its full potential is revealed in a totally different form, one that is out of all proportion to its small beginning.

The size of the shrub is still a long way from the tree in the parables of Matthew and Luke (Mt 13:32; Lk 13:19) and even further from the great tree in the dream Daniel interprets, a tree that reaches all the way to heaven and in which the birds of the air dwell (Dan 4:12; see also Ezek 17:23; 31:6). Mark's shrub is a humbler prospect, yet still the birds are able to make a home in its shade. His imagery stays with a kingdom of insignificance that is generous in providing a home for all comers. Compared to people's grandiose expectations, it may appear inconsequential; but compared to its beginnings, its size is still great. Again there is a note of assurance:

11. Pliny, *Natural History* 29.54.170.

there is greatness at the heart of the ordinary and there is real growth from the smallest of beginnings. The unspectacular beginnings of Jesus' own ministry and the early church should not steal people's hope that much greater results will ensue.

The section on parables closes with Mark's summary, in verses 33-34, of Jesus' teaching in parables. Mark has chosen representative samples of Jesus' parables ('With many such parables ... ') from a larger cycle of tradition. By way of editorial conclusion he repeats his own distinction between Jesus' public proclamation in parables to everyone and his private instruction to the disciples.

The stilling of the storm   4:35-41

[35] On that day, when evening had come, he said to them, 'Let us go across to the other side.' [36] And leaving the crowd behind, they took him with them in the boat, just as he was. Other boats were with him. [37] A great windstorm arose, and the waves beat into the boat, so that the boat was already being swamped. But he was in the stern, asleep on the cushion; and they woke him up and said to him, 'Teacher, do you not care that we are perishing?'

[39] He woke up and rebuked the wind, and said to the sea, 'Peace! Be still!' Then the wind ceased, and there was a dead calm. [40] He said to them, 'Why are you afraid? Have you still no faith?' [41] And they were filled with great awe and said to one another, 'Who then is this, that even the wind and the sea obey him?'

Following on his parable discourse, Mark now moves his narrative forward with a cycle of miracle stories that serve to display Jesus' power over the elements, over the demons, over disease, and over death itself (4:35-5:43). These detailed and colourful stories stand on their own and are not told to illustrate or support any teaching of Jesus; they are connected geographically by the movement of Jesus going back and forth across the Sea of Galilee.

The first miracle story begins by noting the time as evening, after a full day of teaching. Jesus takes the initiative by telling his disciples to cross the Sea of Galilee to the other side. The new group's first voyage together is ordered by Jesus, but no reason is offered why they leave the west shore. The 'other side' in this case means the Gentile territory of the Decapolis, where Jesus' next miracle takes place. Before Jesus and his disciples arrive on Gentile territory there is a storm. Is the storm before ministry to a Gentile itself an image of the rough passage of the early church? Certainly, within this Gospel, Jesus' sea journeys mediate between the Jewish/Gentile opposition.[12] Between the opposing sides lies the sea, and Jesus' mastery of the place traditionally associated with evil powers secures the safe passage of his disciples to what is a new frontier.

The crowds that were Jesus' audience for the parable discourse are left behind. Other boats are mentioned but they play no part in the unfolding drama. As a fierce wind whips up the sea, the waves crash so heavily into the boat that it is filling up. In the midst of all this turmoil there is a portrait of calmness personified: Jesus is asleep on a cushion in the stern of the boat. In dramatic contrast to the sleeping Jesus, the disciples are openly afraid of drowning at sea. They wonder if the presence of a sleeping Jesus means the absence of his concern for their survival, so they wake him with the reprimand: 'Teacher, do you not care that we are perishing?'

Aroused from his sleep, Jesus 'rebuked' the wind, the same verb (*epitmao*) that Mark uses elsewhere to describe Jesus' exorcisms (1:25; 3:12; 9:25). His two commands to the sea – literally, 'be quiet, be muzzled' – are also commands associated with exorcism (1:25). It is as if Jesus exorcises the demonic powers that are responsible for throwing the sea into such dramatic turmoil in the same way that he exorcises them when they create similar disorder and upheaval in the lives of those who are possessed. Both aspects of chaos are subject to the power of Jesus.

The great storm is now replaced by a great calm. In the calm Jesus makes his own rebuke known to the disciples, in the form of two questions: 'Why are you afraid? Have you still no faith?' Their previous experience of Jesus' powerful word has not led them to faith. After the great storm, now in the great calm, the disciples share a great fear. Our translation, 'they were filled with great awe', is misleading, suggesting that the disciples are awe-struck by Jesus' extraordinary powers. As Kelber comments: 'Mark, far from depicting reverential disciples in awe of Jesus, gives us panic-stricken disciples frightened by Jesus' rebuke'[13]

The story finishes with the question the disciples ask them-

12. See E. Struthers-Malban, 'The Jesus of Mark and the Sea of Galilee,' *Journal of Biblical Literature* 103 (1984) pp. 363-377.

13. W.H. Kelber, *Mark's Story of Jesus* (Philadelphia: Fortress Press, 1979) p. 31.

selves: 'Who then is this, that even the wind and the sea obey him?' Their new experience of Jesus leads them to a question, not an answer; it deepens their wonder about the identity of the one who can exercise such authority over the elements. Before this they have seen Jesus as a teacher, exorcist and healer; now there is new revelation in seeing the power of his authoritative word over wind and sea. Thus the miracle story does not finish with the usual acclamation of praise, but with the question: 'Who then is this?'

Mark's readers can answer the question the disciples cannot: Jesus is the Son of God (1:1). The story serves to illustrate the identity and care of Jesus. Behind Mark's miracle story is the weight of Old Testament texts which speak of control of the sea as distinctive of God's sovereign power and faithfulness. We can take two examples from the Psalms.

> O Lord God of hosts,
> who is as mighty as you, O Lord?
> Your faithfulness surrounds you.
> You rule the raging of the sea;
> when its waves rise, you still them. (Ps 89: 8-9)

> For he commanded and raised the stormy wind,
> which lifted up the waves of the sea.
> They mounted up to heaven,
> they went down to the depths;
> their courage melted away in their calamity ...
> Then they cried to the Lord in their trouble,
> and he brought them out from their distress;
> he made the storm be still,
> and the waves of the sea were hushed. (Ps 107:25-29)

Mark's story is so overlaid with ancient imagery that it seems impossible to recover its original source in Stage 1 of the tradition (see Introduction). Neither can we say with certainty that it is a construction of the early church to communicate its new understanding of Jesus. In its present setting Mark's story shows Jesus to be the divine ruler of nature, the one who can exorcise the chaos that causes turmoil and endangers life, the one who remains steadfast in care for his followers. Jesus enables his own community to make the turbulent crossing from their own side to Gentile territory where mighty work will be done in God's power.

In that sense Mark's message is for all Christians. To follow Jesus is to be commanded to leave familiar territory behind and journey to places we would not normally visit; it is to face exposure to storms that threaten to engulf us; it is to wonder fearfully if he has gone to sleep in the midst of chaos that appears to leave him untouched; it is to be challenged to trust in him anew. That continues to be true.

The exorcism of the Gerasene demoniac   5:1-20

They came to the other side of the sea, to the country of the Gerasenes. [2]And when he had stepped out of the boat, immediately a man out of the tombs with an unclean spirit met him. [3]He lived among the tombs; and no one could restrain him any more, even with a chain; [4]for he had often been restrained with shackles and chains, but the chains he wrenched apart, and the shackles he broke in pieces; and no one had the strength to subdue him. [5]Night and day among the tombs and on the mountains he was always howling and bruising himself with stones. [6]When he saw Jesus from a distance, he ran and bowed down before him; [7]and he shouted at the top of his voice, 'What have you to do with me, Jesus, Son of the Most High God? I adjure you by God, do not torment me.' [8]For he had said to him, 'Come out of the man, you unclean spirit!' [9]Then Jesus asked him, 'What is your name?' He replied, 'My name is Legion; for we are many.' [10]He begged him earnestly not to send them out of the country. [11]Now there on the hillside a great herd of swine was feeding; [12]and the unclean spirits begged him, 'Send us into the swine; let us enter them.' [13]So he gave them permission. And the unclean spirits came out and entered the swine; and the herd, numbering about two thousand, rushed down the steep bank into the sea, and were drowned in the sea.

[14]The swineherds ran off and told it in the city and in the country. Then people came to see what it was that had happened. [15]They came to Jesus and saw the demoniac sitting there, clothed and in his right mind, the very man who had had the legion; and they were afraid. [16]Those who had seen what had happened to the demoniac and to the swine reported it. [17]Then they began to beg Jesus to leave their neighborhood. [18]As he was getting into the boat, the man who had been possessed by demons begged him that he might be with him. [19]But Jesus refused, and said to him, 'Go home to your friends, and tell them how much the Lord has done for you and what mercy he has shown you.' [20]And he went away and began to proclaim in the Decapolis how much Jesus had done for him; and everyone was amazed.

After leaving the Jewish side of the Sea of Galilee and surviving the storm, Jesus and the disciples arrive safely on Gentile territory. The Decapolis (the name in Greek literally means a group of ten cities) was a region to the south-east of the sea and was home to a mostly pagan population. The only other miracle connected with a pagan region is the exorcism of the daughter of the Syrophoenician woman, in the region of Tyre (Mk 7:24-30). On that occasion Jesus' attitude to Gentiles is openly hostile, whereas in this story it is not. It would make more narrative sense if that incident, where the woman's persistence succeeds in leading Jesus to change his mind, were placed earlier than the present story.

Mark locates the cure of the demoniac in the 'country of the Gerasenes', the region around the city of Gerasa. This city was some thirty miles from the Sea of Galilee, which hardly fits the present narrative unless the expulsion of the pigs is a later development to the original form of the story. Some manuscripts read 'Gadarenes' (Mt 8:28), but even Gadara was six miles south-east of the sea, while others read 'Gergesenes', following the guess made by Origen that the place was Gergesa, on the east bank of the sea. Most scholars are in agreement that the best manuscript evidence points to the original reading as 'Gadarenes'.[14] This conclusion has consequences for determining the primitive content of the story. As Meier points out:

> Since the story most likely arose on Palestinian soil or adjoining territory, and since presumably the native storyteller would have known that Gerasa was nowhere near the Sea of Galilee, our decision that 'Gerasenes' belongs to the earliest form of the story confirms the view that the original story of the Gerasene demoniac did not include the incidents of the pigs rushing into the Sea of Galilee. In other words, what has often been claimed on form-critical grounds (namely, that the pig-incident is secondary) is likewise supported by our text-critical decision that the primitive story was located near Gerasa – from which not even possessed pigs can jump into the Sea of Galilee.[15]

It seems likely that different venues were suggested later to accommodate the addition of the pig-scene to the story.

14. See B.M. Metzger, *A Textual Commentary on the Greek New Testament* (London: United Bible Societies, third edition, 1971) pp. 23-24, 84f.

15. J.P. Meier, *A Marginal Jew: Rethinking the Historical Jesus* Vol 2 pp. 651, 652.

As the story stands in Mark, it is not easy to uncover the historical core that is free from legendary accretions, apart from the fact that Jesus performed an exorcism in the Decapolis, in the region of Gerasa. The unlikeliness of the geographical setting could argue to a memory of an exorcism performed there, one that became important in the early church as an argument from Jesus' ministry to justify the development of the Gentile mission.

Mark's vivid drama opens with the meeting between Jesus and the Gentile demoniac. After Jesus steps out of the boat, the afflicted man emerges from the tombs to meet him. The tombs were traditionally understood to be the haunt of demons, and this is the man's normal address. The local inhabitants have tried to restrain him with shackles and chains, but he has always managed to break free: no one can tame this maniac who is possessed of a frenzied strength. The two places where he wanders, the tombs and the mountains, indicate his seclusion from normal village and town life. A mad outcast, stripped of clothing and dignity, he wanders night and day, howling and wounding himself with stones.

When he sees Jesus from a distance, he runs to him, bows down, and shouts out Jesus' identity as Son of the Most High God, begging him not to torment him. The reason for this is that Jesus has already commanded the unclean spirit to leave the man. Unlike the Syrophonecian woman, the man wants nothing to do with Jesus, but that does not alter Jesus' stance towards him. Having been identified himself, Jesus asks the man for his name – the only occasion Jesus ever asks a demon's name.

The answer is given without protest: 'Legion, for we are many.' Before it came to mean many, the term 'legion' referred to a large body of Roman soldiers, numbering about six thousand men. The theory that this name is a metaphor for the Romans who possess the land as 'colonialists' might make sense for a Jewish demoniac; but Gerasa was a hellenized city that looked to the Romans to protect them from their Jewish adversaries. Whatever the connection, the man is possessed by a regiment of demons and begs Jesus not to send them out of the country.

The attention of the story shifts to the great herd of swine, feeding freely, cared for by the swineherds. The swine, regarded as unclean by Jews but herded by this Gentile population, are better cared for than the demoniac. Apart from Jesus, everything in this story is unclean: the territory, the demoniac, the spirits, the tombs, the pigs, the inhabitants. The speakers are now the unclean spirits, who are suppliant rather than defiant as they address Jesus: they beg him for permission to enter the swine. When Jesus accedes, the demons leave the man and possess the swine. The herd of about two thousand animals rushes down the bank into the sea, where they are drowned. In one fell stroke, Jesus cleanses the man of the demons and the neighbourhood of the swine.

The account now shifts to the swineherds, suddenly unemployed, who rush off to tell the story in the city and the country. On hearing the story the people come out to see what has happened. Mark focuses on what they see and how they react. They come to Jesus but it is the demoniac they see. The people see a transfiguration: the raving madman whom they could not restrain is now sitting, clothed, and self-possessed. Rather than being overjoyed at the transformation, the people are afraid. The witnesses to the original event tell the story, and on hearing the account the people beg Jesus to leave the neighbourhood.

Jesus does not pause to argue, but gets into the boat. As he does, the healed man begs him again, this time to follow him as a disciple. Jesus refuses his request and commands him not to the usual secrecy but to 'Go home to your friends, and tell (*apaggeillon*) them how much the Lord has done for you, and what mercy he has shown you.' And the healed man goes off and widens the commission to proclaim (*keryssein*) in the Decapolis how much Jesus has done for him. The story, unsurprisingly, concludes with the amazement of everyone.

The command to tell his friends what *God* (*kyrios*) has done is changed to proclaiming to the whole region what *Jesus* has done. As Taylor comments: 'Such a distinction is very primitive and belongs to a time when *kyrios* was not yet used of Jesus in the tradition Mark used.'[16]

The healed man anticipates Christian theology in the content of his proclamation and becomes a missionary in the Gentile region. The story's conclusion has clear echoes of the Gentile mission. The new man turns his experience of Jesus into a message, his new

16. V. Taylor, *The Gospel according to Saint Mark* p. 285.

liberation into proclamation; and the note of amazement that concludes the story is a reaction to his proclamation.

When we focus on the profound change Jesus brings about in this man, from maniac to missionary, the pigs suddenly seem irrelevant. The story manages fine without them. But they can still steal people's attention, in the same way they held the attention of the Gerasenes. The pigs are a distraction. As Jesus dismisses them from the story, we should do likewise.

The daughter of Jairus and the afflicted woman 5:21-43

[21] When Jesus had crossed again in the boat to the other side, a great crowd gathered around him; and he was by the sea. [22] Then one of the leaders of the synagogue named Jairus came and, when he saw him, fell at his feet [23]and begged him repeatedly, 'My little daughter is at the point of death. Come and lay your hands on her, so that she may be made well, and live.' [24]So he went with him. And a large crowd followed him and pressed in on him. [25]Now there was a woman who had been suffering from hemorrhages for twelve years. [26]She had endured much under many physicians, and had spent all that she had; and she was no better, but rather grew worse. [27]She had heard about Jesus, and came up behind him in the crowd and touched his cloak, [28]for she said, 'If I but touch his clothes, I will be made well.' [29]Immediately her hemorrhage stopped; and she felt in her body that she was healed of her disease. [30]Immediately aware that power had gone forth from him, Jesus turned about in the crowd and said, 'Who touched my clothes?' [31]And his disciples said to him, ' You see the crowd pressing in on you; how can you say, 'Who touched me?' [32]He looked all around to see who had done it. [33]But the woman knowing what had happened to her, came in fear and trembling, fell down before him, and told him the whole truth. [34]He said to her, 'Daughter, your faith has made you well; go in peace, and be healed of your disease.'

[35] While he was still speaking, some people came from the leader's house to say, 'Your daughter is dead. Why trouble the teacher any further?' [36]But overhearing what they said, Jesus said to the leader of the synagogue, 'Do not fear, only believe.' [37]He allowed no one to follow him except Peter, James, and John, the brother of James. [38]When they came to the house of the leader of the synagogue, he saw a commotion, people weeping and wailing loudly. [39]When he had entered, he said to them, 'Why do you make a commotion and weep? The child is not dead but sleeping.' [40]And they laughed at him. Then he put them all outside, and took the child's father and mother and those who were with him, and went in where the child was. [41]He took her by the hand and said to her, 'Talitha cum,' which means, 'Little girl, get up!'

⁴²And immediately the girl got up and began to walk about (she was twelve years of age). At this they were overcome with amazement. ⁴³He strickly ordered them that no one should know this, and told them to give her something to eat.

After his dramatic exorcism on Gentile territory, Jesus crosses the Sea of Galilee to the Jewish side where he performs the even more dramatic miracle of raising the daughter of Jairus from the dead. Jesus' power is exercised on both the Jewish and Gentile sides of the Sea, just as earlier, during the turbulent crossing, his power was exercised over the Sea itself. It is as if Mark wants to demonstrate to his readers that Jesus' ministry is neither confined to safe places nor limited by geographical boundaries. The in-breaking of the kingdom can take place anywhere.

Jesus is back on land, by the Sea, surrounded again by a great crowd. Out of the crowd one man emerges, Jairus by name. His name means 'he (God) will enlighten' or 'he (God) will awaken'. As a leader of the synagogue Jairus is a public figure whose function would have been to arrange the services, appoint readers and preachers, and preserve order. But he does not come to Jesus in this official capacity; he comes as a desperate father to plead for his little daughter who is at the point of death. Jairus' love for his daughter makes him into a beggar. His dignity is cast aside; his pleading is expressed in his whole body, fallen at the feet of Jesus. Such is the quality of his desperation, and such is the quality of his faith in Jesus. In response to his repeated pleas, Jesus says nothing, he promises nothing. He goes with Jairus. And the crowds press forward into the new drama.

The walk to Jairus' house is interrupted by a secret sufferer. Mark now inserts the story of the haemorrhaging woman into the story of Jairus' daughter, using the technique of an interval to heighten the tension of the developing drama, one that will have its climax in Jesus' greatest miracle on behalf of another person in the Gospel. In somewhat similar fashion, the fourth evangelist begins the story of the raising of Lazarus with the petition of Martha and Mary that Jesus heal their sick brother (Jn 11:1-3); Lazarus, like the daughter of Jairus, then dies while Jesus delays in coming.

In Mark's story the woman comes up behind Jesus. She suffers from a haemorrhage, an embarrassing affliction that renders her, and anyone she touches, ritually unclean (Lev 15:24-27). She has already exhausted all attempts at a natural cure, and the long and painful treatments have exhausted her savings. She is all spent. Like Jairus, she is desperate; like Jairus, she believes that Jesus will make a difference. She is not disappointed: when she touches Jesus' clothes, she feels in her body she is cured.

But Jesus feels something too, that power has gone out from him. When Jesus asks who touched his clothes, the disciples feel the question is meaningless in the crush of the crowd. Jesus ignores them and continues to look around the crowd. The woman is not going to be allowed to disappear back into the anonymity of the crowd.

The woman comes to Jesus a second time. She comes forward in fear, falls down at Jesus' feet and tells the whole truth. This establishment of personal contact with Jesus distinguishes the story from being merely magical. For all people's faith, Jesus is not be treated as a mobile relic. On hearing her story, Jesus addresses her affectionately as 'Daughter,' compliments her for her faith and allows her to go in peace. Her first coming, to touch Jesus' clothes, brought healing. Her second coming, in open and honest response to Jesus' invitation, brings her the assurance of salvation and the offer of peace. Thus her salvation is something that happens to her in the midst of life, something she contributes to by her own faith in Jesus.

The affliction of twelve long years has stopped, but that good news is interrupted by messengers from Jairus' house with the sad news that the life of twelve short years has come to an end. Jesus' delay has proved fatal. Their advice to Jairus is not to trouble the teacher further, since there is no expectation that Jesus can do anything in the face of death itself. It is one thing to have faith that Jesus will heal; it is another to believe in Jesus' power to raise the dead. This time Jesus speaks to Jairus: 'Do not fear, only believe.' The interrupted journey continues. Jesus goes with Jairus, limiting those who follow him to his three favourite disciples, the ones who will be with him on the mountain of transfiguration (9:2), on the Mount of Olives when he sits facing the Temple (13:3), and in the garden of Gethsemane (14:33).

Arriving at the house, the professional mourners are about their business of ritual wailing. Jesus expresses his belief that the child is not dead but asleep. By way of reaction to what Jesus says, the mourning turns to mockery. Jesus expels the hired mourners from the house and, accompanied by the child's parents and his three disciples, goes into the room of the dead child. Mark preserves the original Aramaic, 'Talitha cum,' which he translates for his readers as 'Little girl, get up.' On Jesus' command she gets up and walks about. The witnesses are overcome with amazement, but they are charged to silence. How they could be expected to tell no one about this, with a crowd waiting outside and the girl herself walking around, is not explained. The scene closes with Jesus' command to give her something to eat.

Some commentators read the words of Jesus literally – 'The child is not dead, but sleeping' – and argue that the girl is not dead but in a coma, thus interpreting the account as another story of healing. Mark's carefully crafted tension throughout the story – from Jairus' initial plea that his daughter was at the point of death, through the fatal delay caused by the afflicted woman, the messengers' news that the girl is dead, their expectation that Jesus could do nothing in the face of death, the mockery of the mourners, the reduction of the number of witnesses, to the words of Jesus in Aramaic and the astonishment of the witnesses – argues for more than another story of healing. Although the contrast is made between 'sleep' and 'death', there seems little doubt that Mark views this incident as a raising from the dead, consonant with Christian belief that sleep is a euphemism for death (Mt 27:52; 1 Cor 11:30; 15:16; 1 Thess 4:11). Mark can declare his belief that *in this instance* death is sleep because Jesus wills death to be as impermanent as sleep by raising the girl to life.[17] In Matthew's account the girl is already dead when Jairus comes to Jesus (Mt 9:18); Luke tells us that the mourners knew she was dead (Lk 8:53), a truth underlined by the fact that when Jesus speaks to the dead girl, 'her spirit returned' (Lk 9:55).

Whatever actually happened in Stage 1 of the tradition, there seems little doubt that Mark understands the story as Jesus raising a dead girl. That the story forms a climax to the series of miracles

17. See C.E. Cranfield, *The Gospel according to Saint Mark* (Cambridge: Cambridge University Press, 1959) pp.188-189; W. Lane, *The Gospel according to Mark* (Grand Rapids: Eerdmans, 1974) pp.196-197.

(4:35-5:43) would likewise argue to its being understood as the supreme miracle of raising someone from the permanence of death. The image of Jairus walking with Jesus, after the messengers tell him his daughter is dead and advise him to trouble Jesus no further speaks its own language of quiet faith. It tells us of someone who has faith in Jesus as more than a healer, someone who can walk towards the unspeakable loss of death with the one who can meet death itself with a power of new life. In the presence of Jesus, death is not the last and permanent word that can be said about anyone. In the presence of Jesus, the good news is that death is as impermanent as sleep.

Rejection in Nazareth   6:1-6a

He left that place and came to his hometown, and his disciples followed him. [2]On the sabbath he began to teach in the synagogue, and many who heard him were astounded. They said, 'Where did this man get all this? What is this wisdom that has been given to him? What deeds of power are being done by his hands! [3]Is not this the carpenter, the Son of Mary and brother of James and Joses and Judas and Simon, and are not his sisters here with us?' And they took offence at him. [4]Then Jesus said to them, 'Prophets are not without honor, except in their home town, and among their own kin, and in their own house.' [5]And he could do no deed of power there, except that he laid his hands on a few sick people and cured them. [6]And he was amazed at their unbelief.

Jesus' rejection in his own home town serves as the conclusion to this section of Mark's Gospel (3:6-6:6a). Earlier in the section the family of Jesus came to restrain him, convinced he was out of his mind (3:20-21); in response Jesus redefined his own family as those who do the will of God (3:31-35). Now Jesus leaves his ministry by the Sea of Galilee and returns to Nazareth, situated in the hills of Lower Galilee. He is followed by his disciples. This is not a private social visit, but part of the Galilean ministry.

Nazareth, the native village of Jesus, is nowhere mentioned in the Old Testament. Pixner, a teacher of archaeology who has worked in Israel for thirty years, writes of Nazareth:

The excavations during recent decades have shown that the population of Nazareth at the time of Jesus could hardly have numbered more than 120-150 people. It is most likely that this rather off the beaten track hamlet in the hills of Galilee belonged to the larger village Japhia, just about a mile away, which was a strongly fortified place that played an important role in the Great War against the Romans (A.D. 66-70) ... one may well take it for granted that most of the inhabitants of Nazareth belonged to the same extended family, that is to say, to the clan of the Nazarene.[18]

In Nazareth everyone would have known everyone else; probably most of the villagers would have been related by blood or marriage.

Jesus takes the opportunity to teach in the local synagogue – although it is only a matter of time before he and the synagogue part company. Mark does not tell us what Jesus teaches, only that many who hear him are astounded. They are not caught by their astonishment for long, however, as they begin wondering about the origin of Jesus' teaching, the source of the wisdom granted to him, as well as the powerful deeds worked through his hands.

They cannot account for this new Jesus. Moving from their unanswered questions, they focus on what they do know. Jesus, they know, is a layman and manual labourer: the Greek word *tekton* means someone who works with wood or metal or stone. The parallel passage in Matthew speaks of Jesus as 'the carpenter's son' (Mt 13:55). They also know that Jesus is 'son of Mary' – a designation only found here in the New Testament – probably an indication that Joseph is already dead.

The 'brothers of Jesus' is a phrase that is interpreted variously, largely depending on the reader's prior position regarding the virginity of Mary. Mark never mentions the virginal conception. Some commentators are sure that brothers (*adelphoi*) and sisters (*adelphai*) can only mean the siblings of Jesus, rejecting any other interpretation as without warrant. Witness Gould: 'There is no more baseless, nor for that matter, prejudiced theory, in the whole range of Biblical study, than that which makes Jesus the only child of Mary.'[19] Happily, this tone, as aggressive as it is assured, has been replaced in modern ecumenical discussions on the subject.[20]

18. B. Pixner, *With Jesus through Galilee according to the Fifth Gospel*, (Israel: Corazin, 1990) pp. 15, 17.
19. E. Gould, *The Gospel according to St. Mark* (1st Impression, 1896. Edinburgh: T & T Clark, 1983) p. 104.
20. See *Mary in the New Testament: a Collaborative Assessment by Protestant and Roman Catholic Scholars*, edited by R.E. Brown and others (London: Chapman, 1978).

Among the patristic writings, Hegesippus, a church historian of
the second century, distinguished between the uncles, cousins and
brothers of Jesus.[21] Likewise the African Church Father, Tertullian
(*ca* 160-225), in asserting the full humanity of Jesus, considered the
brothers of Jesus true brothers.[22] Not until the late fourth century,
in Jerome's tract *Against Helvidius*, do we hear the argument that
Mary was a perpetual virgin and the brothers and sisters of Jesus
were, therefore, 'cousins'. This became the predominant position
of Christianity in the West, and was held during the Reformation
by Luther, Calvin and Zwingli. The view that the brothers and
sisters of Jesus were Joseph's children by a previous marriage,
defended by Epiphanius and Origen, remains the dominant position in the East.

Since the perpetual virginity of Mary is not raised within the
New Testament itself, clearly questions surrounding that subject
cannot be answered by the New Testament writings. And since
Mark himself expresses no belief in the virginity of Mary, the
interpretation of the brothers and sisters of Jesus depends largely on
the authority one accords later church insights.

Jesus' own relatives and neighbours decide against him when he
teaches them in the local synagogue. 'And they took offence at
him' has the meaning that they saw in him a stumbling-block. Their
taking offence gives rise to Jesus' use of a popular proverb –
modified by Matthew, Luke and John – that prophets are without
honour in their own country, among their own relatives, and in their
own house. In the form Mark gives it, the rejection is local and total.
Jesus' application of the proverb to his rejection at Nazareth means
that those now 'outside' include not only his family (3:31-35) but
also his neighbours.

There is a sense in which none of the locals, given their past
experience of Jesus, can see anything extraordinary in his background, in spite of the evidence before their eyes. Their memory of
Jesus' ordinariness, rather than their awareness of his teaching and
his powerful deeds, becomes operative in their judgement of him.
Their new awareness attracts them to Jesus, but their memory of
him repels them. Their static memory proves a useful fiction, fixed

21. In Eusebius, *Ecclesiastical History* 2.23.4; 3.19.1; 4.22.4.
22. Tertullian, *Against Marcion* 4.19.

as it is on Jesus' unexceptional past.

Following the rejection of the people of Nazareth, Mark adds an unusually frank note about Jesus' powerlessness to do any mighty deed there. This is modified only by his reference to Jesus curing a few sick people. The last note of Jesus in his home town focuses on his amazement at his own people's unbelief. Their incapacity to receive Jesus' ministry because they are transfixed by his past leaves them as a people without faith. But their unbelief is not harmless. Their distrust disables Jesus; their rejection renders him powerless; their frozen familiarity leaves him no choice but to move on. And when he leaves Nazareth this time, he never returns.

4

Revelation to disciples

6:6b-8:26

Following the break with Nazareth and his own people, Jesus continues his ministry elsewhere and sends out the twelve disciples on mission. Inserted into the story of the missionary journey is the account of John the Baptist's passion narrative, a foreshadowing of the violent death Jesus will undergo. Although the disciples figure prominently in the section and are first portrayed in a favourable light, it is their lack of understanding that Mark highlights: 'Do you have eyes and fail to see?' (8:18); 'Do you not yet understand?' (8:21) The section ends with the story of a blind man whose sightlessness is successfully but gradually healed by Jesus.

The mission of the twelve   6:6b-13

Then he went about among the villages teaching.[7]He called the twelve and began to send them out two by two, and gave them authority over the unclean spirits. [8]He ordered them to take nothing for their journey except a staff; no bread, no bag, no money in their belts; [9]but to wear sandals and not to put on two tunics. [10]He said to them, 'Wherever you enter a house, stay there until you leave the place. [11]If any place will not welcome you and they refuse to hear you, as you leave, shake off the dust that is on your feet as a testimony against them.' [12]So they went out and proclaimed that all should repent. [13]They cast out many demons, and anointed with oil many who were sick and cured them.

Rejected by the synagogue in Nazareth, Jesus now turns to the villages in the surrounding countryside. It is difficult to know if Mark is using the transition from synagogue to village to indicate that Jesus is now unable to teach in any of the Galilean synagogues: certainly, as the Gospel narrative progresses, we do not see him in a synagogue again. Jesus' theatre of ministry will not be the religious meeting place but wherever ordinary people live.

Earlier, Jesus appointed the twelve 'to be with him, and to be sent out to proclaim the message, and to have authority to cast out demons.' (3:14-15) Having heard Jesus' preaching and witnessed his mighty works, the twelve are now called for the declared purpose of mission. Mark's missionary discourse and brief account of their mission, a tradition attested and amplified by Matthew 10:5-15 and by Luke 9:1-6 and 10:1-16, clearly provide a foundation framework for the later Christian missionary work. The mission of the twelve, however, plays no decisive role in the development of the Gospel: although a modest success is registered, Mark will show how the disciples themselves are no closer to understanding Jesus or the nature of the kingdom of God. That understanding will have to wait until after Jesus' death and resurrection; only then, therefore, can it be proclaimed by the first witnesses.

The twelve are to be sent out in pairs, a practice of Jewish witness that was adopted by the disciples of John the Baptist (see Lk 7:18; Jn 1:37) and is commonly witnessed in the early church. Surprisingly, there is no explicit charge to preach, and the implication of verse 7 is that the sole purpose of the mission is healing. Although Mark says Jesus gives the twelve authority over unclean spirits, the evangelist will mention later how they are unable to cast out a spirit (9:18).

The mission charge enjoins them to take nothing for their journey except a staff. The instructions are influenced by the belief that the final crisis is imminent, so the urgency of the task is its most pressing note. The list of negative commands forbids them to rely on their own resources. Instead, the disciples are forced to rely on the kindness of strangers, on the welcome of those to whom they minister. They are to depend on the authority that has been given them and the hospitality that will be offered them. The opening injunction in Matthew, 'Go nowhere among the Gentiles and enter no town of the Samaritans' (Mt 10:5) is absent. In Mark's account, wherever the disciples are made welcome, they are to stay in the same house and thus avoid wasting time in hunting for better quarters. When they are refused welcome, they are not to force themselves on a reluctant community but shake the dust from their feet and move on. This symbolic action of dissociation, interpreted in the light of the Jewish practice of removing dust from a heathen land before returning to Jewish soil, is a pronouncement that whatever place rejects them is to be considered pagan. The disciples' act of shaking the dust from their feet will also serve as a warning to the community and a summons to repentance.

When the disciples go out, they proclaim, like John the Baptist before them, that everyone should repent. Unlike Matthew and Luke, Mark avoids making the twelve proclaimers of the kingdom of God. Two further actions are specified: they cast out demons and, after anointing the sick with oil, cure them of their affliction. In spite of their manifest unreadiness, their unfinished training, their lack of understanding, their halting convictions, the twelve are sent out. Jesus risks sharing his mission with his vulnerable friends, making them collaborators in his own missionary enterprise. In this preliminary outreach their faith and authority will be tested on the road and in the villages. Mark does not claim too much for them; it is too early to claim anything much on their behalf, as he has yet to explore the full story of their discipleship.

Herod and Jesus 6:14-16

[14] King Herod heard of it, for Jesus' name had become known. Some were saying, 'John the baptizer has been raised from the dead; and for this reason these powers are at work in him.' [15] But others said, 'It is Elijah.' And others said, 'It is a prophet, like one of the prophets of old.' [16] But when Herod heard of it, he said, 'John whom I beheaded, has been raised.'

Mark now slows the pace of his narrative as he turns from focusing on Jesus' activity to dealing with questions about Jesus' identity.

The reputation of Jesus has reached the ears of Herod Antipas. Although Mark calls him a king, probably reflecting common custom, Herod was the tetrarch of Galilee and Perea, territory that he inherited on his father's death in 4 B.C. The second surviving son of Herod the Great, Antipas was raised and educated in Rome, and was initially favoured as the principal beneficiary under his father's will. Although he received only two territories, Antipas managed to hold his title and land secure until 39 A.D. when he travelled to Rome to petition the new emperor, Caligula, for the title of 'king'. His journey into ambition proved his downfall: Caligula deposed him on suspicion of treason and exiled him to France.

Mark does not tell us what Herod heard about Jesus, only that Jesus' name has become known in the region. Mark has, however, already depicted the Herodians as fellow conspirators with the

Pharisees in plotting against Jesus (3:6; see 12:13). Although this note of opposition is given early in the Gospel, it probably reflects the antagonism of Herod. Before giving us Herod's opinion of Jesus, Mark cites three popular theories about Jesus' identity.

The first theory attempts to account for the powerful works done through Jesus by arguing that Jesus is John the Baptist raised from the dead. Although there is no testimony in any of the Gospels that John the Baptist healed or exorcised or was a miracle-worker – in fact it is explicitly denied in John 10:41 – this theory argues that because the Baptist has been raised from the dead, *therefore* miraculous powers are at work in Jesus. Commenting on this verse, Jerome Murphy-O'Connor writes:

> Had Jesus merely been performing miracles, it is hard to say with whom he might have been identified, but certainly it would not have been with John. This is clear confirmation that the pericope is not a pure redactional creation. It is an adaptation of an older source in which a different basis of identification was given.... The mere fact that Jesus had once been a disciple of John would not have sufficed to give rise to such an identification, if his comportment had lacked the distinctive feature of the Baptist's activity. Hence, Jesus must have baptised. Only in such circumstances would it have been natural for the crowds to think 'It is John the Baptist all over again!' and for this to be transmuted in the mind of Herod into 'John I killed, and now it is as if he has come to life again.'[1]

Whether one agrees with this hypothesis or not, the ready identification of Jesus with John in the popular imagination may be an embarrassing witness to the simple truth that Jesus followed John so closely that they were difficult to tell apart.

The second opinion identifies Jesus as Elijah. In 9:11-13 Mark identifies John the Baptist as Elijah, the one who must come first to restore all things (see Mal 2:1,23). For Mark, John is limited to a role within the story of Jesus as his precursor, therefore Elijah is a suitable role for John, not Jesus. Elijah's coming portends the end time; with Jesus, 'the time is fulfilled' (1:15).

1. J. Murphy-O'Connor, 'John the Baptist and Jesus: History and Hypotheses,' *New Testament Studies* 36 (1990) p. 372 .

The third popular estimate about Jesus is that he is prophet, like one of the prophets of old, or it may refer to the prophet like Moses whom God promised to raise 'from among your own people' (Deut 18:15). Mark has already noted Jesus speaking about himself as a prophet in the synagogue in Nazareth (6:4); but Mark's readers know, after reading the prologue, that this is an inadequate title to capture the fullness of who Jesus is.

Herod subscribes to the first theory, that Jesus is John the Baptist raised from the dead. That belief, allied with the information that Herod was responsible for beheading John, leads Mark into a flashback in which he tells the story of John's execution.

Herod and John the Baptist   6:17-29

[17]For Herod himself had sent men who arrested John, bound him, and put him in prison on account of Herodias, his brother Philip's wife, because Herod had married her. [18]For John has been telling Herod, 'It is not lawful for you to have your brother's wife.' [19]And Herodias had a grudge against him, and wanted to kill him. But she could not, [20]for Herod feared John, knowing that he was a righteous and holy man, and he protected him. When he heard him, he was greatly perplexed; and yet he liked to listen to him. [21]But an opportunity came when Herod on his birthday gave a banquet for his courtiers and officers and for the leaders of Galilee. [22]When his daughter Herodias came in and danced, she pleased Herod and his guests; and the king said to the girl, 'Ask me for whatever you wish, and I will give it.' [23]And he solemnly swore to her, 'Whatever you ask me, I will give you, even half of my kingdom.'

[24]She went out and said to her mother, 'What should I ask for?' She replied, 'The head of John the baptizer.' [25]Immediatley she rushed back to the king and requested, 'I want you to give me at once the head of John the Baptist on a platter.' [26]The king was deeply grieved; yet out of regard for his oaths and for the guests, he did not want to refuse her. [27]Immediately the king sent a soldier of the guard with orders to bring John's head. He went and beheaded him in the prison, [28]brought his head on a platter, and gave it to the girl. Then the girl gave it to her mother. [29]When his disciples heard about it, they came and took his body, and laid it in the tomb.

Scholars have difficulty categorising Mark's story of the arrest and execution of John the Baptist, the only narrative in the Gospel that is not directly about Jesus. Part of the difficulty stems from a comparison between two independent sources that have independent purposes. Mark's Gospel, consistent with its theological confession focused on the theme of religious martyrdom, presents the death of John as a direct result of his prophetic criticism of Herod Antipas' marriage with Herodias. Josephus' *Antiquities*, a work that documents the political unrest of first century Palestine, argues that John was executed because his growing popularity among the people had become a political threat to Herod Antipas.[2] Both sources, written from different perspectives, agree on the historical core, that Herod arrested John and had him executed.

Josephus also mentions Herod's marriage difficulties, but he makes no connection between them and the death of John. Herod Antipas had been married to a daughter of Aretas IV, king of Nabatea. The kingdom of Aretas bordered on Herod's southern territory of Perea. As Josephus writes:

> When starting out for Rome, he [Herod Antipas] lodged with his half-brother Herod, who was born of a different mother, namely the daughter of Simon the High Priest. Falling in love with Herodias, the wife of this half-brother ... he brazenly broached to her the subject of marriage. She accepted and pledged herself to make the transfer as soon as he returned from Rome. It was stipulated that he must cast out the daughter of Aretas. The agreement made, he set sail for Rome.[3]

Mark mistakenly identifies Herodias as the wife of Herod Antipas' brother Philip, but since the chart of the Herodian dynasty is a tortuous web of relationships, Mark's confusion is all too understandable.

After Herod Antipas' return from Rome, his wife discovered his pact with Herodias, and asked for permission to travel to the fortress Machaerus, which was on the boundary between the territory of her husband and her father. From Machaerus she returned home to her father and told him of Herod's plans. King Aretas swore vengeance on his former son-in-law, and used a territorial dispute as a pretext for war. Josephus says that when Herod's army was defeated, the Jews interpreted it as a divine vengeance for John the Baptist's execution, which had taken place in the frontier fortress at Machaerus, east of the Dead Sea.[4]

2. Josephus, *Antiquities*, 18.5.4.
3. Josephus, *Antiquities*, 18.5.1.
4. Josephus, *Antiquities*, 18.5.1-2.

Mark's setting for his story is not in Perea but in Galilee, presumably in Herod's new palace in Tiberius. The occasion is a birthday banquet which Herod holds for his courtiers, army commanders and leading men of Galilee. Although Herod fears and respects John, his wife Herodias has nursed a grudge against the prophet and wants to kill him. She bides her hostile time. This is reminiscent of the original Elijah's struggle with King Ahab and his evil wife Jezebel, who persuades her weak husband to have the prophet killed (1 Kgs 19:1-2; 21:17-26).

Mark calls Herod's daughter Herodias, but we know from Josephus that her name was Salome. She pleases Herod and his guests with her dancing, but whether a king's daughter would publicly demean herself in Near Eastern society by dancing solo before a group of partying men is highly doubtful, although it makes interesting copy for storytelling. The gratified Herod commits himself to giving his daughter whatever she wishes, even half his kingdom. As a client-ruler working for imperial Rome, Herod has no 'kingdom' to dispose of, but again the fictional detail heightens the drama. The incident is reminiscent of another royal banquet that the Persian king, Xerxes, gives for all the nobles and governors of his province: 'While they were drinking wine, the king said to Esther, "What is your petition? It shall be granted you. And what is your request? Even to the half of my kingdom, it shall be fulfilled".' (Esth 5:6; see 7:2)

Salome leaves the all-male banqueting hall and asks her mother's advice. The erotic dance of the daughter turns out to be a front for the violent desire of the mother. The answer comes readily to Herodias: the head of John the baptizer. The girl makes her request known, adding that the head should be delivered immediately, on a platter. Although Herod is grieved, he is caught by the reckless promise he made publicly as a solemn oath. His public reputation is more important to him that the life of the prophet he reluctantly admires, so he orders John's execution and his head is brought on a platter and given to the girl. She takes it from the soldier and hands her gruesome prize to her gruesome mother. The whole scene is macabre: the guests who began being pleased with a dancing girl end up looking at the decapitated head of a prophet. Finally, when John's disciples hear what has happened, they take his body and lay it in a tomb.

Why does Mark tell the story? What purpose does it fulfil in advancing the narrative of the Gospel? Mark has inserted the story of John's martyrdom into the story of the apostles' *mission*. This is the first connection between martyrdom and mission, which will be made explicit in 8:31 where Jesus speaks about the destiny of the Son of Man; and the connection between martyrdom and mission becomes the dominating theme of the Gospel. Mark depicts John the Baptist as the forerunner not only of Jesus' mission but also of his death. As John was condemned to death by a vacillating ruler, one whose reluctant admiration for the prophet surrendered to his need to placate the crowd, so Jesus will undergo a similar fate at the hands of Pontius Pilate (15:1-15).

Ironically, the Baptist ends up being a representative and forerunner of Jesus and the disciples. As John preached and was 'delivered up', so Jesus preaches and will be delivered up; so, in turn, the disciples preach and will be delivered up (13:9-13). And if Mark is writing for a persecuted community, no doubt the same passion story keeps on being retold in the lives of his community. In the continuing story of the Gospel communities, martyrdom has a way of inserting itself into mission. Thus Mark's dramatic story of John's arrest and death at the hands of the civil authorities, however weighted with Old Testament reminiscence and legendary accretion, has a worthy theological function to play in the movement of the Gospel.

Feeding the five thousand   6:30-44

[30] The apostles gathered around Jesus, and told him all that they had done and taught. [31]He said to them, 'Come away to a deserted place all by yourselves and rest a while.' For many were coming and going, and they had no leisure even to eat. [32]And they went away in the boat to a deserted place by themselves. [33]Now many saw them going and recognized them and they hurried there on foot from all the towns and arrived ahead of them. [34]As he went ashore, he saw a great crowd; and he had compassion for them, because they were like sheep without a shepherd; and he began to teach them many things. [35]When it grew late, his disciples came to him and said, 'This is a deserted pleace, and the hour is now very late; [36]send them away so that they may go into the surrounding country and villages and buy something for themselves to eat.' [37]But he answered them, 'You give them something to eat.' They

said to him, 'Are we to go and buy two hundred denarii worth of bread, and give it to them to eat?' [38]And he said to them 'How many loaves have you? Go and see.' When they had found out, they said, 'Five, and two fish.' [39]Then he ordered them to get all the people to sit down in groups on the green grass. [40]So they sat down in groups of hundreds and of fifties. [41]Taking the five loaves and the two fish, he looked up to heaven and blessed and broke the loaves, and gave them to his disciples to set before the people; and he divided the two fish among them all. [42]And all ate and were filled; [43]and they took up twelve baskets full of broken pieces and of the fish. [44]Those who had eaten the loaves numbered five thousand men.

The feeding of the multitude is the only miracle story recounted in all four Gospels, and the only one recounted in two variant forms: the second account, the feeding of the four thousand with seven loaves and a few fish, is found in Mark 8:1-10 with a parallel in Matthew 15:32-39. Given six different versions of the story, the literature on the subject is vast,[5] but here we are confined to commenting on Mark's first narrative.

Mark opens his first account with a transitional passage that refers to the sending out of the twelve (6:7-13) and prepares for the feeding of the multitude by moving the action to a deserted place. Mark refers to the returning twelve as *apostoloi*, the only time he applies this term to them, using it not as an exclusive title but as a description of their missionary work. They are *apostoloi* because they were 'sent out' to teach and to heal on behalf of Jesus. This understanding of apostle as Christian missionary reflects the meaning of apostleship in the post-Easter community, particularly in the writings of Paul.

When the apostles tell Jesus what they have done and taught, a report unsupported by any details, Jesus invites them to retire to a wilderness place for a rest. So many people are coming and going that the twelve have no leisure even to eat. Mark makes no connecting link between the withdrawal of Jesus and his previous story of the death of John the Baptist, unlike Matthew who says that the news of John's death prompts Jesus to escape to a deserted place, to be by himself (Mt 14:13).

5. For a detailed study of the comparisons and contrasts in the six accounts, see J.P. Meier, *A Marginal Jew: Rethinking the Historical Jesus* Vol 2 pp. 950-967; R.E. Brown, *The Gospel according to John* Vol 1 pp. 236-250; I. de la Potterie, 'The Multiplication of the Loaves in the Life of Jesus,' *Communio* 16 (1989) pp. 499-516.

The tired fugitives manage to get to a desert place but it is anything but deserted, for the energetic crowd, seeing their departure and anticipating where they were heading, manage to arrive there first 'on foot'. This is not a crossing of the lake to the Gentile side but a change of venue on the Jewish lake-side. Although the pressing need of the crowd does not coincide with the disciples' need for peace, there is no question which has priority. The schedule of care must continue. When Jesus disembarks and sees the expectant crowd, his reaction is one of compassion, for he sees the people as sheep without a shepherd.

This is reminiscent of Moses when he is shown the promised land but told he will not enter it. He asks God to appoint a leader, before his death in the wilderness, to take his place and lead the people into the land, so that they 'may not be like sheep without a shepherd.' (Num 27:17) God appoints a successor to Moses in the person of Joshua, who has the same name as Jesus himself – Jesus being the Greek form of the Hebrew/Aramaic Joshua or Jeshua. Jesus is now seen as the leader of a leaderless people in this wilderness place. Mark will again make use of the image of a leaderless people at the beginning of the passion narrative, when Jesus' prediction will be fulfilled, 'I will strike the shepherd, and the sheep will be scattered.' (14:27) Now he will try to teach his disciples how to exercise their leadership as shepherds over a leaderless people.

Before challenging his disciples to leadership, Jesus first exercises his own authority by teaching the crowd many things. As the day progresses to late afternoon, the disciples remind him of where they are and how late it is. Confronted with such a large crowd in such a lonely place, the disciples have their own pastoral suggestion: send the people away, so that they can provide for themselves by buying food in the surrounding villages. Then Jesus challenges the disciples to exercise their own leadership: 'You give them something to eat.'

The disciples object. They interpret Jesus' challenge to mean that they are to go and buy bread for the crowd. Jesus asks them what they have already, and tells them to check their own resources. After doing this, the disciples come up with the humble fund of five loaves and two fish. In 2 Kings 4:42-44 a man comes bringing the prophet Elisha twenty loaves of barley bread and fresh ears of grain. Elisha orders his servant: 'Give to the people and let them eat.' His servant objects that the food is too little for a hundred people. Elisha repeats his command, adding the prophecy: 'They shall eat and have some left.' The servant 'set it before them, they ate, and had some left, according to the word of the Lord.'

In Mark's story Jesus makes no comment on the meagre resources of the disciples, but orders them to get the people to sit in groups 'on the green grass.' Even though they are in a wilderness place, it is covered in spring green after the winter rains. The disciples do as Jesus asks, arranging the people in groups, to make the distribution of food easier.

Jesus then takes the little the disciples have, the five loaves and two fish, and looks up to heaven. The eucharistic language is strong: 'he took ... he blessed ... he broke ... he gave' (see 14:22; 1 Cor 11:23-24). Jesus gives the loaves to the disciples 'to set before the people'. The disciples now exercise their leadership by feeding the crowd they first wanted to turn away. The people eat until they are satisfied. Indeed twelve baskets, one for each disciple, are collected from what remains. Mark concludes with the note that there were five thousand people. Curiously absent from the miracle story is any reaction of awe or wonder by either the people or the disciples. This is all the more inexplicable when one considers the great impact attributed to a single exorcism, 'At once his fame began to spread throughout the surrounding region of Galilee.' (1:28)

Although this miracle is popularly referred to as 'the multiplication of the loaves', there is no word in the story about multiplication. The miracle is that Jesus takes the little the disciples have and shows how that little is more than enough to meet the hunger of a leaderless crowd. When the disciples share the little they have in the blessing of Jesus, they discover that the crowd is satisfied. There is no need to send anyone away.

Their leadership and ministry will be a sharing from poverty. Poverty of resources is not an excuse to dismiss people; poverty is not a diriment impediment to ministry. Disciples can become fascinated with their own poverty, obsessed by their own apparent inability to do anything of consequence in the face of people's needs. Jesus, however, is never embarrassed by poverty. When disciples share their meagre resources in the name of Jesus, that is always a miracle.

Revelation at sea   6:45-52

[45] Immediately he made his disciples get into the boat and go on ahead to the other side, to Bethsaida, while he dismissed the crowd. [46]After saying farewell to them, he went up on the mountain to pray.
[47]When evening came, the boat was out on the sea, and he was alone on the land. [48]When he saw that they were straining at the oars against an adverse wind, he came towards them early in the morning, walking on the sea. He intended to pass them by. [49]But when they saw him walking on the sea, they thought it was a ghost and cried out; [50]for they all saw him and were terrifed. But immediatly he spoke to them and said 'Take heart, it is I; do not be afraid.' [51]Then he got into the boat with them and the wind ceased. And they were utterly astounded. [52]For they did not understand about the loaves, but their hearts were hardened.

Mark follows the story of the feeding of the five thousand with the account of Jesus walking on the water, and the close connection between the two stories was probably in the primitive tradition Mark used as his source. It is worth noting that the fourth evangelist's independent account follows the same sequence (Jn 6:16-21); Matthew, following Mark's sequence, inserts his own account of Peter trying to walk to Jesus on the water (Mt 14:28-32).[6] Luke omits the story.

After Jesus succeeds in challenging the disciples to exercise their leadership over a leaderless hungry people, he now commands them to go on ahead without him, to cross to the other side on their own initiative. Mark gives their destination as Bethsaida, a small fishing village on the north-east shore of the Sea of Galilee, less than a mile from the Jordan. Bethsaida was in the tetrachy of Philip. About a mile further inland from the village, Philip had built a new city that he named Julias, to honour the daughter of Augustus Caesar. Josephus refers to the whole place as Bethsaida-Julias.[7] John's Gospel provides a reason for Jesus' hasty departure from the territory of Herod Antipas: following the feeding of the multitude,

6. For an extensive treatment of the three accounts, see J.P. Heil, *Jesus Walking on the Sea* (Analecta Biblica 87; Rome: Biblical Institute, 1981).
7. Josephus, *Jewish Wars* 2.9.1; *Antiquities*, 18.4.6.

the excited Galilean crowd wanted to make Jesus king by force (Jn 6:14-15).

Jesus says farewell to the crowd, dismisses them and goes up a mountain to pray. After mentioning the time as evening, Mark underlines Jesus' detachment from his followers. With Jesus alone on the mountain and the disciples all at sea, the separation is established. But they will soon be reunited at the initiative of Jesus. When he sees his disciples struggling at the oars against an adverse wind, he comes towards them, walking on the sea. In the Greek text the time is about the fourth watch of the night – between 3 a.m. and 6 a.m. – which our translation interprets as 'early in the morning'.

Jesus overcomes the separation between himself and his disciples by coming to them, walking on the sea. Mark tells us that Jesus' purpose for performing the miracle was that 'he intended to pass them by.' This means the contrary of what we might suppose: it signifies, in the language and imagery of Old Testament theophanies, that Jesus wished to reveal himself to his disciples by illustrating his dominion over the sea, the place of chaos and evil. In celebrating God's unlimited power over creation, one that no mortal can share, Job described God as the one 'who tramples the waves of the sea' (Job 9:8). Later God spoke to Job out of a whirlwind, listing divine qualities that forever separate him from human beings: 'Have you entered into the springs of the sea, or walked in the recesses of the deep?' (Job 38:16) This power, unique to God, is now applied to Jesus in the Gospel miracle-story.

The phrase 'to pass by' is best understood with the help of the Old Testament. In Exodus, when Moses begs God to reveal his glory, God consents, promising: 'I will make all my goodness pass before you (or by) you, and will proclaim before you the name, "The Lord" ' (Ex 33:19). The Hebrew text uses the verb *'ahar* (to pass by): the Greek Old Testament uses the verb *parerchomai*, the same verb Mark uses to describe the purpose of Jesus, 'He intended to *pass by* them.' In the Exodus story, God keeps his promise, comes down and stands beside Moses, passes by him and reveals his identity in a solemn formula. In Mark's story, Jesus' declared purpose is to pass by his disciples, to reveal himself to them, which he does by coming close to them and proclaiming his identity in the solemn formula: 'Take heart, it is I; do not be afraid.'

Mark emphasises that the declared purpose of Jesus' coming to his disciples on the water is to reveal himself to them. This is a story of Jesus as the epiphany of God, not a rescue story of the disciples at sea. Unlike the story of the stilling of the storm (4:35-41), the disciples are not in grave danger, nor are they crying out to Jesus in fear for their lives. The disciples do not need rescuing. A contrary wind that makes rowing arduous and progress difficult hardly constitutes a serious danger for fishermen; rather, it is an occupational hazard. In this story the disciples are terrified because they think they are seeing a ghost, not because they are afraid of the elements.

At the heart of Jesus' self-revelation is the pronouncement, 'It is I' (*ego eimi*). This reflects God's self-proclamation to Moses (Ex 3:14-15), translated in the Greek Old Testament as *ego eimi ho on* ('I am the One who is'). This proclamation of the mystery and nearness of God is celebrated in Second Isaiah:

Do not fear for I have redeemed you ...
When you pass through the waters, I will be with you ...
For I am the Lord your God ...
Do not fear, for I am with you ...
You are my witnesses, says the Lord, and my servant whom I
    have chosen,
so that you may know and believe me
and understand that I am he ...
I, I am the Lord,
and besides me there is no saviour ...
Thus says the Lord,
who makes a way in the sea
a path in the mighty waters ... (Is 43:1-16)

The words 'I am' are used as a name for God, one that signifies his saving presence among his people. This is not, however, the interpretation of the disciples in Mark's story. When Jesus joins them in the boat, the wind ceases – not by a word of command but by his presence with them. The disciples are utterly astonished, 'for they did not understand about the loaves, but their hearts were hardened.' Matthew concludes his epiphany story with the disciples worshipping Jesus and confessing, 'Truly you are the Son of

God.' (Mt 14:33) This might be the response of Mark's community on reading the story, but Mark now categorises the disciples with the opponents of Jesus, those who grieved him because of 'their hardness of heart.' (3:5) The disciples' lack of understanding is all the more dramatic when we read that on reaching land the disciples disembark and the 'people at once recognised him' (6:54).

Mark's narrative, overlaid as it is with Old Testament themes associated with theophany, is a christological confession of Jesus in the form of a story. While the story might appear more at home in the 'high christology' of John's Gospel, it reflects how early this christology came in as part of the tradition of the church. It demonstrates the belief that Jesus is the epiphany of God, the one who comes among his own people to reveal and to save, even if his coming is not understood by those who might be expected to recognise it and welcome it. This might be a consolation for the early Christians who had to take into account an embarrassing historical fact: not many people believed in Jesus as the unique Son of God.

Healing the sick at Gennesaret   6:53-56

⁵³ When they had crossed over they came to land at Gennesaret and moored the boat. ⁵⁴When they got out of the boat, people at once recognized him, ⁵⁵and rushed about that whole region and began to bring the sick on mats to wherever they heard he was. ⁵⁶And wherever he went, into villages or cities or farms, they laid the sick in the marketplaces, and begged him that they might touch even the fringe of his cloak; and all who touched it were healed.

Having originally set out for Bethsaida, the disciples now land their boat at Gennesaret. The fertile plain of Gennesaret, part of the rift valley, is located on the north-west side of the Sea of Galilee, between Tiberias and Capernaum. According to Josephus, the area was well irrigated by three brooks, allowing the growth of a variety of species including walnut, palm-trees, figs and olives.[8] The region was also well populated, and the *Via Maris* passed through the plain linking the coastal cities and Megiddo with Syria to the north.

Jesus and the disciples, after a sleepless night, have no time to

8. See Josephus, *Antiquities*, 3.5.15-18.

rest when they land at Gennesaret. The people recognise Jesus and start rushing about the whole region, bringing the sick wherever Jesus happens to be. Mark's summary account of Jesus' travels into villages and cities and farms – no synagogues are mentioned – offers no details about where exactly he goes. Neither does Mark give particulars about the sick or their infirmities. No teaching or preaching is mentioned. The only detail offered is that people beg to touch the fringe of his cloak, and those who touch it are healed. This may be a reference to the garment that had tassels called *tzitzit* attached to its four corners, as prescribed by the Torah (Num 15:38; Deut 22:12). In popular belief these fringes were regarded as having the power of a talisman.

The passage, situated between the misunderstanding of the disciples and the hostility of the Pharisees, serves to remind the reader of the popularity of Jesus' healing ministry among the people. Yet Mark's summary also gives the impression that Jesus is moving from place to place, but finding peace nowhere. The rest and retirement he held out to his disciples after their mission (6:31) still await their own time.

The tradition of the elders   7:1-23

Now when the Pharisees and some of the scribes who had come from Jerusalem gathered around him, [2]they noticed that some of his disciples were eating with defiled hands, that is, without washing them. [3](For the Pharisees, and all the Jews, do not eat unless they thoroughly wash their hands, thus observing the tradition of the elders, [4]and they do not eat anything from the market unless they wash it; and there are also many other traditions that they observe, the washing of cups, pots, and bronze kettles.) [5]So the Pharisees and the scribes asked him, 'Why do your disciples not live according to the tradition of the elders, but eat with defiled hands?' [6]He said to them, 'Isaiah prophesied rightly about you hypocrites, as it is written,

"This people honors me with their lips,
but their hearts are far from me;
[7]in vain do they worship me,
teaching human precepts as doctrines."

[8]You abandon the commandment of God and hold to human tradition.'

[9]Then he said to them, 'You have a fine way of rejecting the commandment of God in order to keep your tradition! [10]For Moses said, "Honour your father and your mother": and, "Whoever speaks evil of

father or mother must surely die." [11]But you say that if anyone tells father or mother, "Whatever support you might have had from me is Corban" (that is, an offering to God) – [12]then you no longer permit doing anything for a father or mother. [13]thus making void the word of God through your tradition that you have handed on. And you do many things like this.'

[14]Then he called the crowd again and said to them, 'Listen to me, all of you, and understand: [15]there is nothing outside a person that by going in can defile but the things that come out are what defile.'

[17]When he had left the crowd and entered the house, his disciples asked him about the parable. [18]He said to them, 'Then do you also fail to understand? Do you not see that whatever goes into a person from outside cannot defile, [19]since it enters, not the heart but the stomach, and goes out into the sewer?' (Thus he declared all foods clean.) [20]And he said, 'It is what comes out of a person that defiles. [21]For it is from within, from the human heart, that evil intentions come: fornication, theft, murder, [22]adultery, avarice, wickedness, deceit, licentiousness, envy, slander, pride, folly. [23]all these evil things come from within, and they defile a person.'

This section of controversy and teaching has no discernible link with the previous passage, and Mark makes no suggestion when or where the incident takes place. It precedes Jesus' meeting with the Gentile woman (7:24-30), and this might warrant its present setting. As Kelber notes:

> The author of the Markan Gospel feels and writes from a Jewish perspective. The integration of the Gentiles constitutes a difficult problem for him, which calls for special clarification. Before the acceptance of the Gentiles is formalised, the legal issue has to be settled. This is the function of the abolition of ritual taboos (7:1-23).[9]

The section easily lends itself to a threefold division.

Washing of hands   7:1-8
The narrative opens with the arrival of the Pharisees, who are probably Galilean, together with some scribes who have come from Jerusalem. These opponents, already familiar to us from the series of five conflict stories in 2:1-3:6, now gather around Jesus. Some of the disciples have been eating food without first washing their hands, a practice that is criticised not as unhygienic but as a

9. W.H. Kelber, *Mark's Story of Jesus* p. 37.

violation of ritual cleanliness connected with Pharisaic table fellowship. The washing was to remove defilement produced by contact with profane things. In an editorial note for his Gentile readers, Mark puts the Pharisees together with 'all the Jews,' an indiscriminate association that would seem more appropriate coming from a Gentile writer. As Taylor observes: 'The tone is certainly hostile as throughout the entire passage.'[10]

The tradition of the elders is quoted as the source of the practice of hand washing, and Mark enlists other traditions of ritual cleansing from the same source. This unwritten tradition was handed down by generations of rabbis and treated by the Pharisees as though it was as binding as the written Torah. The oral tradition came to be written down in the second century in the Mishnah and two centuries later in its commentary, the Talmud. The Pharisees want to extend the laws of ritual purity, which originally referred only to priests before entering the sanctuary (Ex 30:19), to all Jews, thus fulfilling the vision of a priestly people.

To the question why his disciples fail to observe the tradition of the elders, Jesus applies the words of Isaiah 29:13 to his opponents, whom he calls *hypocrites*, a Greek word denoting stage actors who assume a role not their own for the benefit of the public. The accusation is levelled against these religious actors that they honour God only with their lips, while their hearts are engaged elsewhere; their worship is useless theatre; their message tries to pass off human precepts as the word of God. Charging them with theological perversity, Jesus claims that they abandon the commandments of God and hold fast to inventions of formal piety.

Jerome Neyrey has analysed all Mark's comments on ritual purity in anthropological terms, showing how the purity rules function as boundary setting mechanisms for the community.[11] He argues that Jesus and the Pharisees are competing for control over the community. The Pharisees, who are defenders of a certain type of community, are attacked by Jesus for their purity regulations and, elsewhere, for their restrictive table fellowship and sabbath traditions. The effect of Jesus' teaching is to widen the boundaries of the community, therefore loosening the norms for its member-

10. V. Taylor, *The Gospel according to St. Mark* p. 335.
11. J. Neyrey, 'The Idea of Purity in Mark's Gospel,' *Semeia* 35 (1986) pp. 91-128

ship. In doing this Jesus creates a community outside the control of their traditions and authority. This interpretation goes some way to explain the deep hostility shown to Jesus, since the argument is not about esoteric matters of ceremonial law, but one that affects the life of community itself.

The question of Corban   7:9-13

In all its irony the opening charge recapitulates the meaning of the previous verses: to secure their traditions, the Pharisees and the scribes are skilled in making a casualty of the commandment of God. Quoting Moses, the prophet who gave the people the divine commandments, Jesus stands firmly in support of the Decalogue. The divine commandment involves honouring one's parents and not holding them in contempt. This stands in sharp contrast to the teaching of the Pharisees and scribes on Corban – a transliteration of the Hebrew *korban*, which means 'an offering' or 'a gift devoted to God'.

In this teaching, a son who declares money or property a gift to God, even though he does not actually give anything to the Temple, legally excludes his parents from the right of benefit. Even when sons vowed their money to God in haste or anger, the rigorous interpretation of the law did not dispense them from their original vow. The misuse of Corban, which is supported uncritically by some religious leaders, is fraudulent piety because it uses God to avoid moral obligation and puts religious custom before people. This destroys the very purpose of God's commandment, to say nothing of common decency. Gould comments:

> The choice in such cases is not between God and man, but between two ways of serving God, the one formal and the other real. Offerings belong to the formal side of worship, whereas God is really served and worshipped in our human duties and affections.[12]

The misuse of Corban is not an isolated example, but typical of many other contraventions of God's word. In the name of human tradition, God's word is being emptied of its spirit and power by the very people who should be its promoters and guardians.

12. M. Gould, *St. Mark* p. 129.

Clean and unclean food   7:14-23

In this passage Jesus calls the people, teaches them in the form of a 'parable' – which in this case probably means a proverbial saying – and then privately explains the saying for the benefit of his disciples (see 4:34). Jesus calls the crowd not only to listen but to understand, but he does not explain the riddle to them. What defiles a person is not what he takes in but what he gives out. Goodness is rooted in the inner disposition, not in the outward observance.

When the disciples are inside the house with Jesus, they ask him about the parable. Again the disciples' failure to understand is noted, reflecting the earlier question that Jesus asked after telling the parable of the sower: 'Do you not understand this parable? Then how will you understand all the parables?' (4:13) Jesus tells them that the material food people consume cannot defile their spiritual selves. Mark's editorial note, that Jesus abrogates the distinction between clean and unclean in matters of food, thus declaring all foods clean, is clearly written from inside the viewpoint of the early Christian church. Mark's narrative has Jesus annul whole sections of the written Law (see Lev 11-15), minutes after criticising the Pharisees for not upholding the same Law. This seems, at best, to be claiming too much.

If in Stage 1 of the tradition, the historical Jesus had so clearly emancipated his followers from all food laws, why did they spend so much time arguing about these matters in the early church? (See Acts 10-11.15; Gal 2; Rom 14:13-23.) Probably the clearest example is Peter's vision prior to his visit to the centurion Cornelius. When Peter sees a large sheet coming down from heaven containing all kinds of animals, he hears a voice commanding him: ' "Get up, Peter, kill and eat." But Peter said, "By no means, Lord; for I have never eaten anything that is profane or unclean." The voice said to him again, a second time, "What God has made clean, you must not call profane." ' (Acts 10:13-15)

This does not mean that Mark's passage is pure invention, but it does suggest that Jesus' original criticism was not as wide-ranging as Mark suggests.

Jesus focuses on a person's inside as the source of good or evil. The implication of Mark's passage is that the Pharisees and scribes who confront Jesus on matters of ritual are themselves defiled by the malice that is within them, while Jesus and his disciples are undefiled because ritually impure food can defile nobody. Placing the passage here, immediately before Jesus' journey into Gentile territory, Mark prepares the ground for a new fellowship between Jew and Gentile.

A Gentile woman comes to Jesus 7:24-30

[24]From there he set out and went away to the region of Tyre. He entered a house and did not want anyone to know he was there. Yet he could not escape notice, [25]but a woman whose little daughter had an unclean spirit immediately heard about him, and she came and bowed down at his feet. [26]Now the woman was a Gentile, of Syrophoenician origin. She begged him to cast the demon out of her daughter. [27]He said to her, 'Let the children be fed first, for it is not fair to take the children's food and throw it to the dogs.' [28]But she answered him, 'Sir, even the dogs under the table eat the children's crumbs.' [29]Then he said to her, 'For saying that, you may go – the demon has left your daughter.' [30]So she went home, found the child lying on the bed, and the demon gone.

Jesus moves farther from the region of Herod Antipas as he travels north to the region of Tyre. Tyre was one of the most ancient cities on the Phoenician coast and a great cosmopolitan centre. Its people were renowned as seafarers and merchants. It first appears in the Old Testament, when Ezekiel imagines its destruction by Nebuchadnezzar. The prophet pictures the mariners of the world lamenting over the greatest city that ever graced the Mediterranean: 'Who was ever destroyed like Tyre in the midst of the sea? When your wares came from the seas, you satisfied many peoples; with your abundant wealth and merchandise you enriched the kings of the earth. Now you are wrecked by the seas, in the depths of the waters'. (Ezek 27:32-34) Isaiah predicted that the wealth of Tyre and Sidon would one day belong to the people of Israel, while Jeremiah lists the two cities among the traditional enemies of Judah (Is 25:22).

In antiquity Tyre was an island, but when Alexander the Great captured the fortress city in 322 B.C., he made it into a peninsula by linking the island to the mainland with a causeway. Although subject to Roman rule from the time of Augustus, Tyre managed to stay relatively free from interference in its traditional mercantile dealings with other nations. Its mainland territory reached south to the borders of Upper Galilee.

With Jesus' journey north to the region of Tyre, the Gospel marks Jesus' definite break from the Pharisees and the scribes in their purity regulations (7:1-23) and the end of the Galilean ministry. Jesus will pass through Galilee again, but he will do so incognito, concentrating his energy on his disciples (9:30). Although the four Gospels and Paul agree that Jesus did not make a programmatic mission to the Gentiles as a group during his lifetime,[13] the turning to Gentile territory in this section (7:34-8:26) will be of special interest to Mark's Gentile-Christian readers, showing them that the saving power of Jesus was not limited exclusively to Jews.

In Mark, Jesus goes into a house, wishing nothing to be known of his presence; there is no mention of the disciples. In Matthew's account (Mt 15:21-28), he walks in the street openly with his disciples. Mark tells us that Jesus has come to the district not for ministry but for privacy, presumably for the rest and reflection that have eluded him and the disciples since the mission of the twelve (6:31). His reputation is known, however, even here – possibly from those who followed him earlier from Tyre and Sidon (3:8). If the house Jesus enters is Gentile, it stands in dramatic contrast to Peter's later statement to Cornelius: 'You yourselves know that it is unlawful for a Jew to associate with or visit a Gentile ... ' (Acts 10:28).

A woman comes to the house where Jesus is staying, and Mark first describes her as a mother whose daughter has an unclean spirit. The woman's attitude of faith, prostrating herself at the feet of Jesus, stands in contrast to the Pharisaic inflexibility described in the previous passage. She is described by her religion and her nationality. She is a Greek, *Hellenis* – our translation gives the meaning as Gentile – and a *Syro*-Phoenician by birth, to distinguish her from the Phoenicians who live in Libya and Carthage, in the north of Africa. When she begs Jesus to cast the demon out of his daughter, he replies that the children should be fed first, since it is unfair to take the children's food and throw it to the dogs. Only Jews have a right to be treated as 'children' of God; the Gentiles, like this woman, are 'dogs'. She is outside the territory of Jesus' pastoral concern.

13. See J. Jeremias, *Jesus' Promise to the Nations* (London: SCM, 1967)

Addressed to a sincere petitioner, the language of Jesus' reply sounds harsh and insulting. He ignores the needs of her afflicted child to concentrate on the rights of the children (the Jews). If Jesus' reply is calculated to dismiss her and so be left in peace, it clearly fails to work. She addresses Jesus as *kyrie* ('sir') – the only time in Mark's Gospel that Jesus is addressed by this title, one that will later bear the weight of Christian theology with its meaning of 'Lord'. The woman refuses to take 'No' for an answer; she refuses to be diverted from her goal by initial rejection; she is steadfastly unimpressed with theological divisions. Ignoring the *separatist* view of Jesus, she makes a witty *connection* between children and dogs: even the dogs under the table eat the children's crumbs. The crumbs of the children become dog-food, something that will satisfy this woman, dog that she might be. Her persistence, which is more developed in Matthew's account (Mt 15:21-28), is rewarded and she succeeds in converting Jesus.

Ironically, this desperate woman is Jesus' teacher. The theological distance that separates Jesus from the woman and the physical distance that separates Jesus from her daughter are now overcome. Jesus yields to the Gentile woman's request and, with no promise of healing or word of command, he assures her that her daughter is already cured.

Mark's focus is not on the exorcism but on the conversation between the woman and Jesus, on the propriety of Jesus the Jew healing a Gentile. It provides Mark with a warrant for the early church's mission to the Gentiles, announced by Paul in his dictum: 'to the Jew first and also to the Greek' (Rom 1:16).

Jesus cures a deaf man   7:31-37

[31]Then he returned from the region of Tyre, and went by way of Sidon towards the Sea of Galilee, in the region of the Decapolis. [32]They brought to him a deaf man who had an impediment in his speech; and they begged him to lay his hand on him. [33]He took him aside in private, away from the crowd, and put his fingers into his ears, and he spat and touched his tongue. [34]Then looking up to heaven, he sighed and said to him, 'Ephphatha,' that is, 'Be opened.' [35]And immediately his ears were opened, his tongue was released and he spoke plainly. [36]Then Jesus ordered them to tell no one; but the more he ordered them, the more zealously they proclaimed it. [37]They were astounded beyond

measure, saying, 'He has done everything well; he even makes the deaf to hear and the mute to speak.'

Jesus leaves one Gentile territory to travel into another. By a strangely circuitous route – twenty miles north from Tyre to Sidon, south-east across the Leontes, continuing to the east of the Jordan, turning south past the east side of the Sea of Galilee and then travelling farther south through the region of the Decapolis – this confusing itinerary may tell us more about Mark's geographical sense than Jesus' actual journey. The important point is that it provides a Gentile setting for the cure of the deaf man and the feeding of the four thousand.

In a previous visit to the Decapolis, when Jesus had cured the Gerasene demoniac, the people had begged Jesus to leave the neighbourhood. The people of the district now come to Jesus in hope, bringing with them a man who suffers from a double affliction: he is deaf and suffers from a speech impediment. They beg Jesus to lay his hand on him. Taking the man apart from the crowd, Jesus performs a cure that seems to be an elaborate magical ritual more easily associated with pagan tradition – which might explain why this story is omitted by Matthew and Luke. The language of signs Jesus uses, however, could simply be explained as conveying his purpose to the man who is otherwise cut off from other means of communication.

Jesus touches the afflicted man, first by placing his fingers into the man's ears, then applying saliva to his lips or tongue. The use of spittle as a curative device was common to both Greek and Jewish healers. Jesus looks up to heaven, sighs either in prayer or in compassion, and then speaks a word of command, which Mark gives in the original Aramaic. With the word of command, the man's ears are opened and he is now able to speak clearly.

The miracle is followed by a command to the crowds to say nothing about the cure, reflecting Mark's insistence that Jesus' identity cannot be fully captured in this healing story and will be revealed only after his death and resurrection. The prohibition proves a useless exercise, since the more Jesus commands the crowd to silence, the more they proclaim what has happened. Mark tells us that their reaction is one of astonishment beyond measure. They speak of Jesus as the one who has done everything well, even making the deaf to hear and the mute to speak.

The phrase 'had an impediment in his speech' translates a single Greek word, *mogilalos*, the only time it occurs in the New Testament. The only occurrence of this word in the Greek Old Testament is in Isaiah 35:6. There is a description of the wonderful events that will happen when God's saving purposes will be fulfilled at the end-time: 'Then the eyes of the blind shall be opened, and the ears of the deaf unstopped; then the lame shall leap like a deer, and the tongue of the speechless (*mogilalos*) sing for joy.' (Is 35:5-6) The cure of the Gentile could serve a symbolic purpose for Mark and his readers: the Gentiles, once deaf and dumb towards God, are now capable of responding to the signs and words of Jesus. Through this veiled revelation among the Gentiles, Mark is clearly suggesting to his readers that the age of messianic salvation has now arrived in Jesus.

Not until Caesarea Philippi, also in Gentile territory, will the proclamation of Jesus' identity as the Messiah be made. Then the ears of the disciples will be opened and their tongues released, so that they can declare through Peter their spokesman, 'You are the Messiah' (8:21).

The feeding of the four thousand   8:1-10

In those days when there was again a great crowd without anything to eat, he called his disciples and said to them, [2]'I have compassion for the crowd, because they have been with me now for three days and have nothing to eat. [3]If I send them away hungry to their homes, they will faint on the way – and some of them have come from a great distance.' [4]His disciples replied, 'How can one feed these people with bread here in the desert?' [5]He asked them, 'How many loaves do you have?' They said, 'Seven.' [6]Then he ordered the crowd to sit down on the ground; and he took the seven loaves, and after giving thanks he broke them and gave them to his disciples to distribute; and they distributed them to the crowd. [7]They had also a few small fish; and after blessing them, he ordered that these too should be distributed. [8]They ate and were filled; and they took up the broken pieces left over, seven baskets full. [9]Now there were about four thousand people. And he sent them away. [10]And immediately he got into the boat with his disciples and went to the district of Dalmanutha.

The proclamation of the Gentile crowd at the close of the previous miracle story concluded a section in the Gospel that began with the feeding of the five thousand in 6:30-44. The story of the feeding of the four thousand begins a cycle of events that parallels the previous section. Mark's arrangement of his material can be seen in the table below.

The feeding of the 5,000 (6:35-44)	The feeding of the 4,000 (8:1-9)
The crossing of the lake (6:45-53)	The crossing of the lake (8:10)
A controversy with the Pharisees (7:1-23)	A controversy with the Pharisees (8:11-13)
The children's bread (7:24-30)	The leaven of the Pharisees (8:14-21)
The healing of a deaf man (7:31-37)	The healing of a blind man (8:22-26)

The episodes between the two feedings can be interpreted as a preparation for the Gentiles to participate in the story of salvation. The first feeding of the multitude took place in Galilee and its beneficiaries were Jews. The twelve baskets in that account could be read to symbolise the twelve tribes of Israel. The second feeding of the multitude takes place in the Decapolis, which was largely a pagan territory, and its beneficiaries are almost certainly Gentiles. The seven baskets could refer to the seven pagan peoples who once inhabited the promised land (Deut 7:1; see Acts 13:19) or to the Gentile mission, that is to the seventy nations of the world, undertaken by the seven Hellenist deacons under the supervision of Stephen in Acts 6:1-7. Certainly, when Jesus later asks the disciples about the different number of baskets in the two feedings (8:19-20), even though they answer correctly, he rebukes them for failing to understand the symbolic meaning of the miracles. The implication is that the different number of baskets has a special significance.

The order of the two accounts, first the feeding of the Jews followed by the feeding of the Gentiles, could be interpreted as a hopeful narrative commentary on Jesus' earlier saying, 'Let the children be fed first' (7:27).

For comment on the Old Testament parallels to the story, see the commentary on 6:30-34.

The crowd have been with Jesus for three days, and they have had nothing to eat. Apparently their eagerness to be with Jesus has postponed their basic need of food. Jesus calls his disciples and speaks to them about the compassion he feels for them and his reluctance to send them home hungry. Some have a long journey of return, and there is a real possibility they will faint on the way. The disciples' objection sounds like a repeat of their earlier one: how can the crowd be fed in a wilderness place? In spite of the previous feeding in a wilderness place, they seem to be suffering either from incredible dullness or from acute amnesia. Their failure to understand is the principal reason that has lead some commentators to argue that the two feeding narratives must be variant accounts of the same incident. When asked this time about their resources, the disciples mention they have seven loaves. Jesus himself orders the crowd to sit down in preparation for the food they will be given. Jesus' actions over the bread closely resemble his actions at the Last Supper (Mk 14:22-23) as can be seen in the following table.

The feeding of the crowd	The Last Supper
over the bread	*over the bread*
HE TOOK the seven loaves of	HE TOOK a loaf of
BREAD	BREAD
AND AFTER GIVING THANKS	AND AFTER BLESSING it
HE BROKE them	HE BROKE it
AND GAVE them	AND GAVE it
TO HIS DISCIPLES	to them

Mention of the fish is artfully postponed until after the disciples have distributed the bread to the crowd, thus heightening the eucharistic significance of the account. Clearly the focus is on the bread, although there is some similarity between Jesus pronouncing a blessing over the fish and doing likewise over the wine at the Last Supper. In both accounts Jesus 'gives thanks' and 'pronounces a blessing' over the two elements of food. After Jesus blesses the few small fish, the disciples distribute them to the crowd. Like the first feeding, Jesus actively involves the disciples in serving the needs of the crowd. It is as if, in some veiled way, they are being initiated into ministry to the Gentiles. Kelber comments:

> Both their feeding of the Jews and their feeding of the Gentiles
> should enlighten them with respect to their own future roles and
> the kind of community for which they were to carry responsibil-
> ity.[14]

The crowd eat and are filled, and the disciples collect seven
baskets full of broken pieces. As in the first feeding, no surprise or
wonder is registered by anyone. After the feeding, Jesus dismisses
the crowd and sets out with his disciples on the boat to the district
of Dalmanutha, a name that appears on no known map.

The demand for a sign   8:11-13

[11] The Pharisees came and began to argue with him, asking him for a
sign from heaven, to test him. [12]And he sighed deeply in his spirit and
said, 'Why does this generation ask for a sign? Truly I tell you, no sign
will be given to this generation.' [13]And he left them, and getting into the
boat again, he went across to the other side.

Jesus has crossed to the west shore of the Sea of Galilee: in the
parallel account in Matthew, the place is given as Magdala (15:39),
which lies approximately one mile north of Tiberias. Jesus has been
absent from Jewish territory since his dispute with the Pharisees
about the tradition of the elders (7:1-23); now on his return, they
come for a new contest. This time they ask him for a sign from
heaven, to test him.

Mark's first comment on the conflict between Jesus and the
religious authorities –'for he taught them as one having authority,
and not as the scribes' (1:22) – summarised the root issue at the
heart of the conflict between Jesus and the authorities who oppose
him. Mark has shown us Jesus exercise his authority by proclaiming the good news of God, calling disciples, healing the sick,
exorcising demons, overriding the tradition of the elders, ministering to Gentiles, and feeding the multitudes. The religious authorities began their opposition to Jesus by way of indirect confrontation
with the disciples of Jesus; now their opposition becomes more
vigorous, as we see in this passage, when they move to direct
confrontation. Kingsbury comments:

14. W.H. Kelber, *Mark's Story of Jesus* p. 39.

The Pharisees, in demanding that Jesus give them a sign from heaven, at last do what their confederates have not previously dared to do: challenge Jesus directly on a matter relating to his own action (8:11-13). At this Mark has so guided events in the middle of his story that the conflict between Jesus and the authorities has intensified to the point where it has become acutely confrontational: attacks are no more indirect but face to face.[15]

Jesus asks a question about why this generation seeks a sign, but he declines to answer his own question. Indeed it must seem puzzling to Mark's readers that after such a litany of miracles, a sign of Jesus' trustworthiness would be regarded as essential. The Pharisees, however, unless they are being utterly perverse, believe that Jesus' mighty works (*dynameis*) are not signs (*semeia*) because the miracles by themselves are ambiguous and do not prove that Jesus is working in the power of God. Earlier in the narrative, the scribes who came from Jerusalem attributed Jesus' exorcisms to the power of Beelzebul (3:22). The issue is still about authority: by what authority does Jesus do what he does? Is he the agent of God or of the devil?

The Pharisees' request for a heavenly sign that will accredit Jesus and his message evokes from Jesus a deep groan. His refusal is as absolute as it is blunt: he will not perform on demand to satisfy his opponents, as if some heavenly demonstration dissociated from his ministry would compel their belief. Jesus cannot compel their belief, or indeed anyone else's; the Pharisees have to make their own journey and arrive at their own judgement. The presumption is that Jesus believes his miracles are self-authenticating, a point that is clarified by reference to the mission of Jonah in the parallel passages of Matthew and Luke (Mt 12:38-42; Lk 11:29-32). For Mark, there is nothing more for Jesus to say, there is nothing more that Jesus can do to satisfy his recalcitrant opponents. So Jesus leaves them behind, climbs into the boat and heads back across the Sea of Galilee to the Gentile side.

15. J.D. Kingsbury, 'The Religious Authorities in the Gospel of Mark,' *New Testament Studies* 36 (1990) p. 55.

The failure of the disciples   8:14-21

[14]Now the disciples had forgotten to bring any bread; and they had only one loaf with them in the boat. [15]And he cautioned them, saying, 'Watch out – beware of the yeast of the Pharisees and the yeast of Herod.' [16]They said to one another, 'It is because we have no bread.' [17]And becoming aware of it, Jesus said to them, 'Why are you talking about having no bread? Do you still not perceive or understand? Are your hearts hardened? [18]Do you have eyes, and fail to see? Do you have ears, and fail to hear? And do you not remember? [19]When I broke the five loaves for the five thousand, how many baskets full of broken pieces did you collect?' They said to him, 'Twelve.' [20]'And the seven for the four thousand, how many baskets full of broken pieces did you collect?' And they said to him, 'Seven.' [21]Then he said to them, 'Do you not yet understand?'

After refusing the Pharisees' demand for a sign, Jesus, accompanied by his disciples, makes his way to the east shore of the Sea of Galilee. As the Sea divides the Jewish and Gentile sides, the boat is used as a way of crossing the divide between opposite shores. The crossing to the Gentile side is the setting Mark provides for drawing together Jesus' complex saying about the yeast of the Pharisees and his severe criticism of the disciples for their failure to understand the miracles of the feeding. The passage, it has to be said, is notoriously difficult to interpret.

The account of the journey opens by noting a problem – the disciples have forgotten to bring sufficient bread with them, but they do have one loaf. Following two miracles in which Jesus fed different crowds, the disciples' concern seems somewhat misplaced. For the moment, nothing is said about this; rather Jesus warns them against the 'yeast' of the Pharisees and the 'yeast' of Herod. What the 'yeast' refers to, Mark does not say. In Matthew's account, he substitutes the Saduccees for Herod, and explains that the yeast refers to their teaching (Mt 16:5-12). This would make little sense in Mark's reading, since Herod is not famous for his teaching.

When Paul writes to the Christian community at Corinth, he warns them that a little yeast leavens the whole batch of dough: 'Clean out the old yeast so that you may be a new batch, as you really are unleavened. For our paschal lamb, Christ, has been sacrificed. Therefore, let us celebrate the festival not with the yeast of malice and evil, but with the unleavened bread of sincerity and truth.' (1 Cor 5:7-8; see Gal 5:9) While not wishing to use Paul's clear imagery to interpret Mark's unexplained imagery, it is probable that Paul's imagery is not his own, but derives from a wider Jewish tradition that explained why, after the Passover, Jews were forbidden to eat any bread that was leavened. In this understanding, Jesus would be warning his disciples against the evil disposition of the Pharisees and of Herod.

The mention of yeast leads the disciples to think that Jesus is complaining about their lack of provisions. Jesus asks the question, 'Why are you still talking about having no bread?' As Beck rightly points out:

> The words *artous ouk echousin* in 8:16 and *artous ouk echete* in 8:17 should not be translated as 'they have no bread' and as 'you have no bread,' but as 'they did not have several loaves of bread' and as 'you do not have several loaves of bread.' 'No bread' as a translation in 8:16 and in 8:17 fails to take into consideration the plural form of the noun in contrast to the singular form 'one loaf' in 8:14. Further, the translation 'no bread' is nonsensical when it has just been stated that they had one loaf with them in the boat.[16]

The point might be that with Jesus present, the one loaf they have is sufficient. Mark's setting has its own teaching: Jesus and the disciples are in the boat. They are in transition between the Jewish and the Gentile shores. *One* loaf is all that is needed. Several, and therefore separate, loaves are not required for uniting Jews and Gentiles in table fellowship.

The series of questions that follows underlines the disciples' failure to understand. In 4:10-12 Jesus separated the twelve and those around him from the 'outsiders' – characterising the latter as those who look but do not see, as those who listen but do not understand. The disciples now seem to be relegated to the outsider group. Jesus' questions concentrate on the two different feeding miracles and their baskets of leftovers. The different words for baskets are preserved, *kophinoi* (baskets of a type used tradition-

---

16. N. Beck, 'Reclaiming a Biblical Text: The Mark 8:14-21 Discussion about Bread in the Boat,' *Catholic Biblical Quarterly* 43 (1981) p. 53.

ally by Jews?) for the feeding of the five thousand, and *spyrides* (ordinary baskets indicating the Gentile world?) for the feeding of the four thousand. It is difficult to uncover what significance, if any, Mark attaches to the different words. While the disciples' memory of the two events corresponds to the written accounts, their correct remembrance of the symbolic numbers seems to be vacant of understanding (see comment on 8:1-10).

Jesus' last question to his disciples ('Do you still not understand?') underlines their continued failure to grasp the significance of the two miracles of feeding. These miracles do not seem to have led the disciples, any more than the mighty works of Jesus have led the Pharisees, to faith in Jesus. As Countryman writes:

> Where faith is to come from, Mark has not yet revealed to us; but we are at least left with one great negative conclusion – it does not come from signs and wonders.[17]

Jesus cures the blind man at Bethsaida   8:22-26

[22]They came to Bethsaida. Some people brought a blind man to him and begged him to touch him. [23]He took the blind man by the hand and led him out of the village; and when he had put saliva on his eyes and laid his hands on him, he asked him, 'Can you see anything?' [24]And the man looked up and said, 'I can see people, but they look like trees, walking.' [25]Then Jesus laid his hands on his eyes again; and he looked intently and his sight was restored, and he saw everything clearly. [26]Then he sent him away to his home, saying, 'Do not even go into the village.'

After their boat journey from the west shore of the Sea of Galilee, Jesus and the disciples land at Bethsaida, on the north-east shore, east of the Jordan River. Recent surveys on the site argue that the Bethsaida referred to by Mark was probably the old fishing village, which acted as a port to Bethsaida-Julias, the new city built a little farther inland by the Herodian tetrarch Philip.[18]

When Jesus and the disciples arrive, some unnamed people from the village come to meet Jesus; they bring a blind man in the hope that Jesus will touch him and cure him. The resemblance between this story and the healing of the deaf man (7:31-37) is striking: in

17. L. Countryman, 'How Many Baskets Full? Mark 8:14-21 and the Value of Miracles in Mark,' *Catholic Biblical Quarterly* 47 (1985) p. 654.

18. See J. Strange, 'Beth-Saida,' *The Anchor Bible Dictionary* Vol 1 pp. 692-693.

both miracle stories, the people come with an afflicted man and ask Jesus to heal him by touch; Jesus takes the man aside and uses spittle; Jesus lays hands on him and cures him, then commands silence; no reaction by the cured man is registered. Both stories are found only in Mark. Taylor sets out the Greek text of the two accounts, underlining their linguistic agreements, but maintains that the differences are sufficiently striking to argue against duplicate accounts of the same incident.[19]

The significant difference in this story is that the miracle is the only one in the Gospels that describes a gradual cure, in two stages. After putting saliva on the blind man's eyes and laying hands on him, Jesus asks, 'Can you see anything?' The man responds that he can see 'people, but they look like trees, walking.' Only partial sight has been restored. Again Jesus goes to work by laying his hands on the man's eyes, and this time the cure is successful. Mark describes the cure in three graphic phrases – the man looks intently; his sight is restored; he sees clearly. Jesus sends him away home; the further command to avoid the village makes little sense if the man has to go home. Other ancient manuscripts have Jesus command him to tell no one in the village; however unrealistic the command sounds, it makes better sense in the light of Mark's editorial concern for secrecy during the public ministry. There is no mention of any reaction from the cured man or his helpers.

The miracle story is omitted by Matthew and Luke, possibly because they found the failure of Jesus to effect an immediate cure with spittle somewhat embarrassing.

The gradual nature of the blind man's cure, however, fits well into Mark's theological scheme. The story marks the end of the second bread-cycle that began with the feeding of the Gentile multitude at 8:10 and ends with the gradual healing of the blind man at 8:26 (see table on commentary of 8:1-10). The first bread-cycle began with the feeding of the Jewish multitude at 6:30 and ends with the cure of the deaf man at 7:37. In the first bread-cycle Mark says of the disciples: 'they did not understand about the loaves, for their hearts were hardened' (6:52). In the second bread-cycle, Jesus bluntly criticises the disciples: 'Do you have eyes, and fail to see? Do you have ears, and fail to hear? ... Do you not yet understand?'

19. V. Taylor, *The Gospel according to St. Mark* pp. 368-373.

(8:18,21) The disciples are blind and deaf to the significance of what Jesus is doing.

Given the story's position in the plan of Mark's Gospel, the healing of the blind man at Bethsaida looks back to the disciples' blindness and looks forward to the gradual opening of their eyes. The healing of the blind man, in two stages, symbolises the disciples' gradual growth to full sight. The first stage, which will be incomplete, will be when Peter as spokesman for the disciples confesses that Jesus is the Messiah (8:27-30). Peter's blurred view of Christ, however, evokes a rebuke from Jesus (8:33). The full vision of who Jesus is will be revealed only in the cross and resurrection, 'after the Son of Man has risen from the dead.' (9:9)

Thus Mark's story of the gradual healing of the blind man plays a pivotal role in the structure of his Gospel. The blindness of the disciples is not an affliction beyond healing, but healing will not be effected all at once. Their journey towards understanding will not be completed immediately. Further effort will be needed by Jesus to open their eyes. In the meantime they will see partially, but what they manage to see will never match the fullness of clarity. That will happen only when Jesus' mission is completed: only when Jesus' destiny is fulfilled on the cross will his true identity be revealed to a human being (15:39). And then it will not be one of his Jewish disciples who will be the first to see, but a Gentile in the service of imperial Rome.

5

The suffering Son of Man

8:27-10:52

The central section of the Gospel follows the geographical route from Caesarea Philippi in the north to the road heading south from Jericho, thus preparing for the entry into the city of Jerusalem. The theological route Mark traces has the same destination: the evangelist invites us to pay attention to how Jesus teaches his disciples about the way of the suffering Son of Man, in preparation for what will happen after their arrival in the city. The Galilean ministry is now over, and the action is directed towards Jerusalem. Mark's way of the cross begins 'on the way' to Caesarea Philippi: throughout this section Jesus, the disciples and, of course, the readers will always be 'on the way.'

The section opens with Peter's declaration about Jesus' identity, a passage that serves as the major turning point of the Gospel. In the first half of the Gospel, the unanswered question 'Who is Jesus?' was raised by Jesus' teaching and his mighty works. The popular guesses, that Jesus was John the Baptist or one of the mighty prophets, have proved wholly inadequate. The only voices to identify Jesus correctly have come from the demons. In the second half of the Gospel, the question about Jesus' identity is answered, but not by the disciples. Jesus reinterprets Peter's confession in terms of the suffering Son of Man: this and the consequences it has for discipleship dominate the remainder of the Gospel. If the way of Jesus is the way of rejection, suffering and death, vindicated by resurrection, that will also prove to be the way of discipleship.

As Jesus gradually and successfully opened the eyes of the blind man to see clearly (8:22-26), he tries to do likewise with his own disciples on the way to Jerusalem. His identity is disclosed progressively, in stages. The disciples' failure to understand Jesus' teaching about the nature of his destiny, however, means that they cannot yet understand who he is. Only when Jesus' destiny of suffering is grasped, is his identity revealed. Who he is and what he must undergo are wrapped inside the destiny of the suffering Son of Man.

Three passion predictions (8:31; 9:31; 10:33-34) help to determine the structure of the section, focusing on the way of suffering that cannot be avoided. The first prediction happens at Caesarea Philippi; the second occurs as Jesus and the disciples pass through Galilee; the third takes place as they are going up to Jerusalem. At three different 'stations' on the way, Jesus speaks to his disciples about the suffering and death he must undergo and also about his resurrection. The three predictions prepare the reader to interpret the death of Jesus: what is going to happen in Jerusalem is not some brutal misadventure, but part of the predetermined plan of God. The section closes, as did the previous one, with the healing of a blind man: this time, however, the blind man follows Jesus 'on the way.'

Peter's declaration   8:27-30

[27] Jesus went on with his disciples to the villages of Caesarea Philippi; and on the way he asked his disciples, 'Who do people say that I am?' [28]And they answered him, 'John the Baptist; and others, Elijah; and still others , one of the prophets.' [29]He asked them, 'But who do you say that I am?' Peter answered him, 'You are the Messiah.' [30]And he sternly ordered them not to tell anyone about him.

Jesus and his disciples head farther north to the villages in the region of Caesarea Philippi, some twenty-five miles north of Bethsaida but still within the tetrachy of Herod Philip. Caesarea Philippi was the name of the city and district situated at the foot of Mount Hermon; the city housed the official residence of Philip. Located between Syria and Palestine, Caesarea was originally called Paneas, receiving its name from a cave and spring dedicated to the nature god Pan. The rock-grotto, at the southern foot of Hermon where one of the sources of the Jordan River rose, was regarded as sacred. Near the rock-grotto, Herod the Great had built a magnificent temple in white marble to honour his patron Caesar Augustus. When Philip inherited the city from his father, he enlarged its boundaries and renamed it *Kaesaria*, to complete his father's honour to Augustus. It came to be known as Caesarea 'of Philip', to distinguish it from Caesarea on the coast.

On the way Jesus asks his disciples again, 'Who do people say that I am?' The answers reflect those given earlier, at the time of

John the Baptist's death (6:14-16). In spite of what has happened since then, no progress in understanding is registered. Jesus moves away from considering what others think of him to asking his own what they think. They are the ones, distinguished from outsiders, about whom Jesus has already said: 'To you has been given the secret of the kingdom of God' (4:11). They are now asked: 'But who do you say that I am?' Peter, as spokesman for the group of disciples, replies that Jesus is *Christos*, the Messiah.

In Matthew's Gospel, Peter's confession, which includes the declaration that Jesus in Son of God, is greeted with enthusiasm and acknowledged as the revelation of the Father (Mt 16:16-20). By contrast, Jesus' immediate reaction in Mark's Gospel appears ambiguous: Jesus sternly orders them to silence. Although the title Peter uses is correct – Mark introduced his Gospel with it (1:1) – the disciples' understanding of it is far from the truth as Jesus' corrective will make clear. The disciples' recognition is an example of seeing without understanding (8:17).

Jesus' question is not unlike the one he asked of the blind man: 'Do you see anything?' Like the blind man, the disciples see faintly and indistinctly. But that in itself is progress, marking a beginning out of blindness.

What exactly Peter might have understood by Messiah cannot be fully recovered. There was no univocal meaning of the term among the variety of Jewish beliefs that existed at the time of the Second Temple period. The notion of 'the Messiah' as understood by Christian theology, as opposed to 'messiahs' recognised by different popular Jewish movements, has its own complex history within Judaism.[1] If 'Messiah' is confined to referring to the anointed king of the Davidic dynasty who was to establish in the world the kingdom intended by God, and if Peter was referring to this in his declaration, then his understanding was not a false one within Judaism. R. E. Brown writes:

> It is inaccurate and unjust to say that the Jews of Jesus' time had corrupted the idea of the Messiah as spiritual saviour by making it secular and nationalistic and that Jesus restored the concept to

1. See R. Horsley, 'Palestinian Jewish Groups and Their Messiahs in Late Second Temple Times,' *Concilium* 1 (1993) pp.14-29; 'Popular Messianic Movements around the Time of Jesus,' *Catholic Biblical Quarterly* 46 (1984) pp. 473-478.

its pristine meaning. The Christian understanding of a spiritual Messiah with a kingdom not of this world represented a change rather than a restoration – a change that Christians believe brought the development of the messianic expectation to a rich fruition, but a change nonetheless.[2]

Mark's understanding of the Messiah has been clearly reworked in the light of Jesus' death and resurrection, an understanding which excludes any political implications. That re-interpretation of messiahship through Jesus' actual career is something that, in this passage, is impossible for Peter to manage. For obvious reasons, Peter cannot be wise in the way that Mark is wise. It is hardly surprising, therefore, that Jesus' reaction to Peter's confession is to instruct the disciples that the Son of Man – not the recently confessed Messiah – is the identity that is going to reveal who he is and why he must undergo a violent death.

The suffering Son of Man   8:31-33

[31] Then he began to teach them that the Son of Man must undergo great suffering, and be rejected by the elders, the chief priests, and the scribes, and be killed, and after three days rise again. [32]He said all this quite openly. And Peter took him aside and began to rebuke him. [33]But turning and looking at his disciples, he rebuked Peter and said, 'Get behind me, Satan! For you are setting your mind not on divine things but on human things.'

The response of Jesus to Peter's confession is first to rebuke the disciples and then to offer a new teaching about the suffering Son of Man. Jesus' teaching about his passion points to a significant change in the narrative. The idea of Messiah has to undergo a radical reinterpretation in the light of Jesus' chosen way of speaking about himself, the Son of Man who must (*dei*) suffer. This teaching avoids referring to the anointed one, but combines the Suffering Servant of Isaiah 53 with that of the Son of Man. Jesus' destiny is under the 'must' of God's governing providence.

In this first prediction of the passion, the movement of the passion is well summarised: 'suffer ... be rejected ... be killed ... rise again.' Without denying that Jesus referred to the inevitability

2. R.E. Brown, *An Introduction to New Testament Christology* (London: Chapman, 1994) p.161.

of his violent death, it is probable that the passion predictions are framed in the light of the passion story. It seems less likely that Jesus referred so explicitly to his resurrection. As Taylor notes: 'The subsequent sharpening of an originally less direct expression is the best explanation of the difficulty.'[3]

The Son of Man sayings are among the most difficult of New Testament problems, and there is no clear consensus among scholars about their origin or meaning.[4] Most readers could join the crowds in John's Gospel who ask Jesus: 'Who is this Son of Man?' (Jn 12:34) No one addresses Jesus by this title; Jesus never explains it; it is not used of him by the early Christians in their creeds. Whereas Jesus never unambiguously claims he is the Messiah, the Son of Man sayings occur, with one exception (Acts 7:56), only on his lips. Initially the phrase *bar nasha* (meaning man, but literally translated into the Greek as 'son of man') was a general Semitic term for a human being. Ninety-three times in the book of Ezekiel, for example, God addresses the prophet by using this term.

The difficulty arises with the 'one like a son of man' in Daniel 7:13. Although the designation here means one like a human being, later reflection in Jewish apocalyptic circles developed a strong image of a heavenly Son of Man, a messianic human figure of heavenly origins who is glorified by God and made a judge.[5] If it is a fair presumption that Jesus did his own thinking about his vocation, it is not wholly unlikely that Jesus thought of himself through this understanding and made the original connection with the Suffering Servant. It is difficult to ascribe the title 'Son of Man' wholly to the invention of the early church, particularly when there is almost no trace of it outside the Gospels among New Testament literature. We are not necessarily being more faithful to historical criticism by stubbornly assuming that Jesus, unlike the early Christian writers, was incapable of originality.

Mark says that Jesus spoke about himself as the Son of Man who must undergo suffering and that he said 'all this quite openly.' In dramatic contrast to the silence enjoined on the disciples about his

3. V. Taylor, *The Gospel according to St. Mark* p. 378.
4. See J.D. Kingsbury, *The Christology of Mark* (Philadelphia: Fortress, 1984) pp. 166-179.
5. See J.J. Collins 'The Son Man in First-Century Judaism,' *New Testament Studies* 38 (1992) pp. 448-466.

Messianic identity, his identity as the suffering Son of Man is revealed without nuance or charge to secrecy. Peter's reaction, however, tells of vehement disagreement with Jesus' confession: he takes Jesus aside and 'rebukes' him. The word 'rebuke' is used of Jesus' command to the demons (1:25; 9:25), to the storm (4:39), to Peter (next verse), and to his disciples (10:13). The same word is translated as 'sternly charged' in Jesus' commands to silence (3:12; 8:30). Peter presumptuously becomes Jesus' teacher as he reverses the roles of master-disciple in trying to correct Jesus. Peter is shocked at Jesus' confession – which must, therefore, have been so unlike the meaning of his own – and tries to dissuade Jesus from following such a pattern of humiliation and persecution, no matter what divine compulsion lies behind it.

Jesus turns and looks at his disciples. And then he uses the strongest language to voice his own rebuke to Peter and, by implication, the disciples: 'Get behind me, Satan!' Nowhere else does Jesus identify a human being as satanic. The dramatic confrontation between Jesus and Peter is reminiscent of the temptation in the wilderness elaborated in Matthew 4:1-11 and Luke 4:1-13. There Jesus is tempted by Satan to abandon the role God sets out for him and adopt that of a popular political messiah, winning power without pain, and achieving glory without suffering. Mark is more original and more daring in naming Peter as the one who tempts Jesus away from the decreed plan of God.

Jesus accuses Peter of setting his mind not on divine things but on human things. By this charge, Peter is obstinately excluding the plan of God from his thinking. If it is the will of God that the Messiah should suffer, no doubt Peter and the others reckon that a similar fate might befall them as disciples. Their objection to Jesus' idea is not limited to opposing Jesus' suffering but protesting against the likelihood of their own. And that probability turns into certainty in the next passage.

Discipleship and loyalty   8:34-9:1

[34] He called the crowd with his disciples, and said to them, 'If any want to become my followers, let them deny themselves and take up their cross and follow me. [35]For those who want to save their life will lose it, and those who lose their life for my sake, and for the sake of the gospel,

will save it. [36]For what will it profit them to gain the whole world and forfeit their life? [37]Indeed, what can they give in return for their life? [38]Those who are ashamed of me and of my words in this adulterous and sinful generation, of them the Son of Man will also be ashamed when he comes in the glory of his Father with the holy angels.'

[9:1]And he said to them, 'Truly I tell you, there are some standing here who will not taste death until they see that the kingdom of God has come with power.'

Mark attaches a series of sayings on discipleship and loyalty to the confrontation between Peter and Jesus. His editorial framework is a teaching addressed to the Gentile crowd as well as the disciples, a further instance of Jesus speaking openly, without parables. Placed after Jesus' revelation about the necessity of Messianic suffering, the sayings deepen the connection between the fate of Jesus and the fate of those who would follow him. Jesus' original call to the first four disciples (1:14-16) emphasised their personal attachment to him and their new direction, one that involved a share in his mission. That fidelity to Jesus will call for courage and sacrifice from his followers, for they will have to tread their own *via dolorosa.*

First on the list is self-denial. For true disciples, the refusal to make themselves the object of their life's interest, rather than the pursuit of self-fulfilment, will be a characteristic trait. This will show itself in the willingness of the disciple to take up his cross and follow Jesus. This call to take up the cross would seem a Christian formulation: at the time of Jesus it would simply have meant, without further explanation, a condemned criminal on his way to the ultimate Roman punishment. Nothing of this has been suggested in the passion prophecy.

Those who are bent on saving their bodily life at the cost of treachery to Jesus and his mission will experience only its loss, whereas those who sacrifice their life for a higher goal, for the sake of Jesus and the gospel, will save their true self.

Profiting by gaining the whole world (having) is judged useless beside forfeiting one's life (being). If a man has literally *spent* his life to gain money, for example, what he has spent is infinitely more precious than what he has gained. The loss is irrevocable, which makes the supposed gain useless beside it. Nothing is more precious than the gift of life itself.

For those who are ashamed of Jesus and his words, the Son of Man will disown them when he comes in glory (see Dan 7:10, 13-14). The Son of Man here is not the suffering Messiah but the future Son of Man who will come in judgement. Later on, in the eschatological discourse, Jesus warns his disciples: 'they will hand you over to councils; and you will be beaten in synagogues; and you will stand before governors and kings because of me, as a testimony to them.' (13:9) The disciples will be sorely tested because of their allegiance to Jesus. The punishment for being ashamed of Jesus will be infinitely greater than any punishment they avoided in their previous apostasy.

Finally, there is the strange promise that some of Jesus' listeners will not die before they see the kingdom of God come with power. This is a difficult verse to interpret. It seems to reflect an unrealised prophecy, namely one that did not actually take place, and it appears all the more strange that Mark has included it. But that Mark himself believes it seems not to be in doubt, since the sentiment is repeated more forcefully in 13:30-32.

Earlier, in the period of Paul, the time between Jesus' death and the parousia had already lengthened into decades, and those surviving had their own questions (1 Thess 4:13-18; 1 Cor 15:51-53). Paul had taught his converts in Thessalonica that Jesus would return soon to establish his kingdom. A problem arose when some of the converts died, leading others in the church to ask Paul if the dead would miss out on the kingdom. Paul replies confidently that 'the dead in Christ will rise first. Then we who are alive, who are left, will be caught up in the clouds together with them to meet the Lord in the air'. The interesting thing is that Paul was so certain that Jesus would return immediately that he had forgotten to teach the Thessalonians that those who died would be raised.

Some commentators argue that Mark intended his readers to see a partial fulfilment of the final coming of the kingdom in the transfiguration story, which follows immediately on the prophecy. This seems somewhat artificial: a momentary vision of heavenly glory six days later, experienced by three disciples who do not understand its significance, hardly constitutes a foretaste of the definitive coming of the kingdom of God that would include the Gentiles.

By contrast, Trocmé translates the meaning of Mark 9:1 as mercilessly ironic: 'Among those here present there are cowards who would never be willing to die before the end of the world, who avoid taking risks so that they may be alive to see the great Day come!'[6] While solving the problem of unfulfilled prophecy, this reading appears more ingenious than credible. The more difficult reading, supported by 13:30-37, is the more likely.

Obviously this collection of sayings is aimed to challenge and console Mark's persecuted community; the words are directed not only to the leaders but also to the whole crowd (v.34). To stay loyal to Christ in the face of persecution and condemnation will require enormous courage and self-sacrifice. To remain constant to the way of suffering and humiliation, refusing to disavow Christ for a faithless freedom, will demand nothing less than life itself. To remain steadfast, Mark says, is to walk in the footsteps of the suffering Christ himself, whose own journey will end in glory.

Finally, Mark encourages those who are concerned about the unexpected lengthy delay of the parousia with the promise that some of them will live through the present time of hostility to experience the kingdom come in power.

The transfiguration 9:2-8

[2] Six days later, Jesus took with him Peter and James and John, and led them up a high mountain apart, by themselves. And he was transfigured before them, [3] and his clothes became dazzling white, such as no one on earth could bleach them. [4] And there appeared to them Elijah with Moses, who were talking with Jesus. [5] Then Peter said to Jesus, 'Rabbi, it is good for us to be here; let us make three dwellings, one for you, one for Moses, and one for Elijah.' [6] He did not know what to say, for they were terrified. [7] Then a cloud overshadowed them, and from the cloud there came a voice, 'This is my Son, the Beloved; listen to him!' [8] Suddenly when they looked around, they saw no one with them any more, but only Jesus.

The story opens with a precise note about time, 'six days later' – presumably about a week after Peter and Jesus had their strong disagreement over the meaning of their different confessions. The temporal note serves to bind those two different ways of under-

6. E. Trocmé, *The Formation of the Gospel according to Mark* (London: SPCK, 1975) p. 123.

standing Jesus' identity and destiny to the most important confession in the Gospel: the confession of God who will proclaim Jesus as his Son and command people to attend to his words. Jesus' own words have just been opposed by Peter and the disciples; now, for the first time, a divine proclamation states that Jesus speaks with the authority of God.

What Mark means to teach his readers by the transfiguration story can be readily understood from his Gospel account, but the more difficult question to answer is: what actually happened in Stage 1 of the tradition? Some scholars argue that this question is unanswerable. Beare states:

> The story as we have it is unquestionably a literary creation, not a fragment of tradition shaped by the processes of oral transmission. There is not the slightest hope of recovering any element of historical fact that might conceivably lie behind it.[7]

Other scholars argue that it is a misplaced resurrection account; a vision accorded to Peter (or the three disciples); a historical event in the ministry of Jesus; a symbolic story depicting Jesus as the heavenly Son of Man in the glory of the parousia. The list goes on. Fitzmyer comes to a cautious conclusion:

> Given the diversity of the way in which the incident is reported, no real historical judgement can be made about it; to write it all off as mythical is likewise to go beyond the evidence. Just what sort of an incident in the ministry of Jesus – to which it is clearly related – it was is impossible to say.[8]

Jesus takes his three favourite disciples – those who were with him in the house of Jairus and will be closest to him in Gethsemane – and leads them up a high mountain, to be by themselves.

Traditionally the mountain has been identified as Mount Tabor, which lies ten miles south-west of the Sea of Galilee and overlooks the Jezreel valley. It is a majestic landmark that can be seen from great distances. Mount Hermon can be seen from its summit, a feature reflected by the psalmist: 'Tabor and Hermon joyously praise your name.' (Ps 89:12) From earliest times Hermon was

7. F.W. Beare, *The Gospel according to Matthew* (Oxford: Blackwell, 1981) p. 361.
8. J. Fitzmyer, *The Gospel according to Luke* I-IX (New York: Doubleday, 1981) p. 796.

regarded as a sanctuary and cultic site. As Arav writes:

> Hittite and biblical records support the use of Hermon as a
> dwelling-place for the gods.... More than twenty temples have
> been surveyed on Mt. Hermon and its environs.[9]

In Mark's account, since the disciples are still in the region of
Caesarea Philippi, Mount Hermon would seem a more likely
candidate than Tabor as the setting for the story.

The structure of the transfiguration has some similarity with that
of the baptism story, being told through a simple and a wonderful
element (see comment on 1:9-11). The simple element consists of
Jesus taking his three disciples up a mountain, to be by themselves.
Luke says that Jesus goes up the mountain to pray (Lk 9:28-29).
The wonderful element happens in the transfiguration of Jesus, the
appearance of Moses and Elijah, and the heavenly voice proclaiming the identity of Jesus. Unlike the story of the baptism, the
wonderful element is now revealed to the bystanders, in this case
the three disciples. Jesus is transfigured '*before them*'; Moses and
Elijah appear '*before them*'; a cloud *overshadows them*; the voice
is no longer addressed to Jesus – 'You are my Son' – but to the
witnesses, '*This* is my Son'.

Mark makes no reference to Jesus' face (see Mt 17:2; Lk 9:29),
but describes a metamorphosis of Jesus' entire person that even
extends to his clothing. Jesus' clothing becomes brilliantly white,
a whiteness impossible to attain by any natural means. Elijah and
Moses appear – Mark reverses the normal order – and the disciples
see the heavenly visitors talk with Jesus. Luke adds that they talk
to Jesus about his *exodos* (departure) which he is about to accom-
plish in Jerusalem (Lk 9:31). Both Mark and Luke emphasise the
actual presence of Moses and Elijah, while Matthew explains that
what the disciples see is a vision (Mt 17:9).

The presence of Moses and Elijah, both of whom received a
revelation from God on Mount Sinai (Horeb), is traditionally seen
to represent the Law and the Prophets respectively. In Exodus
Moses took three friends with him up the mountain, and the cloud
covered the mountain: 'The glory of the Lord settled on Mount
Sinai for six days; on the seventh day he called to Moses out of the

---

9. R. Arav, 'Mount Hermon,' *The Anchor Bible Dictionary* Vol 3 pp. 158,159.

cloud.' (Ex 24:16) Both Moses and Elijah were believed to have been taken up into heaven; one or both, depending on different traditions in Judaism, were expected to return in the last days. Their presence at the transfiguration confirms the unity of God's revelation in Christ through Moses and all the prophets.

Peter responds by addressing Jesus as 'Rabbi', a strange title if he perceives this as a christophany. He impulsively suggests a building programme of three dwellings. Mark explains that Peter did not know what to say, for the three disciples were terrified. Peter's suggestion, however foolish, rings a familiar bell: 'If in doubt, build something.'

A cloud, the revealing yet veiling vehicle of God's presence, covers the disciples in its shadow. Out of the cloud the confession of God is proclaimed, which speaks more directly to us than either the confession of Peter or the confession of Jesus. The voice proclaims the true identity of Jesus and commands the disciples to attend to him: 'This is my Son, the Beloved; listen to him.'

When the disciples look around, there is no one with them any more except Jesus. He alone, not the great figures from the past, stands as God's Son and spokesman.

It has to be acknowledged that neither the three disciples nor the other followers of Jesus appear to benefit from the revelation as the Gospel story unfolds. Although Mark gives the three disciples a central part in what is happening, he makes no claim that they understand what is going on. No change is discernible in their attitude to Jesus. When Jesus again foretells his death and resurrection, the disciples' reaction remains the same as it was prior to the transfiguration: 'But they did not understand what he was saying and they were afraid to ask him.' (9:32)

If, on the mountain, Peter did experience the awesome truth that Jesus was the Son of God, his steadfast bewilderment about Jesus' identity and his wholesale denial of Jesus during the passion seem incredible.

Although Mark places the transfiguration at the centre of his Gospel, he is careful not to claim too much on behalf of the disciples: there is no recognition of Jesus' identity by his followers. Whatever happened on the mountain and however the story is interpreted, Mark's theological scheme remains secure: no one will recognise Jesus' identity as the Son of God until his destiny is fulfilled on the cross.

Thus, in the larger context of the Gospel, it is the death and resurrection, not the transfiguration, that will reveal who Jesus is to his followers. For the disciples of any age in history, Christ can only be understood in the light of the cross.

The descent from the mountain   9:9-13

[9] As they were coming down the mountain, he ordered them to tell no one about what they had seen, until after the Son of Man had risen from the dead. [10] So they kept the matter to themselves, questioning what this rising from the dead could mean. [11] Then they asked him, 'Why do the scribes say that Elijah must come first?' [12] He said to them, 'Elijah is indeed coming first to restore all things. How then is it written about the Son of Man, that he is to go through many sufferings and be treated with contempt? [13] But I tell you that Elijah has come, and they did to him whatever they pleased, as it is written about him.'

Immediately following the transfiguration, the imagery returns to the suffering Son of Man. As Jesus and the three disciples descend the mountain, Jesus charges them to silence until the Son of Man has risen from the dead. The first prophecy of the passion and resurrection (8:31), which provoked such vehement opposition from the disciples, is tied to the transfiguration. The disciples are no wiser, however, because they do not understand what Jesus means.

A difficult discussion ensues, one that appears somewhat disjointed. The focus suddenly moves to Elijah, as the disciples quote the teaching of the scribes that Elijah must come first. This probably refers to the prophecy, 'Lo, I will send you the prophet Elijah before the great and terrible day of the Lord comes.' (Mal 4:5) Malachi does not say that Elijah must come before the Messiah, but must come to prepare the way for God himself. Faierstein and Fitzmyer maintain that there is no firm proof that the idea of Elijah preparing the way for the Messiah has any support in pre-Christian Judaism.[10] If their argument is true, then Mark's passage is an attempt to reconcile the Jewish tradition about Elijah

10. M Faierstein, 'Why do the Scribes Say that Elijah Must Come First?' *Journal of Biblical Literature* 100 (1981) pp. 75-86; J. Fitzmyer, 'More about Elijah Coming First,' *Journal of Biblical Literature* 104 (1985) pp. 295-296.

returning to restore all things and the Christian proclamation about the suffering Son of Man. Mark's understanding seems to be that as Jesus was the secret Messiah, so John the Baptist was the secret Elijah.

Mark is clearly arguing for the early church when he tries to settle the critical question: how can John the Baptist, who was put to death by Antipas and Herodias, be seen as the reappeared Elijah? Mark argues that the fate of John the Baptist is not an argument against his being considered Elijah. Elijah has come again, but his reappearance did not protect him from the grasp of fate, for 'they did to him whatever they pleased'. The fate that Jezebel had planned for Elijah has befallen John through Herodias. The violent death of John the Baptist not only relates back to Elijah but, more importantly, looks ahead to the fate of the Messiah. In his violent death John the Baptist is the precursor of the suffering Messiah.

Mark makes the Christian argument that John the Baptist is the perfect forerunner for *the kind of messiah* Jesus turned out to be. Given that Jesus has to endure the fate of the suffering Son of Man, John the Baptist proves to be the perfect forerunner. Before Jesus went the way of suffering, John travelled that route himself. What has proved true of the forerunner will prove true of the Messiah himself.

The healing of the epileptic boy 9:14-29

[14]When they came to the disciples, they saw a great crowd around them, and some scribes arguing with them. [15]When the whole crowd saw him, they were immediately overcome with awe, and they ran forward to greet him. [16]He asked them, 'What are you arguing about with them?' [17]Someone from the crowd answered him, 'Teacher, I brought you my son; he has a spirit that makes him unable to speak; [18]and whenever it seizes him, it dashes him down; and he foams and grinds his teeth and becomes rigid; and I asked your disciples to cast it out, but they could not do so.' [19]He answered them, 'You faithless generation, how much longer must I be among you? How much longer must I put up with you? Bring him to me.' [20]And they brought the boy to him. When the spirit saw him, immediately it convulsed the boy, and he fell on the ground and rolled about, foaming at the mouth. [21]Jesus asked the father, 'How long has this been happening to him?' And he said, 'From childhood. [22]It has often cast him into the fire and water, to destroy him; but if you are able to do anything, have pity on us and help us.' [23]Jesus said to him,

'If you are able! – All things can be done for the one who believes.'
[24]Immediately the father of the child cried out, 'I believe; help my
unbelief!' [25]When Jesus saw that a crowd came running together, he
rebuked the unclean spirit, saying to it, 'You spirit that keeps this boy
from speaking and hearing, I command you, come out of him, and never
enter him again!' [26]After crying out and convulsing him terribly, it came
out, and the boy was like a corpse, so that most of them said, 'He is
dead.' [27]But Jesus took him by the hand and lifted him up, and he was
able to stand. [28]When he had entered the house, his disciples asked him
privately, 'Why could we not cast it out?' [29]He said to them, 'This kind
can come out only through prayer.'

The movement from the mountain of transfiguration to the plain of
the everyday world is a descent from revelation to argument. The
nine disciples who were not with Jesus are arguing with a group of
scribes. The dispute is probably about the disciples' inability to
heal the stricken boy. We are not told why scribes should be so far
north in Gentile territory; their presence seems curious, for they do
not speak to Jesus or play any part in the rest of the story. Only Mark
has the story of healing set in the context of controversy, which
might reflect a discussion within Mark's community on the effectiveness of the ministry of deliverance. When the crowd see Jesus,
Mark says 'they were immediately overcome with awe' – an
expression which stands in dramatic contrast to the three disciples'
reaction to the transfiguration, 'they were terrified'. The crowd
leave the argument and run to Jesus, to greet him. When Jesus asks
them what they have been discussing, a father blurts out his
problem.

In detail reminiscent of the case of the Gerasene demoniac (5:5),
the state of the sufferer is recited graphically. The struggle in this
story, however, is not a supernatural one between the demon and
Jesus; it is a pastoral struggle between a desperate father who has
his own doubts and Jesus who demands faith as a condition for the
exorcism. The father, addressing Jesus as teacher, explains that he
brought his son to him in the hope that Jesus could heal the boy
possessed of a demon. The details of the son's seizures are
consistent with epilepsy, but the boy's illness is attributed to a deaf
and dumb spirit. The father explains that the disciples were unable
to heal his son. This remark draws from Jesus a lament that goes far
beyond the present situation: he responds by castigating the whole

faithless generation of Israel, including the disciples, and wonders how longer he must live among a people who are so spiritually dull and unsympathetic. That done, he calls for the afflicted boy to be brought into his presence.

The boy goes into convulsions – falling on the ground, rolling about, and foaming at the mouth. When Jesus asks the father how long the boy has suffered from this condition, the father explains that from childhood the evil spirit has cast his son into fire and water, attempting to destroy him. The father moves from explanation to a heartfelt plea, 'But if you are able to do anything, have pity on us and help us.' Given the recent failure of the disciples, the father's request is duly cautious. Jesus recalls the doubt expressed by the anxious father, 'If you are able!' and redefines the problem: the issue is not if Jesus can cure but if the man can believe. Alongside doubt, Jesus places the omnipotence of faith. The father's eloquent plea, 'I believe; help my unbelief!' appeals not to the strength of his own faith but to the compassion of Jesus. The faith of the boy is not an issue. The father has displayed a measure of faith in bringing his son to Jesus and a measure of doubt in his desperate request. He becomes a spokesman for every Christian community living in tension between belief and unbelief.

Seeing a larger crowd approaching, Jesus delays no longer but commands the spirit to leave the boy and never return again. After being freed from the spirit, the boy lies on the ground like a corpse, so that everyone thinks he is dead. Earlier, the disciples had their own question about the meaning of rising from the dead (9:10). Now the power of Jesus is made manifest as he takes the son by the hand, lifts him up, and the boy is able to stand.

When Jesus and the disciples are alone again, the disciples ask him why they were unable to cast out the demon. They have already been given the power to cast out demons and they used it successfully (6:7,13). Jesus replies that this kind can only be cast out by prayer. This private teaching is made available to the Christian reader of the Gospel. Stock notes: 'It may be that the answer to the disciples' question was directed against a shallow ritualism, which depended for its supposed success on some external action or healing method.'[11]

11. A. Stock, *The Method and Message of Mark* (Wilmington: Glazier, 1989) p. 253

That is possible, but it would seem more likely that Mark is deliberately shifting the focus of his teaching from faith to prayer for his own purposes. Mark's community is being given a lesson in the primary place of prayer in the lives of those who follow Jesus and minister to others. For any disciple of Jesus, to be prayerless is to be powerless. The source of all ministry, including that of Jesus, is an attitude of utter dependence on God. If faith places absolute trust in the power of God to act in a beneficent way, prayer deepens and confirms that original reliance on the one who makes all things possible.

Second prophecy of the death and resurrection 9:30-32

[30]They went on from there and passed through Galilee. He did not want anyone to know it; [31]for he was teaching his disciples, saying to them, 'The Son of Man is to be betrayed into human hands, and they will kill him, and three days after being killed, he will rise again.' [32]But they did not understand what he was saying and were afraid to ask him.

This is the second of Jesus' three solemn predictions of his death and resurrection (see 8:31 and 10:32-34). The passage opens with a geographical statement: Jesus and the disciples leave 'from there' – the region of Caesarea Philippi – and travel south through Galilee. Passing incognito through his own region, Jesus uses the secret journey as an opportunity to instruct the disciples on the suffering Son of Man. The ministry in Galilee is now over; the crowds are avoided as Jesus devotes his energy to his disciples; the focus of his teaching is on the schedule of death and resurrection that awaits him in Jerusalem.

This is the shortest, and perhaps the oldest, of the passion predictions. There is a play on words in the prophecy: the Son of Man (the one who represents God) will be delivered into the hands of *men* (the faithless generation who opposes God). The passive verb 'will be delivered (*paradidotai*)' – rendered as 'betrayed' in our translation – intimates that God is the principal agent of the passion, just as he is the hidden principal agent in 'he has been raised' (16:6). This note suggesting God's initiative is more evident in Paul's language: 'If God is for us, who is against us? He who did not withhold his own Son, but gave him up for all of us, will he not with him also give us everything else?' (Rom 8:31-32). The act of delivering Jesus or handing him over will continue in the passion story: Judas will deliver Jesus into the hands of the Sanhedrin; the Sanhedrin will deliver him into the hands of Pilate; under pressure from the crowds, Pilate will hand Jesus over to the soldiers, to be crucified. The whole passion narrative is a story of Jesus being handed over.

Mark tells us that the disciples do not understand Jesus' saying, and that their fear prevents them from asking for an explanation. Luke 9:45 excuses the disciples because the meaning is concealed from them; Matthew 17:23 omits any mention of misunderstanding, saying only that the disciples were grieved. For Mark, Jesus' teaching is again lost on his disciples. Instead of staying with Jesus' difficult saying, they move the conversation from suffering to power as they discuss which of them is the greatest.

Discussion about the greatest   9:33-37

[33]Then they came to Capernaum; and when he was in the house he asked them, 'What were you arguing about on the way?' [34]But they were silent, for on the way they had argued with one another who was the greatest. [35]He sat down, called the twelve, and said to them, 'Whoever wants to be first must be last of all and servant of all.' [36]Then he took a little child and put it among them; and taking it in his arms, he said to them, [37]'Whoever welcomes one such child in my name welcomes me, and whoever welcomes me welcomes not me but the one who sent me.'

The sequel to the second passion prediction is the discipleship discourse (9:33-50) which is often described as a chain of stray sayings linked together by catchwords. In his study of this discourse Fledderman argues that Mark does more than take over a group of traditional sayings, but modifies them for his own purposes.[12]

The first passage is a dispute about greatness, which has obvious similarities with the request of the two sons of Zebedee to secure the places of honour in the kingdom (10:35-45). The story opens with Jesus and the disciples reaching Capernaum. This is where Jesus began his ministry (1:21), where he taught in the synagogue, where he moved around freely and ministered in the open to so

---

12. H. Fleddermann, 'The Discipleship Discourse (Mark 9:33-50)' *Catholic Biblical Quarterly* 43 (1981) pp. 57-75.

many people. Jesus and the disciples now move indoors. The scene unites Jesus with the disciples and separates them as a group from the rest of the people. Inside the house, Jesus asks his disciples what they were talking about on the road – a note suggesting a further separation between Jesus and the disciples after the second passion prophecy. They were travelling together on the way, but separately. The disciples are too ashamed to answer the question, since their argument had been about which of them was the greatest. In spite of their silence, Jesus addresses what gave rise to their argument: their hunger for power.

Jesus sits down and calls the twelve. Mark is hardly making a distinction here between the disciples and the twelve, since Jesus' teaching is an answer to the disciples' dispute. He is probably only making a formal introduction to Jesus' teaching. Paradoxically, Jesus does not criticise the disciples' original ambition to be first, however tactless their ambition might appear in the face of Jesus' talk about his forthcoming death. Instead, Jesus says that whoever wants to be first must be last of all and be servant of all. If that is the condition for holding leadership in Jesus' community, it might result in no contenders for primacy. Who is ambitious for the last place? Who seeks after the role of being the servant of all?

In Jesus' earlier confrontation with Peter, the accusation was voiced, 'You are setting your mind not on divine things but on human things.' (8:33) The disciples' passion for power is related to their idea of the Messiah who is beyond suffering and death. Their ambition is set in this context, where primacy means power and authority and control. Jesus' kind of ambition is set within the context of the kingdom, therefore ambition is redefined as a reversal of conventional wisdom: a disciple's ambition is tied to the values of the kingdom, not to his personal desire for dominion. If the language of greatness is to be used about discipleship, its meaning is defined as service.

A child is now introduced to the story as a visual aid. Jesus allies himself with the child whom he takes in his arms; then he challenges the disciples who sit around him to welcome this little one. The scene dramatises the inclusiveness of the new community that welcomes the insignificant into its centre. The disciples are not exhorted to be like children (see Mt 18:3), but to welcome the lowly ones. These are the weakest members of the community who receive little attention, the ones who are easily overlooked by those whose energy is devoted to their own advancement in power. Whoever welcomes the lowly in the name of Jesus welcomes Jesus himself. Just as the messenger of a king represents the king himself, so the lowly ones, not disciples preoccupied with power, represent Jesus, as Jesus himself in his lowliness represents the One who sent him.

The lowly one is at the centre of Jesus' community, not outside the circle of importance. And the next story will illustrate the difficulty the disciples have in welcoming one who does not already belong to their group.

The strange exorcist   9:38-41

> [38] John said to him, 'Teacher, we saw someone casting out demons in your name, and we tried to stop him because he was not following us.' [39]But Jesus said, 'Do not stop him; for no one who does a deed of power in my name will be able soon afterward to speak evil of me. [40]Whoever is not against us is for us.[41]For truly I tell you, whoever gives you a cup of water to drink because you bear the name of Christ will by no means lose the reward.'

In the previous passage Jesus challenged the disciples to welcome the little ones 'in my name' – a phrase that makes the connection to the present story of a stranger who exorcises in the name of Jesus. There is an interesting Old Testament parallel in the story of Eldad and Medad, who are criticised for their irregular prophesying (Num 11:26-30). Joshua appeals to Moses, 'My lord Moses, stop them!' But Moses refuses: 'Are you jealous for my sake? Would that all the Lord's people were prophets, and that the Lord would put his spirit on them.' Moses refuses to limit God's freedom of speech to those who currently enjoy official approval.

In the present story John tells Jesus that when the disciples saw an outsider exorcising in the name of Jesus, they tried to stop him 'because he was not following us.' Mark has already described an incident where the disciples of Jesus were unable to exorcise the destructive spirit from a boy whose father had brought him to the disciples to be cured (9:14-29). Now, confronted with an unauthorised exorcist who is successfully ministering in the name of Jesus, the disciples are indignant and try to put a stop to his ministry.

As Jesus rejected the self-seeking of the disciples, he now rejects their exclusivism and commands them not to stop the strange exorcist. If someone does a deed of power in Jesus' name, it is unlikely that he will then speak evil about Jesus. More importantly, the principal reason for this tolerance is enshrined in the maxim: 'Whoever is not against us is for us.' Jesus does not require personal attachment to his group as a prior condition for ministry. The fact that the exorcist is ministering in the name of Jesus, even though he does not belong to the followers of Jesus, is enough for Jesus. He recognises and confirms the identity of the exorcist. Unlike the disciples, he is not instinctively intolerant to those not of his company. In this, Jesus displays a remarkably catholic attitude to all who do good to others. In terms of the previous passage, this exorcist is one of the lowly ones who needs to be accepted by Jesus' inclusive community.

Finally, the saying in 9:40 focuses on the ones who welcome the disciples because they 'bear the name of Christ' – a phrase that is clearly a formulation of the early church. The smallest act of kindness to one who is attached to Christ will surely be rewarded by God. This kindness to disciples highlights the disciples' own hostile attitude to the exorcist. Rejecting outsiders who work in the name of Jesus, while enjoying the acceptance of strangers, is a bizarre way for a disciple to live. Acceptance and hospitality are not only to be enjoyed by the disciples; these are kindnesses the disciples are expected to extend to others. Disciples are not just beneficiaries of other people's tolerance, but are expected to promote tolerance in their dealings with others.

Various sayings   9:42-50

[42] 'If any of you put a stumbling block before one of these little ones who believe in me, it would be better for you if a great millstone were hung around your neck and you were thrown into the sea. [43]If your hand causes you to stumble, cut it off; it is better for you to enter life maimed than to have two hands and to go to hell, to the unquenchable fire. [45]And if your foot causes you to stumble, cut it off; it is better for your to enter life lame than to have two feet and to be thrown into hell. [47]And if your eye causes you to stumble, tear it out; it is better for you to enter the kingdom of God with one eye than to have two eyes and to be thrown

into hell, [48]where their worm never dies, and the fire is never quenched. [49] 'For everyone will be salted with fire. [50]Salt is good; but if salt has lost is saltiness, how can you season it? Have salt in yourselves, and be at peace with one another.'

The discipleship discourse concludes with a series of miscellaneous sayings that have some verbal connections. As D. Taylor observes:

> The end of chapter 9 of Mark's Gospel is an untidy and haphazard jumble, but we are extraordinary lucky to have it. Nothing like it survives elsewhere in this or in any other Gospel; but it is likely that the bulk not only of Mark's Gospel but also of the Q material came to the evangelists in this form, and that all three of them were faced with the task, first of unpicking the separate sayings, and then rearranging them in a more literary and acceptable form. Why didn't Mark, then, unpick this passage with all the rest? I suggest because as the gospel now stands he has no section where any of this material would be specially appropriate, so he leaves it as he finds it.[13]

The first saying is a warning against scandalising the little ones 'who believe in me' – probably a reference by Mark to Christians who have a simple and uncomplicated faith in Jesus. The great millstone (*mylos onikos*) literally means a donkey millstone. In most households the crushing of grain was done by women using a hand mill. The large rotary mill, consisting of a base stone surmounted by an upper grinding slab, was commonly driven by a donkey. The great millstone refers to the heavy upper stone of the rotary mill: to hang this dead weight around the neck of someone and then throw him into the sea would make his death doubly certain – drowning by stoning. If giving scandal means putting a stone in someone's path and causing them to stumble, attaching a great millstone to the culprit and hurling him into the sea serves as a dramatic image of overkill.

The next group of three sayings (verses 43-47) refers to causes of sin in oneself. The purpose of the sayings is to impress on the reader that no sacrifice is too small in order to secure wholeness of

13. D.B. Taylor, *Mark's Gospel as Literature and History* (London: SCM, 1992) p. 231.

life. The vivid details of the imagery, as Nineham points out, 'should not be overpressed, though they may perhaps to some extent reflect the old Hebrew concept of "diffused consciousness", according to which each organ was the seat of some one of the psychological forces which go to make up the total personality.'[14] The imagery puts in graphic form a simple teaching: that it is better to lose a limb, however important its function, than life itself.

All three sayings mention Gehenna, which our translation renders as 'hell'. The word *Gehenna*, in Hebrew *ge-hinnom*, means 'Valley of Hinnom' – a narrow gorge that curves along the west and south sides of Jerusalem. The valley was the scene of the idolatrous worship of the gods Molech and Baal: the act of worship consisted in sacrificing children, by passing them through fire on Topheth (the sacrificial site) and into the hands of the gods (Jer 7:31; 19:4-5; 32:35). As part of his reform programme, Josiah had the sacrificial site defiled (2 Kgs 23:10)

The valley's association with fire arose not only from the sacrificial cult of Molech but from the fires that continually burned there when the valley became a refuse dump. Isaiah prophesies the threat of Topheth being readied for Molech himself (Is 30:33), and he speaks about a devouring fire and everlasting burnings, of an unquenchable fire prepared for the wicked (Is 33:14; 66:24). By the first century A.D. there was a metaphorical understanding of Gehenna as the place of judgement and fire for all the wicked.

Gehenna became divorced from its geographical location as a rubbish dump, scene of perpetual fires and perpetual decay, to become hell itself.

The three sayings in verses 49-50 are placed together presumably because they each contain the word 'salt'. Divorced from their original setting, they are almost incomprehensible. 'For everyone will be salted with fire' brings together the destructive/purifying element of fire and the preservative/purifying element of salt. Does it mean that everyone will be tried and purified by the fire of suffering or persecution? Does the fire have anything to do with Gehenna? Is it a saying that would have special meaning in a church suffering from persecution?

The next saying asks, if salt loses its particular quality as a spice,

14. D. Nineham, *Saint Mark* p. 255.

what can restore its lost saltiness? While we know that salt cannot lose its savour, is Jesus telling the disciples to retain their difference from the rest of the world, because their difference gives a season that the world lacks? The meaning is clearer in the parallel in Matthew 5:13: 'You are the salt of the earth ... '

Finally there is the injunction, 'Have salt in yourselves, and be at peace with one another.' Is Jesus telling the disciples to have the purifying element within them, rather than being dependent on outside agencies? Possibly, except that that interpretation sounds too individualistic. In the Old Testament salt is a symbol of the covenant: 'You shall not omit from your grain offerings the salt of the covenant with your God, with all your offerings you shall offer salt.' (Lev 2:13) If the background to this idea lies in the sharing of salt at a meal, the religious image is that to share salt with someone is to share fellowship with them.

The discipleship discourse began with exploring two situations of conflict – the disciples' argument about which of them was the greatest and the rejection of the unauthorised exorcist. It now ends with an appeal to share peace in covenant fellowship.

Teaching about divorce   10:1-12

[1] He left that place and went to the region of Judea and beyond the Jordan. And crowds again gathered around him; and, as was his custom, he again taught them.

[2] Some Pharisees came, and to test him they asked, 'Is it lawful for a man to divorce his wife?' [3]He answered them, 'What did Moses command you?' [4]They said, 'Moses allowed a man to write a cerificate of dismissal and to divorce her.' [5]But Jesus said to them, 'Because of your hardness of heart he wrote this commandment for you. [6]But from the beginning of creation, "God made them male and female." [7]"For this reason a man shall leave his father and mother and be joined to his wife, [8]and the two shall become one flesh." So they are no longer two, but one flesh. [9]Therefore what God has joined together, let no one separate.'

[10]Then in the house the disciples asked him again about this matter. [11]He said to them, 'Whoever divorces his wife and marries another commits adultery against her; [12]and if she divorces her husband and marries another, she commits adultery.'

Jesus' ministry in Galilee is now at an end, and he continues his journey southwards towards Jerusalem, to face the destiny fixed for him. The whole chapter is set against the vague background of a journey through Judea 'and beyond the Jordan.' The region beyond the Jordan refers to Perea, in the dominion of Herod Antipas, where John the Baptist had exercised his powerful prophetic ministry. Jesus no longer travels incognito, as he did through Galilee while teaching his disciples, and the crowds gather round him again. His response, Mark says, it to teach them as he customarily did. The section 10:1-31 is probably part of an early catechetical unit that deals with marriage, children, and possessions.

Jesus is confronted by a group of Pharisees who test him with the question whether it is lawful or not for a man to divorce his wife. This seems a strange question coming from Pharisees, since the prescription in Deuteronomy 24:1-4 clearly supposes that a husband could divorce his wife:

> Suppose a man enters into marriage with a woman, but she does not please him because he finds something objectionable about her, and so he writes her a certificate of divorce, puts it in her hand, and sends her out of the house ...

Because nothing is said about what constitutes valid reasons for divorce, the argument within Judaism turned on the interpretation 'because he finds something objectionable about her'. First century Pharisees and their successors were divided into two schools or houses, named after the great sages Hillel and Shammai, who flourished towards the end of the first century B.C. The school of Shammai demanded a grave pretext for divorce, such as adultery of the wife, while the school of Hillel maintained that trivial causes sufficed for a husband to divorce a wife who failed to satisfy him (bad cooking, ugliness, tediousness).

Jesus questions the Pharisees about Moses' command and they reply that Moses permitted a man to write a woman a certificate of dismissal and so divorce her. The certificate of dismissal was intended as *a letter of protection for the woman,* so that she could remarry with impunity, but the obvious danger was that male privilege could abuse the practice so that the certificate could be used as *a letter of freedom for the man* whenever he wanted a ready release from the marriage. The certificate could thus be used to support a male lifestyle of serial monogamy.

While not questioning the Law, Jesus reinterprets the divorce legislation by setting it against Genesis 1:27; 2:24. Jesus argues that the provision for divorce did not reflect God's original design but was made because of the Israelites' hardness of heart. The dispensation for divorce was permitted because of people's stubborn failure to live up to God's original vision contained in Genesis. Jesus goes on to recall God's original plan for humankind in creating two sexes, male and female. The primary intention for creating difference was that the man and woman should become one flesh: the whole person of each becomes united in one enduring bond of communion. This original community of the man and the woman enshrines the purposes of God, and no one has a right to separate what God has by design joined together.

No reaction by the Pharisees is registered in the story. Instead, Jesus opens up to his disciples in private the full significance of what he has taught in public. That Jesus' teaching has to be explained further in this appendix suggests that cases of divorce had arisen in the early church. The exception mentioned by Matthew 19:9 – 'except for unchastity' – is not mentioned by Mark.

The thought is carried further now when Jesus states that remarriage after divorce is adultery. Orthodox Jewish practice did not allow a woman to divorce her husband. As Taylor comments: 'In respect of impotence, denial of conjugal rights, and unreasonable restriction of movement, a wife could sue for divorce, but even so divorce was the husband's act.'[15]

Jesus' distinctive teaching now affirms the equality of the sexes. Jesus upholds the rights of the first wife in saying that the husband who divorces her is committing adultery 'against her' – thus going beyond Jewish Law where a man could only commit adultery against a married man, when he had sexual relations with the latter's wife. The woman is also bound by the same teaching. Although Jewish Law did not allow a woman to divorce her husband, Roman Law did. For Mark, therefore, this appendix to Jesus' public teaching clarifies Christian instruction on marriage for the Jewish and the Gentile world.

When one considers the abuse of male prerogative within

15. V. Taylor, *The Gospel according to St. Mark* p. 420.

certain sections of the Jewish tradition, something that is certainly not peculiar to that tradition, Jesus' teaching particularly opposes the practice of men managing their own divorces and using male privilege to banish women into obscurity. In recalling God's original intention for marriage, Jesus insists that God's vision should be given its primary place in human consideration. This is not to punish people with legalism, an attitude Jesus has already criticised in his opponents, but to recall that marriage has a larger purpose than an individual's self-fulfilment. Williamson comments on Jesus' teaching:

> The answer was – and is – shocking. As absolute as Jesus' teaching on selling all one's goods and giving to the poor or denying oneself and taking up one's cross, this word, like those, was heard literally by a church that expected the end of history within the span of their current generation. It set the early church counter to easy and selfish views of the marriage relationship in the surrounding culture.[16]

In underlining the sanctity of marriage and the equal dignity of the partners, Jesus' teaching challenges husbands and wives to return together to the roots of marriage and see their commitment to one another in the light of God's seeing.

Jesus blesses little children   10:13-16

[13] People were bringing little children to him in order that he might touch them; and the disciples spoke sternly to them. [14]But when Jesus saw this, he was indignant and said to them, 'Let the little children come to me; do not stop them; for it is to such as these that the kingdom of God belongs. [15]Truly I tell you, whoever does not receive the kingdom of God as a little child will never enter it.' [16]And he took them up in his arms, laid his hands on them, and blessed them.

Following on Jesus' teaching about marriage, there is a pronouncement story about children and the kingdom. The setting is one of conflict between Jesus and his disciples. People (presumably parents or relatives) are bringing children to Jesus so that the great rabbi and healer might touch the little ones. The over-zealous disciples believe that Jesus needs to be protected from this bother-

16. L. Williamson, *Mark* (Louisville: John Knox, 1983) p. 178.

some business, and they speak sternly to the adults responsible. Jesus is indignant when he sees what his disciples are doing in his name, and the story proceeds as an interaction between Jesus and his own followers.

The strong reaction noted by Mark – this is the only instance in the Gospels where indignation is ascribed to Jesus – is dropped by Matthew and Luke in their accounts. Jesus commands the disciples to do the opposite of what they are trying to manage, and allow the children freedom to approach him. Jesus' teaching is addressed to his followers: 'for it is to such as these that the kingdom of God belongs.' Earlier, after the disciples had been discussing which of them was the greatest, Jesus introduced a child into their circle and challenged them to welcome the little one into what should be an inclusive community (9:33-37). That lesson is repeated here: the kingdom of God is not an exclusive community of adults who leave children on the outside, rather it belongs to the likes of them, the lowly and the vulnerable and the overlooked.

In an adult world children cannot count on any achievements of their own; they are powerless to influence the course of events or effect change. Children are life's natural beggars who depend on the gift and bounty of others, on the kindness and attention of those who choose to care from them. Without that favour they die. Paradoxically, Jesus makes the child into a teacher of the disciples rather than the one they can readily dismiss as unimportant. The disciples are challenged to receive the kingdom of God as a little child, so that they can enter it. In this understanding the kingdom is gift and favour, not something that can be made or constructed by serious adult management. Jesus then acts out the welcome of a community that is inclusive and open to the little ones in society: he takes the children in his arms and blesses them by placing his hands on them.

In addition to including men and women, Jew and Gentile, Mark's picture of the Christian community also includes children. This inclusion may explain why this passage was later used for another purpose, in defence of infant baptism.[17] Although this is clearly not the purpose of the passage in Mark, it is easy to see how

---

17. See A. Richardson, *An Introduction to the Theology of the New Testament* (London: SCM, 1979) pp. 360-361.

Jesus' open attitude towards children would serve those who argued that children should be welcomed into the community of faith through the sacrament of baptism.

Riches and discipleship   10:17-31

¹⁷ As he was setting out on a journey, a man ran up and knelt before him, and asked him, 'Good teacher, what must I do to inherit eternal life?' ¹⁸Jesus said to him, 'Why do you call me good? No one is good but God alone. ¹⁹You know the commandments: "You shall not murder; You shall not commit adultery; You shall not steal; You shall not bear false witness; You shall not defraud; Honor your father and mother".' ²⁰ He said to him, 'Teacher, I have kept all these since my youth.' ²¹Jesus, looking at him, loved him and said, 'You lack one thing; go, sell what you own, and give the money to the poor, and you will have treasure in heaven; then come, follow me.' ²²When he heard this, he was shocked and went away grieving, for he had many possessions.

²³ Then Jesus looked around and said to his disciples, 'How hard it will be for those who have wealth to enter the kingdom of God!' ²⁴And the disciples were perplexed at these words. But Jesus said to them again, 'Children, how hard it is to enter the kingdom of God! ²⁵It is easier for a camel to go through the eye of a needle than for someone who is rich to enter the kingdom of God.' ²⁶They were greatly astounded and said to one another, 'Then who can be saved?' ²⁷Jesus looked at them and said, 'For mortals it is impossible, but not for God; for God all things are possible.'

²⁸ Peter began to say to him, 'Look, we have left everything and followed you.' ²⁹Jesus said, 'Truly I tell you, there is no one who has left house or brothers or sisters or mother or father or children or fields, for my sake and for the sake of the good news, ³⁰who will not receive a hundredfold now in this age – houses, brothers and sisters, mothers and children,and fields with persecutions – and in the age to come eternal life. ³¹But many who are first will be last, and the last will be first.'

After the previous story, where the disciples are challenged to receive the kingdom like a little child, Mark has three units on the theme of discipleship and riches: the rich man (vv. 17-22); wealth and the kingdom (vv. 23-27); renunciation and gain (vv. 28-31). The motif of the journey to Jerusalem is repeated in the opening sentence: Jesus is resuming his road to destiny. Mark has already noted how Jesus' call to the first disciples took place as he 'passed along the Sea of Galilee' (1:16), and the call to Levi 'as he was walking along' (2:14). Jesus is on the move again and he will call another prospective disciple to join him on his journey.

Mark's writing is vivid as he tells us how the journey is unexpectedly interrupted by a man who runs up to Jesus, falls upon his knees, and asks him: 'Good Teacher, what must I do to inherit eternal life?' The man is portrayed as impetuous in his behaviour and effusive in his speech. Jesus first responds to the flattering title the man uses by objecting to the term 'good' as a proper description of himself. In traditional Jewish piety, absolute goodness is a quality that belongs to God alone, who is the benevolent source of eternal life. Mark's text distinguishes between Jesus and God, and this embarrassing contrast probably accounts for Matthew's clarification: 'Why do you ask me about what is good?' (Mt 19:17)

Jesus goes on to answer the suppliant's question, what must I do to receive eternal life in the presence of God? In calling the man to account before the Law, Jesus focuses on the second table of the Decalogue, which deals with human relationships. He quotes the commandments in random order. The man's response – this time he addresses Jesus only as 'Teacher' – indicates that he has honoured these commandments from his *bar-mitzvah*, when he assumed adult responsibility before the Law. Clearly, this blameless enthusiast is looking for more than the doing of what is required. It is his dissatisfaction with perfection under the Law that has led him running to Jesus. He is looking for more to life than being accounted a virtuous man; it would appear that his moral self-assurance has led him to believe that higher expectations are asked of him.

Jesus' reaction is one of graciousness and tenderness: he is instinctively drawn to this earnest petitioner and he looks on him with love, a poignant detail omitted by Matthew and Luke. In Mark's Gospel, this man is the beloved would-be disciple (see Jn 13:23). According to Jesus' view, the man can resolve his inner feeling of dissatisfaction by liberating himself from his possessions. Paradoxically, what he lacks is what he owns. Jesus challenges him to go and sell what he has and give the money to the poor. The challenge is issued in a litany of verbs: *go, sell, give, come, follow*. Having dispossessed himself of everything and freed himself from the securities that bind him, he is then invited to follow Jesus in his vagabond way of life.

Jesus does not make renunciation of possessions and almsgiving a precondition for discipleship (see 5:19; Acts 5:4). But for this particular man, in his particular situation, this is the one thing needed for following Jesus. His riches are what disable him from freely following Jesus, just as for others there will be different attachments that prevent them from joining Jesus on the way. The cost of discipleship varies with each individual.

The rich man's response is one of shock, and he goes away grieving, regretting that he cannot fulfil Jesus' one condition. This is the only story in the Gospels in which the invitation to discipleship is refused. However compelling the call of Jesus, it does not overpower people to such an extent that they cannot respond according to their own preference. In refusing Jesus' invitation, the rich man leaves behind him a missed opportunity, a road not taken, a lost adventure in personal attachment to Jesus. And, like so many characters who people the pages of the Gospel, nothing is heard of him again.

In the second unit, verses 23-27, the idea of wealth as an obstacle to following Jesus becomes a general warning that riches are a serious hindrance to those who would enter the kingdom of God. The rich man's sorrowful departure becomes the occasion for a teaching to the disciples, but again they are confused by what Jesus says. Their bewilderment probably follows on the popular belief within Judaism that riches were a sign of God's favour, not a burden to be set aside.

While he insists that it is particularly hard for the rich to enter the kingdom, Jesus goes on to make the point that is difficult for anyone to do so, a hard teaching that is softened by addressing the disciples affectionately as children. Jesus uses a comical image to illustrate his teaching: it is easier for a camel – the largest beast of burden – to pass through the eye of a needle – the smallest opening – than for the rich to enter the kingdom of God. Taylor comments: 'Attempts to soften the rigour of the saying are to be deprecated, especially the exegetical fancy that there was a door in the walls of Jerusalem through which with difficulty a camel might perhaps squeeze.'[18] The very absurdity of the metaphor is what makes the point.

The disciples' reaction to this teaching is undisguised shock,

18. V. Taylor, *The Gospel according to St. Mark* p. 431.

and they openly wonder if anyone can be saved. Mark's phrasing of Jesus' reply is reminiscent of the theology of Paul, focusing as it does on the supreme power of God in the matter of salvation. No one can save or justify himself. Salvation is not something we can manage for ourselves, no matter how morally upright we are – a saying that has particular reference to the previous story. Salvation is the gift of God alone, for whom all things are possible.

Peter, as spokesman for the group, appeals to Jesus on behalf of the disciples: 'Look, we have left everything and followed you.' Although the everything the disciples have left behind them does not compare to the many possessions the rich man was called to abandon, an individual's everything is still everything. Nothing must stand in the way of the disciple's exclusive relationship with Jesus. Jesus reassures his group that anyone who leaves home and family and property for his sake and the sake of the good news will be doubly recompensed. (The identification of Jesus and the gospel is clearly a product of primitive Christian thinking.) Disciples will receive a hundredfold in their own time and eternal life in the age to come.

The hundredfold, however, includes 'with persecutions' – an addition by Mark that would have been particularly appropriate for his community, living in the time of suffering and persecution. Suffering makes its own fellowship, and enduring affliction for the sake of the good news makes a community of witnesses from those who remain deeply attached to the person of Jesus.

Earlier, when Jesus' family stood outside the house and called for him, Jesus looked at those sitting around him and said: 'Here are my mother and my brothers! Whoever does the will of God is my brother and sister and mother.' (3:33-34) The thought is extended here: when Jesus' disciples leave behind their relatives, they will inherit a new family of brothers and sisters, mothers and children. Their separation from old ties will not find them abandoned in a world without relationships, for their attachment to Jesus will inevitably mean affinity with new people. They will become part of a wider family whose kinship is formed not by blood but by bonds of shared commitment and trial. Thus the story of discipleship is told not only in the painful experience of separation and loss, but in the unexpected gladness of new attachment and gain.

Third prophecy of the death and resurrection 10:32-34

[32]They were on the road, going up to Jerusalem, and Jesus was walking ahead of them; they were amazed, and those who followed were afraid. He took the twelve aside again and began to tell them what was to happen to him, [33]saying, 'See, we are going up to Jerusalem, and the Son of Man will be handed over to the chief priests and the scribes, and they will condemn him to death; then they will hand him over to the Gentiles; [34]they will mock him, and spit upon him, and flog him, and kill him; and after three days he will rise again.'

The third prophecy of the death and resurrection is set within the context of the journey up to the high ground of Jerusalem, and the tension in the narrative is clearly evident. The southward journey that began in the region of Caesarea Philippi is nearing its completion, and Mark now names Jerusalem as the final destination. Jesus is portrayed as the one who takes the lead by walking ahead, consciously and resolutely heading for the centre of hostility where he will suffer condemnation and death. Mark's narrative is unclear about who comes after Jesus. There appears to be two distinct groups: the twelve and unnamed others who follow him. One group is said to be amazed, while the other group follows in fear.

The description of how both groups face the ascent to Jerusalem stands in dramatic contrast to the solitary determination of Jesus, who takes the twelve aside to tell them again what is to happen to him. This serves to instruct the reader that Jesus is not about to be overtaken by disaster, but is going knowingly and willingly to his place of execution.

The third prophecy is more detailed than the previous two (8:31; 9:31) and in all probability its contents reflect knowledge of what subsequently happened. Although none of the prophecies specifies crucifixion, the vivid details of the third prophecy and its vocabulary correspond accurately to the historical progress of the passion narrative and function as a brief summary: handed over to the chief priests and the scribes (14:53); condemned to death by the chief priests (14:65); handed over to the Gentiles (15:1); they will mock him, spit on him, and flog him (14:65, 15:15, 16-20); they will kill him (15:24,37); after three days, he will rise again (16:1-8).

This prophecy opens up, before the coming events, the significance of what Jesus will undergo in Jerusalem. However painful the agenda set out for Jesus, Mark tells us that it must be interpreted within the overall plan of God. Jesus is not heading for an accident, but for the fulfilment of his messianic identity.

The request of James and John   10:35-45

³⁵ James and John, the sons of Zebedee, came forward to him and said to him, 'Teacher, we want you to do for us whatever we ask of you.' ³⁶And he said to them, 'What is it you want me to do for you?' ³⁷And they said to him, 'Grant us to sit, one at your right hand and one at your left, in your glory.' ³⁸But Jesus said to them, 'You do not know what you are asking. Are you able to drink the cup that I drink, or be baptized with the baptism that I am baptized with?' ³⁹They replied, 'We are able.' Then Jesus said to them, 'The cup that I drink you will drink; and with the baptism with which I am baptized, you will be baptized; ⁴⁰but to sit at my right hand or at my left is not mine to grant, but it is for those for whom it has been prepared.'

⁴¹ When the ten heard this, they began to be angry with James and John. ⁴²So Jesus called them and said to them, 'You know that among the Gentiles those whom they recognize as their rulers lord it over them, and their great ones are tyrants over them. ⁴³But it is not so among you; but whoever wishes to become great among you must be your servant, ⁴⁴and whoever wishes to be first among you must be slave of all. ⁴⁵For the Son of Man came not to be served but to serve, and to give his life a ransom for many.'

After the second prophecy of the passion and resurrection, Mark noted how the disciples failed to understand what Jesus was saying; instead of asking him what he meant, they argued among themselves which of them was the greatest (9:32-34). In placing the request by James and John for positions of power after the detailed third prophecy of the passion, Mark again underlines the chronic dullness of the disciples. Despite the three predictions, in which Jesus attempts to initiate his disciples into his identity and destiny, the disciples seem no nearer to understanding Jesus or his destiny. Jesus has already said that those who would be his disciples must take up their cross and follow him (8:34), but that teaching seems senseless compared to the real and resolute desire for power.

The sons of Zebedee, who are already part of the inner circle of three, approach Jesus to make their sweeping request that he will do whatever they ask him. Jesus responds graciously to their imprecise request by inviting them to specify what it is he can do for them. Their petition is to ensure that they have the two highest places of honour, one at Jesus' right hand and one at his left, when Jesus assumes his glory. Matthew covers up the raw ambition of the two brothers by putting the request in the mouth of their mother (Mt 20:20), while Luke omits all references to the embarrassing request. Jesus' reply contains its own warning that they do not know what they are asking.

Paradoxically, at the crucifixion, two criminals will assume the positions the brothers have requested, 'one on his right and one on his left' (15:28), although the brothers' request is timed not for suffering but for glory at the messianic banquet.

In referring to the cup that he must drink and the baptism that he must undergo, Jesus is referring to the passion that awaits him. Although the cup is a familiar Jewish symbol for an experience of joy (Ps 116:13; Jer 16:7), more frequently it is used as a figure for disaster or punishment – 'the cup of the wine of wrath' (Jer 24:15), 'a cup of horror and desolation' (Ezek 23:33). The image of the cup as a symbol for profound suffering will be used in Gethsemane, when Jesus, isolated from his disciples, will throw himself on the ground and beg God to take the cup away from him (14:36).

The symbol of baptism expresses the same idea. The baptism does not refer to the familiar act of repentance but is used as a metaphor to express the thought of being flooded or overwhelmed by calamity – 'all your waves and your billows have gone over me' (Ps 42:7). Luke uses the figure clearly as a symbol of affliction when Jesus says: 'I have a baptism with which to be baptised, and what stress I am under until it is completed.' (Lk 12:50)

If James and John did not know what they were asking, it is even more unlikely that they understand the weight of Jesus' reply. Nevertheless, they claim readily that they can follow Jesus in drinking the cup and in undergoing the baptism. Since the Gospel evidence suggests that the disciples believed that Jesus' messianic restoration of the kingdom would be the historic empire of King David, the presumption is that James and John understand Jesus to mean that they would have to suffer in this cause. It is one of Mark's major themes in the Gospel that no matter how much Jesus explains his own messianic destiny in terms of suffering, the disciples are incapable of understanding that teaching, and, consequently, the meaning of their own discipleship.

On his own terms, Jesus agrees that the brothers, like him, will indeed face great tribulation and suffering. This saying has been interpreted as a prophecy of their martyrdom, but this is too narrow an interpretation. As Taylor comments: 'Although James was martyred, martyrdom is not exclusively meant, or even necessarily implied, for the New Testament does not use the imagery of baptism in this sense, and it is not found in Christian usage until the turn of the second century.'[19]

While promising to James and John a share in his suffering, Jesus tells them that positions of honour at his right and left are not his to grant: they lie outside his competence. In any case, discipleship is not an automatic entitlement to privilege or reward. The places of privilege are within the Father's gift. This saying, like Jesus' refusal to accept the rich man's description of him as good, implies a subordination of Jesus to the Father (see also 13:32).

When the ten hear of the brothers' exclusive plea for power, they become angry with their ambitious confrères. Jesus confronts all this by calling them together to give a lesson in humble service and to explain the purpose of his own death. Yet again Jesus tries, as they near the end of their journey, to do what he failed to manage at the beginning of the journey: convince his disciples of the different nature of his kingdom, and, therefore, of the different nature of leadership within it.

Jesus speaks about what they know and what they apparently long for – leadership after the Gentile model. As the disciples are aware, Gentile rulers exercise authority by lording it over their underlings – the greater they are, the more tyrannical is their exercise of power. More hopeful than descriptive is Jesus' saying, 'But it is not so among you'. Jesus forbids his followers to adopt the worldly style of leadership that is characterised by control and dominance. If there is to be ambition for greatness among disciples, that ambition must show itself in service, not autocratic control. And if any of the disciples would seek after the first place, their job description might give them pause: they are to become the slave of all. The slave is the one who enjoys no personal freedom, but who is at the beck and call of those he serves.

The thinking is that as discipleship itself is formed by following

19. V. Taylor, *The Gospel according to St. Mark* , p. 441.

Jesus, so leadership in Jesus' community is formed by following Jesus' style of leadership as the one who came to serve, not to be served. The use of the title 'Son of Man' serves to highlight the importance of the one who nonetheless serves humanity. Again, authentic discipleship is inseparably linked to the model Jesus has already established in his own ministry – otherwise it is fake.

The final thought, 'to give his life as a ransom for many', introduces a new theme of the redemptive significance of Jesus' death, and it is regarded by a number of scholars as a development from the Pauline theology of redemption (see 1 Tim 2:6). The word *lytron* (ransom) was originally a commercial term, referring to money that was paid to secure the release of a prisoner, the emancipation of a slave, or the recovery of property. The saying is probably related to the fourth song of the Suffering Servant: 'When you make his life an offering for sin' (Is 53:10). But scholars have engaged in strange acrobatics when they consider to whom Jesus pays his life in ransom. Beare writes:

> Undoubtedly the thought that the life is offered in sacrifice is present, and a sacrifice can only be offered to God (it is staggering to think that Christian theologians should ever have seriously imagined that in offering up his life, Christ paid a ransom to the devil!). But in the context created for the saying in Mark, and adopted without change by Matthew, the 'ransom' – the giving of life – is the final complete act of service.[20]

Placed as it is before the entry into Jerusalem, this concludes the instruction of the disciples on the way, one that began in 8:31 in the region Caesarea Philippi.

The healing of blind Bartimaeus   10:46-52

[46] They came to Jericho. As he and his disciples and a large crowd were leaving Jericho, Bartimaeus son of Timaeus, a blind beggar, was sitting by the roadside. [47]When he heard that it was Jesus of Nazareth, he began to shout out and say, 'Jesus, Son of David, have mercy on me!' [48]Many sternly ordered him to be quiet, but he cried out even more loudly, 'Son of David, have mercy on me!' [49]Jesus stood still and said, 'Call him here.' And they called the blind man, saying to him, 'Take heart; get up, he is calling you.' [50]So throwing off his cloak he sprang up and came

20. F.W. Beare, *The Gospel according to Matthew* p. 409.

to Jesus. [51]Then Jesus said to him, 'What do you want me to do for you?' The blind man said to him, 'My teacher, let me see again.' [52]Jesus said to him, 'Go; your faith has made you well.' Immediately he regained his sight and followed him on the way.

Before Jesus began his journey to the villages of Caesarea Philippi, he registered his complaint to his disciples: 'Do you have eyes, and fail to see?'(8:18) Immediately following this, an unnamed blind man was brought to him for healing: Jesus restored the man's sight gradually, in two stages, and commanded him to keep his healing a secret (8:22-26). The restored man did not follow Jesus. Immediately after this incident, Peter's spiritual blindness to the true identity of Jesus was partially healed when he was able to confess, however inadequately, that Jesus was the Messiah. On the way, Jesus impressed on his disciples the necessity of his death and resurrection, but in spite of three passion predictions, the disciples remained spiritually blind to this second stage of insight, that Jesus is the suffering, dying, and rising Son of Man.

In the story of Bartimaeus, which stands at a pivotal place in Mark's Gospel, the blind man actively seeks out Jesus, is healed instantly, and becomes a disciple of Jesus on the way. Bartimaeus' recovery of full sight and willingness to follow Jesus on the way of discipleship are set in dramatic contrast to the disciples' persistent misunderstanding displayed during the journey. The healing, which happens before Jesus' entry into the city, foreshadows the second stage of the disciples' inner sight that will take place after the resurrection: 'But go, tell his disciples and Peter that he is going ahead of you to Galilee; there you will see him, just as he told you.'(16:7) Only then will Peter and the other disciples see the truth that Jesus is the risen Son of Man.

Mark begins the story by noting the arrival of the wayfarers in Jericho. The ancient city, west of the present town, was located in the wide plain of the Jordan valley, about six miles north of the Dead Sea, and had the distinction of being the lowest inhabited place in the world. Jerusalem was about seventeen miles north-east and some three thousand feet above the mounds of Jericho. Because of the climate and easy access to water, Herod the Great had built three winter palaces in Jericho, the third one decorated by an elaborate sunken garden and a huge pool. E. Netzger, an archaeologist who worked for many years on the excavations in Jericho, notes:

> It can be assumed that Second Temple Jericho was spread over the plain's irrigated areas, probably in the character of a garden city, side by side with the royal estates. Jericho as a whole functioned not only as an agricultural centre and a crossroad, but as a winter resort for the Jerusalem aristocracy.[21]

For pilgrims coming south from Galilee, Jericho was the last post on the pilgrimage route up to Jerusalem. The scene of the story is set as Jesus and his disciples and a large crowd are leaving the garden city on the final stage of their journey to the holy city. Bartimaeus, a blind beggar, is well positioned to catch the pilgrims leaving Jericho on their way to celebrate the feast of Passover, when Jews were expected to be generous in almsgiving. When he hears that it is Jesus of Nazareth who is passing by, he shouts out: 'Jesus, Son of David, have mercy on me!' Many of the pilgrims do not want to be disturbed by this desperate plea, so they order the one-man disturbance to be quiet. Refusing their peremptory advice, the blind beggar increases the volume of his plea: 'Son of David, have mercy on me!'

Jesus does not continue his journey; he stands still and challenges his companions to bring the afflicted man to him: '*Call* him here.' Their tone changes as they now *call* the blind man by encouraging him to take heart: 'He is *calling* you.' At the invitation, Bartimaeus throws off his cloak, springs to his feet and comes to Jesus. When asked by Jesus how he can help, the blind beggar addresses Jesus as *Rabbouni* (Aramaic for 'my teacher') and asks that he might see again. Jesus does not touch him, but commands him to go, for his faith has made him well. That said, Bartimaeus immediately regains his lost sight and follows Jesus on the way.

As Achtemeier observed about the account: 'A healing is present in the story, but in such abbreviated form that it appears to have been subordinated to some other intention.'[22] He goes on to argue that the account is a form of call story, which Steinhauser has taken a step further by arguing that the form of the Bartimaeus

21. E. Netzer, 'Jericho,' *The Anchor Bible Dictionary* Vol 3 p. 739.
22. P. Achtemeier, '"And he followed him": Miracles and Discipleship in Mark 10:46-52,' *Semeia* 2 (1978) p. 121.

narrative is modelled after the Old Testament form of the call stories of Gideon and Moses.[23] Certainly, this is the only healing miracle in the Synoptic tradition that contains the proper name of the person healed (Matthew and Luke omit the name from their retelling). But just as Jericho is mentioned twice, the naming of Bartimaeus, and its translation for a largely Gentile audience, can be better explained if the account is considered a call story in which the individual is explicitly named.

Bartimaeus first calls Jesus by his personal name, the first time this has happened in the Gospel. He calls out to Jesus twice with the unusual title 'Son of David'. The title seems strange, particularly since the messianic king of Judaism was not expected to perform miracles of healing. Meier's comment is worth noting:

> By the first century A.D., King Solomon – who was the only individual reigning monarch to be called Son of David in the Old Testament – had acquired a reputation in Jewish circles as a great exorcist and healer.... It is against this Jewish background that the blind Bartimaeus' appeal to Jesus as 'Son of David,' i.e., as miraculous healer, makes sense. Indeed the combination of Jesus as wise teacher, exorcist, and healer would make the address 'Son of David' (= a latter-day miracle-working Solomon) natural to a fellow first century Jew in need of healing, all the more so if some idea of Jesus' being of Davidic descent circulated among the common people of the day.[24]

No New Testament text connects Solomon with the title 'Son of David' or with healing, and the early Christian community interpreted Jesus' Davidic connection in terms of the enthronement of the Davidic Messiah, not with Solomon. This may indicate that the Bartimaeus story, as Meier argues, is not a product of a later Christian theology but of a an early tradition, preserved in this account, of how some Palestinian Jews looked on Jesus, as a miracle-worker and teacher in the tradition of Solomon, Son of David.

The story of Bartimaeus is a vivid and moving end to this central section of Mark's Gospel that has focused on how Jesus has tried

23. M. Steinhauser, 'The Form of the Bartimaeus Narrative (Mark 10:46-52),' *New Testament Studies* 32 (1986) pp. 583-595.

24. J.P. Meier, *A Marginal Jew: Rethinking the Historical Jesus* Vol 2 p. 689.

to open the eyes of his disciples to his destiny as he led them on the way. Before meeting Jesus, the blind Bartimaeus sat beside the way, a figure of beggarly immobility, depending on the kindness of passing strangers. When he hears Jesus' call to him, he throws away his cloak, leaps up, and comes to Jesus in faith, certain that Jesus can liberate him from a world of darkness. His energetic faith is rewarded and continues to show itself. The man who now sees Jesus is the man who now freely follows him on the way that inevitably leads to Jerusalem.

6

Ministry in Jerusalem

11:1-13:37

The sixth section of the Gospel deals with the final period of Jesus' ministry in Jerusalem and the surrounding neighbourhood, focusing on Jesus' dealings with the Temple. The section forms a prelude to the passion narrative and has three clear divisions: the events preceding the ministry (11:1-25); teaching and controversy with the Jewish hierarchy in Jerusalem (11:27-12:44); the apocalyptic discourse (13:1-27). According to Mark's chronological arrangement, the events and discourses prior to the passion and resurrection take place over a period of three days. This compression of events is obviously artificial, limiting Jesus final days to the liturgical equivalent of a 'passion week' in Jerusalem.

On each of these three days, Jesus journeys to the Temple. On Jesus' first journey, his entry into the city of Jerusalem is not triumphant. His destination is the Temple (11:11) which he looks at and leaves. His second journey finds him in the Temple again (11:15), where he drives out the buyers and sellers and provokes the Temple authorities to look for ways to kill him. Jesus' third journey to Jerusalem ends in the Temple (11:27) where he is seen again in controversy with the religious authorities. When he leaves the Temple for the last time, he predicts its downfall (13:1-2).

By the conclusion of this section, Jesus' rupture with the Temple and the religious authorities is complete and irreversible. As Kelber observes:

> Jesus' mission in Jerusalem was primarily designed to make the point that the temple was not to be the site of the Kingdom of God, neither in Jesus' own time nor in Mark's time. Jerusalem, far from being the place of the Kingdom, was to become the site of a double trauma, the death of Jesus and the death of the Temple.[1]

Unlike the prediction of Jesus' death, there is no notice of resurrection for the Temple.

1. W.H. Kelber, *Mark's Story of Jesus* p. 70.

Entry into Jerusalem 11:1-11

When they were approaching Jerusalem, at Bethphage and Bethany, near the Mount of Olives, he sent two of his disciples ²and said to them, 'Go into the village ahead of you and immediately as you enter it, you will find tied there a colt that has never been ridden; untie it and bring it. ³If anyone says to you, "Why are you doing this?" just say this, "The Lord needs it and will send it back here immediately." ⁴They went away and found a colt tied near a door, outside in the street. As they were untying it, ⁵some of the bystanders said to them, 'What are you doing, untying the colt?' ⁶They told them what Jesus had said; and they allowed them to take it. ⁷Then they brought the colt to Jesus and threw their cloaks on it; and he sat on it. ⁸Many people spread their cloaks on the road, and others spread leafy branches that they had cut in the fields. ⁹Then those who went ahead and those who followed were shouting,
'Hosanna!
Blessed is the one who comes in the name of the Lord!
¹⁰Blessed is the coming kingdom of our ancestor David!
Hosanna in the highest heaven!'
¹¹ Then he entered Jerusalem and went into the temple; and when he had looked around at everything, as it was already late, he went out to Bethany with the twelve.

The fateful journey to Jerusalem, which has formed the framework for the central section of Mark's Gospel, is now nearing its completion. Mark notes the final approach to the city of destiny by referring to two villages, Bethphage and Bethany, on the slopes of the Mount of Olives. Mark gives them in the reverse order to the way they would be approached from Jericho, probably because he is not acquainted with the local geography. Bethphage (the name literally means 'house of figs') was a suburb of Jerusalem and, although closer to the city than Bethany, it was probably situated off the ancient Roman road that led from Jericho to Jerusalem. Bethany (meaning 'house of dates') marked the last station for the pilgrim travelling on the main road from the east to Jerusalem; the village, about two miles from the city, is used as Jesus' headquarters during these final days of his ministry.

The Mount of Olives itself is a small ridge about two miles long, rising to a height of almost three thousand feet at the highest point. It rises to the east of Jerusalem, running north to south across from the Kidron Valley. According to Zechariah 14:4, God was expected to appear on the Mount of Olives at the end time, to judge the enemies of Israel; according to Josephus, the Messiah was expected to appear there.[2]

Jesus' instruction to two unnamed disciples, to go into the village ahead (probably Bethphage) and bring back the colt they will find there, suggests either Jesus' supernatural knowledge or that he is implementing a previous arrangement made with the colt's owner. The text itself would seem to lean towards the former interpretation, serving to underline a point that Mark has previously made: that Jesus is going knowingly and willingly towards his destiny. Both Matthew and John make it explicitly clear that the foal of an ass, rather than the foal of a horse, is meant. The choice of an unused animal suggests a sacred purpose.

If anyone questions the disciples about taking the animal, they are instructed to say that the Lord needs it and assure the questioner that it will be returned immediately. It is unclear if *kyrios* (meaning 'Lord' or 'Master') refers to Jesus, God, or the colt's owner. Mark never uses the title for Jesus anywhere in his writing, and it seems strange that this solitary incident would prompt its usage. Taylor argues that the name refers to the owner: 'the consideration that a message to the effect that the owner wanted his colt and would return it shortly would be likely to win the response described.'[3] From the evangelist's perspective, however, it seems an appropriate title for Jesus at the beginning of his final week.

Mark makes no explicit reference to the prophecy of Zechariah 9:9:

> Rejoice greatly, O daughter Zion!
> Shout aloud, O daughter Jerusalem!
> Lo, your king comes to you;
> triumphant and victorious is he,
> humble and riding on a donkey,
> on a colt, the foal of an ass.

This oracle, probably composed for the entry of Alexander the Great into Jerusalem in 322 B.C., is shown by Matthew to be literally fulfilled in the life of Jesus (Mt 21:5). It stands behind Mark's narrative, but unlike the Macedonian conqueror on his war horse, the Messianic king approaches the city riding on a donkey.

---

2. Josephus, *Antiquities* 20.8.6 See also Ezekiel 11:23; 2 Samuel 15:30.
3. V. Taylor, *The Gospel according to St. Mark* p. 455.

In Mark's story, Jerusalem does not shout to welcome its king; no crowds come out of the city to greet him; the entrance to the city itself is hardly described in terms of victory and triumph. The final part of the prophecy, however, reflects the modest Messiahship that Jesus claimed: not warlike and political, but spiritual and peaceful.

After the two disciples untether the colt and answer the bystanders' objection satisfactorily, they bring the colt to Jesus and throw their cloaks on it for use as a saddle. The band of pilgrims accompanying Jesus enter into the spirit of the event by spreading their cloaks before him, reminiscent of an earlier drama when 'they all took their cloaks and spread them for him, on the bare steps; and they blew the trumpet, and proclaimed, "Jehu is king".' (2 Kgs 9:13) Others lay 'leafy branches' (leaves and twigs and rushes) on the road as tokens of honour to Jesus, just as the crowds sang songs and laid branches when Simon Maccabeus entered the citadel of Jerusalem (1 Macc 13:51) – actions which were repeated during the annual feast of Dedication.

Some scholars argue that the festival the pilgrims are celebrating is not the spring feast of Passover but the autumn feast of Dedication, which celebrated the recleansing of the Temple by Judas Maccabeus in 165 B.C. This festival involved the carrying and waving of green branches by the people and recitation of the *Hallel* (praise) psalms, Pss 113-118. Thus a band of pilgrims approaching the city for the feast of Dedication, waving branches and singing psalms, would not have posed any particular threat to the civil or religious authorities, but would have passed unnoticed. Mark's modest procession, which appears to interest only those taking part, would seem to fit into this particular context well.

The first part of the pilgrims' acclamation, 'Hosanna! Blessed is the one who comes in the name of the Lord!' is a quotation from Psalm 118:25-26. This was the last of the *Hallel* psalms sung by pilgrims as they approached the Temple for the feast of Dedication. The cry 'Hosanna!' (literally meaning 'Save us') now becomes a shout of joy for the one who enters in the name of the Lord. The second part of the acclamation does not explicitly name Jesus as King or Son of David.

At the centre of all this Jesus rides on in enigmatic silence, allowing his band of followers their traditional pilgrim approach to the city. The coming kingdom they acclaim is a world away from the kingdom Jesus has proclaimed. Luke 19:41-44 tells the reader that Jesus weeps over the city and predicts its destruction. In Mark's account Jesus is the silent figure surrounded by enthusiasts who look to Jesus to restore the fortunes of Jerusalem and reclaim the lost splendour of the Davidic kingdom. Mark notes the entrance to the city in passing, but his focus is on the Temple. As B. van Iersel comments: 'In this part of the book Jerusalem seems to consist only of the temple buildings.'[4]

At the end of the account, the focus is on what Jesus does; but instead of the story reaching a climax in the cleansing of the Temple as it does in Matthew and Luke, it ends abruptly. There are no crowds, no acclamations, no cleansing, no disturbance. All seems quiet now. Jesus looks around at everything. Nothing more is done. Nothing is said. As it is already late, he leaves the Temple and the city and heads back with the twelve to Bethany on the Mount of Olives.

The end of the Temple   11:12-21

[12] On the following day, when they came from Bethany, he was hungry. [13]Seeing in the distance a fig tree in leaf, he went to see whether perhaps he would find anything on it. When he came to it, he found nothing but leaves, for it was not the season for figs. [14]He said to it, 'May no one ever eat fruit from you again.' And his disciples heard it.

[15] Then they came to Jerusalem. And he entered the temple and began to drive out those who were selling and those who were buying in the temple, and he overturned the tables of the money changers and the seats of those who sold doves; [16]and he would not allow anyone to carry anything through the temple. [17]He was teaching and saying, 'Is it not written,

"My house shall be called a house of prayer for all the nations"?
But you have made it a den of robbers.'

[18]And when the chief priests and the scribes heard it, they kept looking for a way to kill him; for they were afraid of him, because the whole crowd was spellbound by his teaching. [19]And when the evening came, Jesus and his disciples went out of the city.

[20] In the morning as they passed by, they saw the fig tree withered away to its roots. [21]Then Peter remembered and said to him, 'Rabbi, look! The fig tree that you cursed has withered.'

4. B. van Iersel, *Reading Mark* (Edinburgh: T & T Clark, 1989) p. 144.

Unlike Matthew and Luke, Mark encloses the story of the cleansing of the Temple within the framework of another story, the curse of the fig tree. This deliberate technique tells us that by putting the story of the fig tree on either side of the cleansing of the Temple, Mark wants the two stories to interpret one another: the fate of the withered tree is connected with that of the Temple. Both stories are prophecies-in-action, both foretelling God's judgement on the Temple. In this Mark is capitalising on Old Testament prophetic imagery, which uses the fig tree and its fruit to depict God's coming to judge Israel.[5]

On his way from Bethany to the Temple, Jesus is hungry. In the distance he sees a fig tree in full foliage and he approaches it expectantly, in the hope of finding food. He discovers nothing but leaves. Mark adds that it was not the season (*kairos*) for figs – which became ripe usually from June. Jesus proceeds to address the fig tree with a curse, 'May no one ever eat fruit from you again.' His disciples hear the curse, thus preparing for the observation the following morning that it has taken effect (11:21).

Why curse a tree for not providing fruit out of season? Ill-tempered disappointment hardly fits the portrait of even a hungry Jesus. This is the only miracle performed by Jesus in Jerusalem; moreover, it is the only miracle among all the Gospels that is punitive and involves cursing. The real question is what Mark seeks to teach us by telling the story as he does and situating it where he has. The story is obviously symbolic: behind it may have been something like Luke's parable of the barren fig tree (Lk 13:6-9) or an incident involving Jesus' comments on a withered fig tree that stood by the wayside between Bethany and Jerusalem.

The clue to Mark's meaning is in his use of the word *kairos*, translated as 'season'. *Kairos* is a spiritual term referring to the right time, one that Jesus used in his programmatic announcement of the kingdom of God (1:14-15). The Temple, the centre of Israel's worship, has not availed itself of the opportunities provided by the *kairos* of Jesus' ministry. R. Hiers points to the belief among Jews that in the messianic age the fertility of nature would yield an

5. For a detailed study of this subject, see W.R. Telford, 'The Barren Temple and the Withered Tree' (*Journal for the Study of the New Testament* – Supplement Series 1: Sheffield, 1980) pp. 128-250. See also D. Juel, *Messiah and Temple* (Montana: Scholars Press, 1977) pp. 135-156.

abundant harvest, so that trees and vines would be always fruitful.[6] The condition of the fig tree – a fine show of leaves but no actual fruit – is a symbol of the Temple religion. The fate of the fig tree is used as a symbol for the fate of the Temple: both are rejected for their deceptive, fruitless show, and Jesus will not only 'cleanse' the Temple but prophesy its total destruction (13:1-2).

When Jesus returns to Jerusalem, again his destination is the Temple. In the outer court of the Temple, open to Gentiles as well as Jews, the business of buying and selling was conducted to support the sacrificial system of worship. Unblemished animals – oxen, sheep, goats, pigeons – were for sale, together with other items necessary for the requirements of the cult – incense, wine, salt, and oil. Money-changers were needed, for the Temple authorities would accept only the local Tyrian coinage, the nearest equivalent to the old Hebrew shekel. Everyone was obliged to exchange Roman and Greek coinage, which carried either the head of the reigning emperor or pagan symbols, for 'the shekel of the sanctuary' (Num 3:47). This arrangement was useful for the multitude of pilgrims coming from near and far, and was instituted by Caiaphas as a more convenient arrangement than buying the animals from one of the four markets on the Mount of Olives. These four markets were under the jurisdiction of the Sanhedrin, while the huge market in the Court of the Gentiles was under the jurisdiction of the high priest and was supposed to be conducted in the interests of the pilgrims.

Jesus begins a one-man riot, expelling merchants and pilgrims alike. He then *overturns* the money tables and the seats – a symbol of destruction. In refusing anyone passage who was carrying anything, it appears that Jesus wants to bring the whole sacrificial system of the Temple to a halt. Beare comments:

> Such a general expulsion of merchants and money-changers as is attributed here to Jesus would have made the continuance of sacrificial worship in the temple impossible.... The modern reader hardly realises how great a disturbance would be involved. The animals for sacrifice would number in the thousands, and there would be even more pigeons. Naturally, these

6. R. Hiers, 'Not the Season for Figs,' *Journal of Biblical Literature* 87 (1968) pp. 294-400.

would require very large numbers of attendants, to feed and water them, apart from the merchants who sold them. Most of the pilgrims had come there precisely to offer sacrifices – are we to imagine that they would all, or any great number of them, be gratified to see Jesus remove the means necessary for the fulfilment of their pious intentions? ... All this is not merely implausible; it is utterly incredible.[7]

It seems more likely that Jesus' activity, which attracted neither the attention of the Temple police nor the intervention of the soldiers from the Antonia fortress overlooking the Temple precincts, was a much more modest affair than appears in Mark's account. Whatever trouble the incident originally caused, it is not raised as evidence against Jesus at his trial.

Jesus justifies his activity by first quoting from Isaiah 56:7, which assures the Gentiles that they will have their own place of prayer in the Temple. Jesus' concern is that the Temple be a house of prayer for all people and his activity is aimed at purging everything that makes prayer and worship difficult or impossible for the Gentiles in the only place they are admitted. The second quotation takes the phrase 'den of robbers' from Jeremiah 7:11, which was written between 608-605 B.C., shortly before the destruction of Jerusalem. Jeremiah protested against using religious observance as a cover for sinful behaviour and then proceeded to predict the destruction of the Temple itself.

There is no overt opposition to Jesus. Mark tells us that when the chief priests and scribes hear what Jesus has said, they keep looking for ways to kill him. Mark notes how the Temple administrators hear Jesus' prophetic critique, thus preparing for their challenge to Jesus' authority the next day. They are afraid of Jesus and nervous of the support he attracts from the ordinary people. For the moment, the crowd is beyond their control. The Temple authorities, representing the whole sacrificial system, know that Jesus is, by implication, criticising their moribund spiritual leadership. Their leadership, like ritual sacrifice, is dated. That the fig tree is seen 'withered away to its roots' the next morning is a dramatic image of what will surely befall the whole Temple system. Thus the story

7. F.W. Beare, *The Gospel according to Matthew* p. 416.

of the fig tree taken together with the cleansing of the Temple tells us that Jesus was not urging the reform of the Temple so that it could function in a new way; he was making a prophetic pronouncement about its final repudiation and doom.

Stray sayings   11:22-25

[22]Jesus answered them. 'Have faith in God. [23]Truly I tell you, if you say to this mountain, "Be taken up and thrown into the sea," and if you do not doubt in your heart, but believe that what you say will come to pass, it will be done for you. [24]So I tell you, whatever you ask for in prayer, believe that you have received it, and it will be yours.

[25] 'Whenever you stand praying, forgive, if you have anything against anyone; so that you Father in heaven may also forgive you your trespasses.'

These verses on faith, prayer, and forgiveness that immediately follow on Peter's recognition of the curse's effect are stray sayings that Mark has included here. They circulated independently in the early Church and have a variety of forms and contexts (e.g. Mt 6:14-15; 17:20; Lk 17:6; Jn 14:13-14; 15:7; 16:23; 1 Cor 13:2). In Mark the sayings are obviously not well integrated into the section of the cursing of the fig tree and the cleansing of the Temple, and have the effect of interrupting the flow of the action. As Meier notes: 'In particular, the stipulation that forgiveness is a necessary condition for having one's prayers heard (v.25) strikes the reader as a strange commentary on Jesus' destructive curse of a tree that symbolizes the temple.'[8] By *placing* the sayings here, however, Mark makes his own contribution to the discussion by moving the narrative from public to private devotion. After the repudiation of the sacrificial system, these verses effectively replace that ritual mechanism with a new piety, that of faith, prayer, and forgiveness.

Jesus first urges his disciples to have faith in God. Their prayer must be permeated with a profound confidence in God. Jesus then states boldly that if they believe in their heart what they say, they can move mountains into the sea. This sounds like an early argument for positive thinking: believe and it will happen; believe that you have received it, and it will be yours. It brings the goal to be achieved into the present tense as a sign of the faith-filled

8. J.P. Meier, *A Marginal Jew: Rethinking the Historical Jesus* Vol 2 p. 888

assurance of the petitioner. 'Removing mountains' was a popular metaphor for doing things that were particularly difficult, and obviously is not meant to be taken literally.

Jesus counsels his disciples to have a basic attitude of forgiveness whenever they pray. Matthew has a liturgical context for prayer and forgiveness: 'leave your gift there before the altar and go; first be reconciled to your brother or sister, and then come and offer your gift.' (Mt 5:24) Mark's text makes no mention of an altar, since the connection between prayer and the Temple has been severed. The power of prayer no longer resides in the Temple but in the disciples who have faith. In this Mark seems a world away from the Temple-centred climate in Acts 1-5; for him, the Christian community has replaced the rejected Temple establishment.

Finally, it could be said that this catechesis, particularly in the final verse, is a way of presenting the various challenges of the Our Father, which is not found in Mark. As Doohan notes: 'For a community undergoing persecution, the Our Father must not be merely recited, but rather must be embodied in concrete attitudes of faith and discipleship.'[9]

Jesus' authority is questioned   11:27-33

[27] Again they came to Jerusalem. As he was walking in the temple, the chief priests, the scribes, and the elders came to him [28]and said, 'By what authority are you doing these things? Who gave you this authority to do them?' [29]Jesus said to them, 'I will ask you one question; answer me, and I will tell you by what authority I do these things. [30]Did the baptism of John come from heaven, or was it of human origin? Answer me.' [31]They argued with one another, 'If we say, "From heaven," he will say, "Why then did you not believe him?" [32]But shall we say, "Of human origin"?' – They were afraid of the crowd, for all regarded John as truly a prophet. [33]So they answered Jesus, 'We do not know.' And Jesus said to them, 'Neither will I tell you by what authority I am doing these things.'

Mark's Gospel contains two prominent controversy sections: the first takes place in Galilee (2:1-3:6) and the second in Judea (11:27-12:40). Just as Jesus' authority is the issue in the first Galilean controversy (2:10), a matter broached by Jesus himself, so too in this first narrative of the Judean cycle the question concerns the

9. L. Doohan, *Mark: Visionary of Early Christianity* (Santa Fe: Bear, 1986) p. 101.

legitimacy of Jesus' power, except that this time Jesus' opponents take the initiative. The three groups mentioned by Mark were first noticed in the passion prediction (8:31) and they will be Jesus' principal antagonists during the passion drama (14:43,53; 15:1). In this story they confront Jesus about the nature and source of his authority.

On Jesus' return to the city, he goes again to the Temple where he walks around like a peripatetic teacher. A deputation from the Sanhedrin, chief priests and scribes and elders, approach Jesus to question him about his authority. This triple alliance of religion, law and politics represents the officially designated authority that oversees the sacred system. Jesus has no authority comparable to theirs, so they ask him first, 'By what authority do you do these things?' The expression 'these things' probably refers primarily to Jesus' recent attack on the sacrificial system of the Temple, when he expelled the merchants and money-changers, but the phrase is sufficiently vague to refer to the whole of Jesus' independent ministry. The second part of their interrogation seeks an answer to the question, 'Who gave you the right to do what you do?' Clearly these representatives of the supreme tribunal do not wish to admit that anyone outside their system could exercise authoritative leadership.

Instead of replying to their double question, Jesus asks a counter-question – a popular form of reply in rabbinic debates. Jesus chooses the example of John the Baptist, who could point to no human authorisation for his ministry, and frames his question in such a way that it includes two mutually exclusive sources of authority: was John's baptism from heaven or earth? Because they did not submit themselves to the baptism of John, the religious authorities have no wish to expose themselves to the charge of unbelief by ascribing heavenly authority to John. Because the ordinary people recognise John as a prophet sent by God, the Jerusalem officials are afraid to deny John that divine authority.

The interesting point to note is how Jesus allies himself with John when questioned about his own authority. Jesus himself had no difficulty recognising John's divinely inspired authority and submitting to his baptism for the repentance of sins. John's natural sanctuary was the wilderness, not the Temple; his ritual act centred around the water of the river Jordan, not around the priestly altar of sacrifice. Jesus' model of authentic religious authority was John, not the Sanhedrin. Over against the 'institutional' authority of the Temple administrators, John and Jesus enjoyed 'charismatic' authority – one that did not depend on the appointment of religious officialdom. Since neither of them was appointed by the constituted authorities, neither of them could be dismissed at their command. Since neither of them enjoyed official sanction, neither of them looked for official approval. Both John and Jesus were independent prophets whose authority came from God.

In replying that they do not know the source of John's authority, the officials from the highest court in Judaism abdicate their authority to pronounce judgement on a critical religious question. It is as if Mark is deliberately displaying the sterility of their leadership before the reader. Jesus' refusal to answer by what authority he acts throws the hearers and, therefore, the readers of the Gospel back to a basic question in religion: 'How do you discern what comes from God?' Jesus' imperative holds good: 'Answer me.' If in looking at the things Jesus does, people cannot see with the eyes of faith that his authority is divine, Jesus' own pronouncement on the matter will make no discernible difference. The readers of the Gospel must provide the missing answer for themselves.

The parable of the wicked tenants   12:1-12

Then he began to speak to them in parables. 'A man planted a vineyard, put a fence around it, dug a pit for the wine press, and built a watchtower; then he leased it to tenants and went to another country. [2]When the season came, he sent a slave to the tenants to collect from them his share of the produce of the vineyard. [3]But they seized him, and beat him, and sent him away empty-handed. [4]And again he sent another slave to them; this one they beat over the head and insulted. [5]Then he sent another, and that one they killed. And so it was with many others; some they beat, and others they killed. [6]He had still one other, a beloved son. Finally he sent him to them, saying, "They will respect my son." [7]But those tenants said to one another, "This is the heir; come, let us kill him, and the inheritance will be ours." [8]So they seized him, killed him, and threw him out of the vineyard. [9]What then will the owner of the vineyard do? He will come and destroy the tenants and give the vineyard to others. [10]Have you not read this scripture:

> "The stone that the builders rejected has become the cornerstone;
> [11]this was the Lord's doing,
> and it is amazing in our eyes"?'
> [12] When they realized that he had told this parable against them, they wanted to arrest him, but they feared the crowd. So they left him and went away.

Having just been questioned by a hostile delegation from the Sanhedrin – chief priests, scribes and elders – Jesus now takes the initiative and confronts them by way of a parable. The parable seems to look back, rather than forward, to the death of Jesus: from the perspective of the early church and its conflict with Judaism, it places the passion of Jesus in the larger context of the fate experienced by God's previous messengers. The parable reflects the interpretation of the death of Jesus in relation to the whole history of Israel as it is articulated in Stephen's speech before the Sanhedrin: 'Which of the prophets did your ancestors not persecute? They killed those who foretold the coming of the Righteous One, and now you have become his betrayers and murderers.' (Acts 7:52)

In its present form the parable contains a substantial strain of allegory; this factor alone has led some scholars to argue that it is a product of the early church. Efforts to reconstruct the primitive form of the parable used by Jesus are necessarily speculative, and we have to interpret the parable Mark sets before us. Some features in the parable (the hedge, the winepress, the tower) serve the details of the narrative and have no allegorical equivalent. The allegorical features can be readily identified, although it is not clear who the 'others' are meant to be: the owner of the vineyard is God; the vineyard is Israel; the tenant farmers are the religious leaders; the servants are God's messengers; the beloved son is Jesus; and the others may well be the Gentiles.

The vocabulary used to describe the vineyard is based on the Song of the Vineyard in Isaiah 5:1-7 from the Greek translation of the Hebrew Bible, one which would have been used only in a Greek-speaking community in the early church:

> My beloved had a vineyard on a very fertile hill.
> He dug it and cleared it of stones,
> and planted it with choice vines

he built a watchtower in the midst of it,
and hewed out a wine vat in it;
he expected it to yield grapes,
but it yielded wild grapes ...
For the vineyard of the Lord of hosts is the house of Israel,
and the people of Judah are his pleasant planting.

The house of Israel and the people of Judah are not tenants, as in the parable, but the vineyard itself; and the punishment is not that the vineyard is given to others, but that it is utterly destroyed (vv. 5-6).

The parable reflects conditions of life in rural Galilee, where estates owned by absentee landlords were let out to local tenants whose rental was paid in kind from the produce of the land. Before leaving, the man plants a vineyard, puts a fence around it to protect it from wild animals, digs a pit to receive the juices from the trodden grapes, and builds a watchtower to accommodate the vinedressers and provide a vantage point from which intruders could be spotted. The owner leases the vineyard and goes abroad. When the time comes to collect his due, he sends a succession of three servants to collect his share of the produce.

The tenants rebel by beating the first servant and dismissing him, wounding the second servant in the head and insulting him, and killing the third servant. The second servant's wounding in the head may be an oblique reference to the death of John the Baptist. The owner keeps sending servants, all of whom suffer either beating or death. The point made is that throughout the history of Israel God has repeatedly and graciously sent his messengers, who have been rejected habitually and violently by the leaders of the people.

After this litany of catastrophes, you would think that the owner's repeated loss would make him wise, but not so: allegory has taken over, leaving the story's plausibility well behind it. The owner remains stubbornly and inexplicably hopeful as he decides to send the one he has left, thinking they will treat him differently and respect him. In what seems the last reckless act of many, he sends his 'beloved son'. Mark, followed by Luke 20:13-14, stresses the identity of the son as beloved – clearly a figure for Jesus himself, who has been recognised as such in Mark's accounts of the baptism (1:11) and the transfiguration (9:7). The tenants react to the visit of the owner's son by magically thinking that if they kill the son they will, therefore, be the inheritors. They kill him and throw his body outside the vineyard. In Matthew 21:39 the son is first dragged out of the vineyard, then killed. The idea of throwing the son outside the vineyard may be connected to the location of Jesus' death outside the walls of Jerusalem. (See Hebrews 13:12: 'Jesus suffered outside the gate'.)

The question 'What then will the owner of the vineyard do?' receives an answer that most people would have supplied much earlier in the story: he will come and destroy the tenants. After such a disastrous experience in leasing his vineyard, repeating the process again seems somewhat unreal, but it is required by the actualities of the Gentile mission. Again allegory presses its own logic on the story.

The parable is followed immediately by a verbatim quotation from the Greek translation of Psalm 118:22-23. The imagery shifts abruptly from a vineyard to a building. The absence of any note of resurrection or exaltation in the parable is now corrected: the Psalm is given a Christian application as a prophecy of the death and exaltation of Christ. Crossan notes:

> The citation from Ps.118 was an obvious necessity of the allegorical situation. The end could not be the death of the son, even when his murder had been amply punished. The end would have to be the triumph of the son. The apologetic of the stone rejected by the builders but made the cornerstone by act of God is well known from the preaching of the early church. This quotation is now added to effect this victorious conclusion.[10]

The leaders hear the parable as one addressed specifically to them – interpreting the wicked tenants to refer not to the whole people of Israel but to themselves as religious leaders. Their ready ability to understand the parable appears in sharp contrast to the point Mark insisted on earlier, that 'those outside' could not perceive or understand the meaning of Jesus' parabolic teaching (4:11-12). The religious hierarchy want to arrest the storyteller –

10. J.D. Crossan, *In Parables: the Challenge of the Historical Jesus* (New York: Harper & Row, 1973) p. 90.

speaking in parables is proving to be a deadly business for Jesus – but their fear of the people prevents them. They leave Jesus and go away. As the next narrative reveals, however, they do not abandon their case against him.

The question about the poll tax   12:13-17

[13] Then they sent to him some Pharisees and some Herodians to trap him in what he said. [14] And they came and said to him, 'Teacher, we know that you are sincere, and show deference to no one; for you do not regard people with partiality, but teach the way of God in accordance with truth. Is it lawful to pay taxes to the emperor, or not? [15] Should we pay them, or should we not?' But knowing their hypocrisy, he said to them, 'Why are you putting me to the test? Bring me a denarius and let me see it.' [16] And they brought one. Then he said to them, 'Whose head is this, and whose title?' They answered, 'The emperor's.' [17] Jesus said to them, 'Give to the emperor the things that are the emperor's and to God the things that are God's.' And they were utterly amazed at him.

The Galilean cycle of conflict stories concluded with the early notice that the Pharisees conspired with the Herodians about how to destroy Jesus (3:6). Now, in this second conflict story of the Judean cycle, the unusual alliance is back in play on behalf of the Sanhedrin or unnamed others. For all their differences, the Pharisees and the supporters of the house of Herod have common cause in trying to entrap Jesus.

Before the challenge is articulated, a disarming compliment is offered. Their flattering overture praises the independence of Jesus as an upright man who shows deference to no one, a teacher of God's way who is concerned only with the truth. Without meaning to, Jesus' adversaries speak the truth about him as someone who refuses to tailor his message according to his audience. No doubt they are maliciously hoping that Jesus' independent attitude, already demonstrated against the Temple authorities, will extend itself to the ultimate civil authority in Tiberius Caesar.

They ask Jesus if it lawful to pay taxes (*kenson*) to the emperor or not. The Greek word *kenson* is a transliteration of the Latin *census*, which refers specifically to the poll tax. This tax was particularly unpopular among the Jews because it was not levied for the expenses of local government but paid directly into the imperial treasury. The poll tax, demanded of all inhabitant of

Judea, Samaria and Idumea, was imposed in 6 A.D. by Coponius, the first Roman procurator, who replaced the deposed Archelaus. Before the introduction of the tax, a census had to be made: the Zealot, Judas the Galilean, interpreted this as an affront to the sovereignty of God.[11] The Zealots refused to pay the tax because it acknowledged Caesar's dominion over the people of God, the Pharisees resented its imposition but agreed to pay, while the Herodians gave it their support in principle. The question is skilfully devised because an affirmative answer from Jesus would alienate him from ordinary people, while a negative reply would be regarded as a threat to public order by the Roman authorities. Either way, it appears that Jesus has to compromise himself.

Since both the Pharisees and the Herodians had paid the poll tax for a long time, Jesus sees that their apparently anxious question is not one that currently troubles their conscience. He names what is happening: they are putting him to the test. He asks his opponents for a denarius, the small silver Roman coin that had to be used for paying the poll tax. The denarius was engraved with the emperor's head and the abbreviated inscription, *Ti(berius) Caesar Divi Aug(usti) F(ilius) Augustus* – Tiberius Caesar Augustus, Son of the Divine Augustus. On the reverse side was written *Pontif(ex) Maxim(us)*. Apart from the poll tax itself, the denarius was regarded as offensive since it bore the image of Tiberius (14-37 A.D.) and contained a blasphemous claim to divinity. When Jesus asks them whose head is engraved on the denarius, they answer that it is the emperor's. Then Jesus makes his pronouncement, to render to the emperor what belongs to him, and to God the things that are God's.

Most commentators interpret the reply as a teaching on honouring one's temporal and religious obligations: one must pay tribute to Caesar and to God. But this reflects the modern division between church and state and makes little sense within traditional Judaism, which believed that power was one and indivisible precisely because the people belonged to a theocracy. Thus Jesus does not specify the things that belong to Caesar, for the emperor does not possess anything independently of God; Jesus does not need to specify the things that belong to God, since everything does. As

11. See Josephus, *Antiquities* 18.1.11.

Cassidy writes:

> Our interpretations is that, instead of positing the existence of two realms, Caesar's and God's, Jesus really taught and acted in terms of only one realm: *God's*. Far from having any kind of independent existence of its own, Caesar's realm, the social order of the Roman empire, was in Jesus' view a part of the larger order of creation, whose only author was God. Therefore the Romans' social patterns were to be evaluated against the standard of the social patterns desired by God, and supported or not on that basis.... Thus, the only areas in which Caesar can expect allegiance are those in which his patterns are in conformity with God's desired patterns.[12]

This interpretation does not make Jesus into a political radical or a Zealot: it simply avoids making him into an uncritical supporter of whatever government or military power happens to be in possession at a given moment. *All* authority and power, including religious hierarchy, has to be evaluated in the light of God's plan. Jesus' opponents would hardly have been utterly amazed at his reply if the only thing he managed to do was avoid their question. In his reply Jesus gives his own teaching, in line with traditional Judaism: it is for people to evaluate whether in demanding the poll tax, Caesar is reflecting the things of God. That evaluation, which is always a complex one, continues in every age.

The question about the resurrection 12:18-27

[18] Some Sadducees, who say there is no resurrection, came to him and asked him a question, saying, [19]"Teacher, Moses wrote for us that "if a man's brother dies, leaving a wife but no child, the man shall marry the widow and raise up children for his brother." [20]There were seven brothers; the first married and, when he died, left no children; [21]and the second married her and died, leaving no children; and the third likewise; [22]none of the seven left children. Last of all the woman herself died. [23]In the resurrection whose wife will she be? For the seven had married her.'

[24]Jesus said to them, 'Is not this the reason you are wrong, that you know neither the scriptures nor the power of God? [25]For when they rise from the dead, they neither marry nor are given in marriage, but are like

12. R. Cassidy, *Jesus, Politics and Society* (New York: Orbis, 1978) p. 58.

angels in heaven. [26]And as for the dead being raised, have you not read in the book of Moses, in the story about the bush, how God said to him, "I am the God of Abraham, the God of Isaac, and the God of Jacob"? [27]He is God not of the dead, but of the living; you are quite wrong.'

In Mark's arrangement of the Judean conflict stories, it seems as if the different religious authorities are queuing up to oppose Jesus. It is now the turn of the Sadducees. Their name probably derives from Zadok, who was the high priest at the time of David and Solomon. Little is known about them as a group within Judaism apart from their rejection of the belief in the resurrection and their acceptance only of the Pentateuch, the five books of Moses. They came from the governing class, but the degree of their influence is difficult to establish. Saldarini comments:

> In view of a common misunderstanding in New Testament scholarship it must be emphasised that neither Josephus nor the New Testament claims that all or most of the chief priests, elders and other members of the governing class were Sadducees, only that Sadducees, however few or numerous, were mostly drawn from that class.[13]

After the destruction of the Temple in 70 A.D. the Sadducees disappeared as a group from the religious scene, suggesting that their base of power and privilege was closely connected with the Temple.

Because the affirmation of Jesus' resurrection was central for the early Christians, the characteristic of the Sadducees that engaged them most fully was the Sadducees' rejection of life after death. (Belief in the resurrection was a late arrival in Judaism, and is reflected in the Old Testament only in late post-exilic passages. These passages – Isaiah 25:8; 26:19; Psalm 73:24-25; Daniel 12:1-3 – are not part of the Pentateuch and so were not accepted as authoritative by the Sadducees.) This controversy between the Sadducees and Jesus is the only mention Mark makes of them in the Gospel. The conflict, with parallels in Matthew and Luke, together with the argument between the Pharisees and Sadducees provoked by Paul in the Sanhedrin (Acts 23), all depend on the denial of the resurrection.

13. A.J. Saldarini, *Pharisees, Scribes and Sadducees in Palestinian Society* (Edinburgh: T & T Clark, 1989) p. 154.

Their question is calculated to disparage Jesus as a teacher. They quote the law of levirite marriage – the term deriving from the Latin word *levir*, brother-in-law. According to this law (Deut 25:5-10), when a man dies without leaving a son, his widow is forbidden to marry outside the family. Her husband's brother must take her in marriage and perform the duty of a brother-in-law (*levir*). The first son that she bears will be accounted to the dead brother, 'so that his name may not be blotted out of Israel.' (Deut 25:6). According to the Sadducees, this law presupposes that the only way one survives after death is through the lives of one's offspring. By way of a riddle, they give the imaginary case of a woman who marries seven brothers in turn, all of whom die childless. Eventually she dies. Their question, 'In the resurrection whose wife will she be?' is meant to suggest that belief in the resurrection is manifestly an absurdity.

In reply Jesus tells the Sadducees bluntly that they are wrong because they know neither the scriptures nor the power of God. They do not appreciate the power of God to overcome death and give new life. Present human relationships do not persist in resurrection life, for the resurrected are like the angels in heaven. In the resurrection God's power establishes a new creation that is not limited by previous human ties. No description of the afterlife is given, just a notice that it will be radically different from this one.

Finally, Jesus turns his attention to the truth of the resurrection itself. The proof is one Jesus infers from the canon of scripture the Sadducees do accept, the Pentateuch, indeed from a passage of classic importance. Jesus instances God's self-revelation to Moses in Exodus 3:6, 15-16. God revealed himself as the God of Abraham, Isaac, and Jacob at a time when the patriarchs were no longer alive according to the flesh. Originally this passage was understood simply to mean that the God who was speaking to Moses identified himself to be the same God who had spoken to the patriarchs – namely, that he was the ancestral God of Israel. Jesus, however, gives the passage a completely new interpretation. Precisely because God is the God of the living, the patriarchs continue to enjoy the kept promise of God's covenant relationship. God cannot be the God of the dead: that is not a relationship but the absence of one. Whatever the appeal of Jesus' argument on the reader, the important point for Mark is the representation of Jesus' own belief in the resurrection.

The two great commandments   12:28-34

> [28]One of the scribes came near and heard them disputing with one another, and seeing that he answered them well, he asked him, 'Which commandment is the first of all?' [29]Jesus answered, 'The first is, "Hear, O Israel: the Lord our God, the Lord is one; [30]you shall love the Lord your God with all your heart, and with all your soul, and with all your mind, and with all your strength." [31]The second is this, "You shall love your neighbor as yourself." There is no other commandment greater than these.' [32]Then the scribe said to him, 'You are right, Teacher; you have truly said that "he is one, and besides him there is no other"; [33]and "to love him with all the heart, and with all the understanding, and with all the strength", and "to love one's neighbor as oneself," – this is much more important than all whole burnt offerings and sacrifices.' [34]When Jesus saw that he answered wisely, he said to him, 'You are not far from the kingdom of God.' After that no one dared to ask him any question.

Mark connects this incident with Jesus' controversy with the Sadducees by showing how a scribe, impressed by the answer he has heard Jesus make, now makes his own enquiry about which commandment is the most important. Mark identifies the attitude of the scribe as positive and concludes the story with Jesus' commendation, 'You are not far from the kingdom of God.' By contrast, Luke and Matthew both stress the adversarial spirit of the encounter (Lk 10:25,29; Mt 22:35) and omit Jesus' final affirmation of the lawyer.

The question about the most important commandment was a popular way of capturing the essentials of a rabbi's teaching. How would you summarise the essence of the 613 commandments of the Torah in one statement? One of the best known examples is that of Hillel (*ca* 40 B.C.-10 A.D.) when he was asked by a Gentile to 'teach me the whole Torah while I stand on one foot.' Hillel gave his reply: 'What you yourself hate, do not do to your neighbour: this is the whole Law, and the rest is commentary. Go and learn it.'[14] Jesus' reply quotes the beginning of the *Shema* (from the first word, 'Hear, O Israel ... ', of the Hebrew text of Deuteronomy 6:4). The *Shema* was the equivalent of a basic creed that every pious Jew

14. Babylonian Talmud, *Shabbath* 31a.

recited as part of morning and evening prayer. In common with the monotheism of his Jewish heritage and in contrast to the pagan traditions, Jesus affirms the oneness of God. This confession of faith moves into affirming the love of God as the ground of human existence. Being one, God demands an undivided love. The four-fold imperative of loving God with heart and soul and mind and strength sets a demand for total integrity and allegiance. Nothing in the person is to be excluded from the unqualified love of God.

This is the only instance in the Synoptics that speaks of human love for God, the stress throughout the scriptures being on God's radical love for his people, a love that is unearned and undeserved. Here Judaism and Christianity share the same ground for living a life of faith: we are called to respond wholeheartedly to the love that has first loved us. Moses and Jesus, Torah and Gospel, resound together.

Jesus links a second commandment to the total love of God: 'You shall love your neighbour as yourself.' This commandment presupposes that people have a healthy self-esteem, so that they can esteem others in the same way. Scholars have asked if Jesus' combination of these separated texts is original or derived from earlier sources. The Jewish scholar Vermes responds to this question:

> While the bond between the two loves is unquestionably present in inter-testamental and rabbinic thought, its simple expression by means of coupling Deut. 6:5 with Lev 19:18 is characteristic of the New Testament, and probably of Jesus himself. In doing so, he succeeded in coining a single principle, incorporating all the theological and ethical contents of the Torah.[15]

The scribe's expansive answer expresses wholehearted agreement with Jesus' teaching. More importantly, he draws out the implications of Jesus' teaching by expressing one further idea. This theologian of the Temple establishment goes on to speak of the primacy of love over ritual sacrifice. Paradoxically, the whole business of burnt offering and sacrifices is downgraded in the very place where it is conducted.

Jesus' response to the sympathetic scribe is one of affirmation.

15. G. Vermes, *The Religion of Jesus the Jew* p. 43.

'Not far from the kingdom of God' is a compliment that the scribe is near, not a complaint that he has not yet arrived. The response acts as Mark's editorial conclusion to a series of questions asked by representatives of the religious authorities. The responses to Jesus' teaching have moved from hostility (12:12) to amazement (12:17) to silence (12:27) to admiration (12:27). Of the aftermath of Jesus' exchange with the scribe, Mark says that 'no one dared to ask him any question.' That allows Jesus to take his own initiative and become the questioner himself.

The question about David's Son   12:35-37a

[35] While Jesus was teaching in the temple, he said, 'How can the scribes say that the Messiah is the son of David? [36]David himself, by the Holy Spirit, declared,
> "The Lord said to my Lord,
> 'Sit at my right hand,
> until I put your enemies under your feet.' "
[37]David himself calls him Lord; so how can he be his son?'

The setting for this story continues to be the Temple and the controversy between Jesus and the religious authorities continues, except that now Jesus provokes it himself. Neither Mark nor Luke identifies the listeners, while Matthew speaks of Jesus addressing his question to the Pharisees who are 'gathered together' (Mt 22:41). In Mark's account, Jesus is presumably teaching the crowds when he poses a question about the scribes' messianic understanding.

Jesus seems to cast doubt on the popular idea that the Messiah would be a son of David – that he would *necessarily* be of Davidic descent. That the Messiah would be of Davidic descent is a belief strongly attested in the Old Testament (see Is 9:2-7; 11:1-9; Jer 23:5-6, 33:14-18, etc.). This, however, does not settle the question how the phrase 'son of David' was understood at the time of Jesus, especially if the Davidic house had been destroyed by the Persians during the exile. Mann states the problem well:

> But what is not at all clear is whether by the time of Jesus the designation 'son of David' meant a physical descendant of the Davidic house or whether the term would be applied to anyone who effectively established a claim to be the messiah. The

question asked by Jesus does not offer us any help at this point. At the same time it is uncertain whether Jesus is in *any* sense claiming to be '*son of David*' either by physical descent or by messianic claim. The claim of Davidic sonship is made for Jesus in early Christian writing (cf. Rom 1:3; 2 Tim 2:8, and in the genealogies of Matt 1:1-17 and Luke 3:23-38), but once again we cannot be absolutely certain that the term 'son of David by human descent' in Rom 1:3 refers to physical genealogy and is not an honorific designation.[16]

Jesus' question is immediately followed by a reference to what David said under the inspiration of the Holy Spirit. This reflects the popular but mistaken belief of the rabbis that Psalm 110 was written by David under divine inspiration. In the opening verse of the Psalm a court poet is addressing the king, claiming that he has heard an oracle from God (the Lord) to the effect that the king (my lord) is about to be victorious over his enemies. When King David is assumed to be the speaker, the interpretation is obviously different: speaking as a prophet, David says that God (the Lord) says to another figure greater than himself (my Lord), 'Sit at my right hand, until I put your enemies under your feet.' If the figure greater than David is the Messiah, how is it possible for the Messiah to be both 'son' of David and 'lord' of David?

Whatever the allusive argument may have meant in the mouth of the historical Jesus, the early Christian community understood Jesus to be making a claim to Davidic descent and Messiahship. The multiple uses of Psalm 110 in the New Testament writings suggests that it was thought to be particularly applicable to Jesus (Acts 2:34, 7:56; Rom 8:34; 1 Cor 15:25; Eph 1:20; Col 3:1; Heb 1:3, 8:1, 10:12; Rev 3:21). Perhaps it was the very allusiveness of Jesus' remarks that gave the early church the freedom to use Psalm 110:1 in the way they did.

Jesus denounces the scribes   12:37b-40

And the large crowd was listening to him with delight.
    [38]As he taught, he said, 'Beware of the scribes, who like to walk around in long robes, and to be greeted with respect in the marketplaces,

16. C.S. Mann, *Mark* (New York: Doubleday, 1986) p. 485.

³⁹and to have the best seats in the synagogues and places of honor at banquets! ⁴⁰They devour widows' houses and for the sake of appearance say long prayers. They will receive the greater condemnation.'

This passage contains Jesus' final public teaching to the crowds. Jesus is still instructing the pilgrims in the Temple; the religious authorities have not yet moved against him because of the crowd's enthusiasm for his teaching (11:18; 12:12). Jesus' final teaching to the Jews is a denunciation of his principal adversaries, the scribes. Having already criticised the teaching of the scribes, he now condemns their conduct as he warns his listeners against them. Although the insistent tone of what appears to be Jesus' anti-clericalism sounds harsh, the content is moderate compared with the unrelieved vituperation of Matthew 23.

In attacking the scribes' lifestyle as one dedicated to personal power and prestige, Jesus is not attacking them for being scribes. As he opposed his disciples for using religion for their own advancement, for their vacant dreams of honour and positions of power, so he does with the scribes. In that sense his criticism is levelled against all religious people who use their influence for their own peculiar advantage.

Jesus first castigates the scribes for actively seeking special recognition by walking around in long robes (*stolai*) and expecting deference to be paid to them because of their supposed religious superiority. Mark does not explain to his Gentile readers what exactly the long robes were: guesses have ranged from an early form of the prayer mantle to special Sabbath clothing. Whatever the clothes looked like – Mark stresses their *length*, which suggests the dress of dignitaries – the point is that they were worn to distinguish the scribes from other mortals, reflecting the scribes' desire for their authority to be recognised. Early on in the Gospel, Mark noted that Jesus taught the crowds 'as one having authority, and not as the scribes.' (1:22) At the beginning of his ministry in Jerusalem, Jesus walked around the Temple (11:27), but it was his teaching that distinguished him, not his long robes.

The scribes are criticised for preferring the best seats in the synagogue – these were the benches that stood on a podium and were situated in front of the ark containing the scrolls. The scribes who sat there faced the congregation and were, therefore, highly visible ornaments throughout the service. They are censured for seeking the places of honour at banquets, on the right of the host. This hunger for prestige and adulation is in dramatic contrast to Jesus' advice to his disciples, 'Whoever wants to be first must be last of all and servant of all.' (9:35) The scribes' behaviour epitomises the opposite of true discipleship.

Jesus charges that the scribes devour widows' houses. Derret argues that this refers to an abuse of Jewish inheritance law, where the trustee, instead of administering the estate on behalf of the widow or orphan, uses up the legacy for his own benefit.[17] The connection between preying on the trust of credulous widows and long prayers for appearance's sake is an intriguing one. The prayer can hardly refer to prayer in private; neither can it refer to prayer in the synagogue, which was primarily a place for instruction. It probably refers to the Temple, the highest place of worship where prayers and sacrifices were made. Fleddermann argues:

> Mark can use the term 'prayer' as his term for worship. In the Isaiah quotation, 'My house shall be called a house of prayer for all nations' (11:17), the term 'prayer' seems equivalent to 'worship.' The reference to 'long' prayers could be Mark's way of describing the constantly repeated, never-ending sacrifices of temple-worship.'[18]

This interpretation would comply with the whole anti-Temple motif that Mark has developed throughout his account of Jesus' ministry in Jerusalem.

The whole passage illustrates the difference between Jesus *who has a unique authority but does not seek honour* with the scribes *who have no comparable authority but still seek honour*. The bill for their greed is paid for by defenceless women and is reckoned to advance the cause of religion.

Jesus' public warning concludes with a judgement that effectively says that these lawyers will receive the greater condemnation in the highest court. While the judgement on the scribes is a harsh one, it is not comprehensive. It stands in painful contrast to Jesus'

17. J.D. Derret, "Eating up the Houses of Widows': Jesus' Comment on Lawyers?' *Novum Testamentum* 14 (1972) pp. 1-9.

18. H. Fleddermann, 'A Warning about the Scribes (Mark 12: 37b-40),' *Catholic Biblical Quarterly* 44 (1982) p. 66.

earlier statement to the honourable scribe who believed that love of God and love of neighbour were more important than the ritual sacrifice of the Temple: 'You are not far from the kingdom of God.' (12:34)

For Mark's community, this close of Jesus' public ministry illustrates the irreparable break with official Judaism. Although Jesus' bond with the Jewish crowds is still alive, they will become vulnerable to the manipulative Temple leadership that Jesus has so consistently criticised. In the passion narrative the religious establishment and the crowds will speak with one voice as they demand that Jesus be crucified (15:11-15).

The widow's offering   12:41-44

> [41]He sat down opposite the treasury, and watched the crowd putting money into the treasury. Many rich people put in large sums. [42]A poor widow came and put in two small copper coins, which are worth a penny. [43]Then he called his disciples and said to them, 'Truly I tell you, this poor widow has put in more than all those who are contributing to the treasury. [44]For all of them have contributed out of their abundance; but she out of her poverty has put in everything she had, all she had to live on.'

The rapaciousness of the scribes in devouring the property of widows is now illustrated as Mark shows one of their victims, a poor widow, who has nothing left after contributing to the upkeep of the Temple. Jesus sits down opposite the treasury, which formed part of the Court of Women in the Temple. In the treasury there were thirteen collection boxes – all shaped like trumpets – for offerings of various kinds. Marshall comments:

> Evidence is also adduced ... that gifts were offered for various purposes, especially in relation to vows, and the offerer declared the amount and purpose of the gift to the officiating priest. In these circumstances it is not surprising that Jesus knew how much the various people were offering.[19]

Jesus notices that many rich people put in large contributions. A poor widow comes and donates two copper coins (*lepta*), the

19. H. Marshall, *The Gospel of Luke: a Commentary on the Greek Text* (Exeter: Paternoster, 1978) p. 751.

copper coin being the smallest unit of money in circulation. She could have kept one of the coins but did not. Calling his disciples, Jesus comments that the poor widow's contribution is worth more than all the others, since the rich gave from their superfluity, but she has given out of her poverty all that she had to live on. The widow makes a real sacrifice by giving everything she has to support the Temple. But the unanswered question remains: was her sacrifice worth it?

Mark's context is important for understanding the story. We saw earlier how the story of the fig tree taken together with the cleansing of the Temple tells us that Jesus was not urging the reform of the Temple so that it could function in a new way; he was making a prophetic pronouncement about its withering to the roots. Having compared the Temple to a dead fig tree, having thrown out the merchants and money changers who were essential for the sacrificial cult to continue, having dismissed the Temple leaders in the parable of the wicked tenants, having just castigated the scribes for supporting the Temple system by sacrificing the property of widows, Jesus does not appear to be subscribing to the Temple system. On leaving the Temple, Jesus dismisses his disciples' admiration for the magnificence of the Temple buildings: 'Do you see these great buildings? Not one stone will be left here upon another; all will be thrown down.' (13:2) Given the sustained critique of the Temple surrounding the story of the widow's offering, it appears that Mark is really showing this poor woman as yet another victim of the scribes as she wastes her life in supporting a religious system that is already doomed.

After reviewing traditional interpretations of the story, Wright observes:

> The story does not provide a pious contrast to the conduct of the scribes in the preceding section (as is the customary view); rather it provides a further illustration of the ills of official devotion. Jesus' saying is not a penetrating insight on the measuring of gifts; it is a lament: 'Amen, I tell you, she gave more than all the others.' Or, as we would say: 'One could easily fail to notice it, but there is the tragedy of the day – she put in her whole living.' She has been taught and encouraged by religious leaders to donate as she does, and Jesus condemns the value

system that motivates her action, and he condemns the people who conditioned her to do it.[20]

The story illustrates something Jesus has previously condemned: the Temple, doomed for destruction, eats up the livelihood of poor widows. By the time the Temple system is finished with them, they are left with nothing. That is reason for lamentation, not praise.

The apocalyptic discourse of Chapter 13

The form Mark has given this chapter, a lengthy speech by Jesus addressed to a select number of disciples, seems to have more parallel with the lengthy discourses in John's Gospel than with Mark's usual narrative style of pressing his story onwards. The plot seems to come to a standstill. Nowhere else in Mark's Gospel does Jesus speak at such length as in this section, which acts as a conclusion to the public ministry and a preface to the passion narrative. The scattered fragments that make up the discourse form a unified theme – everything lies in the future of Jesus' lifetime.

In the chapter Mark uses two readily available literary forms, the farewell speech and the apocalyptic discourse. The farewell speech was the form of a last will and testament attributed to great figures. Before they died, these leaders called their families or disciples or subjects to review the past, look to the future, and offer words of consolation and encouragement to the listeners. There are ready examples in Jacob (Gen 49), Moses (Deut 31-32), Joshua (Josh 23-24), Samuel (1 Sam 12), David (1 Chr 28-29), Jesus (Jn 14-16), and Paul (Acts 20). At the close of the public ministry, Jesus is seen to warn his followers about the necessity of persecution and suffering, while exhorting them to stand steadfast in the conviction that the climax of history will be the coming of the Son of Man.

In apocalyptic literature the author reveals a vision to his readers that encodes contemporary or impending events. The guarded language is a way of referring indirectly to what is happening, particularly at a time of persecution, since a transparent description is obviously dangerous for the writer if his account falls into the wrong hands. A good example can be seen in the book of Daniel.

20. A.G. Wright, 'The Widow's Mites: Praise or Lament? A Matter of Context.' *Catholic Biblical Quarterly* 44 (1982) p. 262.

Writing in the second century B.C., Daniel tells stories about Nebuchadnezzar, who was king of Babylon from 604-562 B.C. The ruthless monarch besieged Jerusalem and destroyed the city, including the Temple and the palace, and forced the survivors into exile in Babylon. People who read chapter 11 when it first appeared, however, would have known that the stories really referred to Antiochus IV (175-164 B.C.) who attacked Jerusalem, killed most of the male population, enslaved the women and children, and prohibited all Jewish rites. Daniel uses a past biblical story, not a vision of the future, to describe the pain and destruction of a current event.

In Mark 13 two principal ideas are joined together: the prophecy of the destruction of Jerusalem – an event that happened about thirty-five years after the death of Jesus – and the end of world, when Jesus would return to sit in judgement over it. There is no obvious connection between these two events, and their conjunction here might simply reflect that both images appear in the apocalyptic writing of Daniel – 'an abomination that desolates' (Dan 9:27, see Mk 13:14) and 'one like a son of man coming with the clouds of heaven' (Dan 7:13, see Mk 13:26).

It seems probable that although Daniel's writing was principally, though covertly, referring to his own time, Jesus thought of Daniel's writing as referring to future events. D. Taylor notes:

> It seems likely, and chapter 13 of Mark is quite good evidence for this, that he (Jesus) understood all the predictions of Daniel as still awaiting fulfilment in the future, and as being literally intended for his own time ... All the prophecies could once again be taken seriously as predictions of an awaited future, and it makes best sense of the Marcan material to suppose that this is how Jesus in fact regarded them.[21]

The destruction of the Temple   13:1-4

[1] As he came out of the temple, one of his disciples said to him, 'Look, Teacher, what large stones and what large buildings!' [2] Then Jesus asked him, 'Do you see these great buildings? Not one stone will be left here upon another; all will be thrown down.'
[3] When he was sitting on the Mount of Olives opposite the temple,

21. D.B. Taylor, *Mark's Gospel as Literature and History* pp. 295, 296.

202 THE GOSPEL OF MARK

Peter, James, John, and Andrew asked him privately, ⁴'Tell us, when will this be, and what will be the sign that all these things are about to be accomplished?'

Having already made a prophetic pronouncement about the inevitable doom of the Temple by comparing it to a dead fig tree, having repudiated the sacrificial system and criticised the moribund leadership of the Temple authorities, Jesus now leaves the Temple for the last time. An unnamed disciple expresses his admiration for the architectural wonder of the Herodian Temple. Given Jesus' recent judgement on the whole Temple system, the disciple's admiration seems, at best, inappropriate.

The response of Jesus is the prediction that not one of these stones will be left upon another, for all will be thrown down. As the fig tree had withered from the roots up, so the Temple will be completely destroyed. While some scholars argue that Jesus' prediction is history dressed up as prophecy, it can also be argued that Jesus' prediction has a precedent in the prophecies of Jeremiah and Micah (Jer 26:6,18; Mic 3:12). Jeremiah spent twenty years of his life warning the people against a disaster they could not believe would occur, the destruction of Jerusalem. The turbulent political climate of Jesus' time would have provided him with sufficient grounds to make such a prediction (see Jn 11:48). Besides, a prophecy after the event would hardly have failed to mention the burning of the Temple, which Josephus reports was the means Titus chose for its destruction in 70 A.D.[22]

The scene moves east to the Mount of Olives, which Mark notes is opposite the Temple. The change of geographical location from the Temple to the opposite side reflects the theological shift that has already been noted. It is worth mentioning also that the Mount of Olives/Jerusalem antithesis has significance in the biblical tradition: the Mount of Olives is the place to which the glory of God retires from a degenerate Jerusalem (Ezek 11:23) and the place where God will pass judgement on Jerusalem (Zech 14:4).

Jesus' disciples are mentioned only once, and then only four are said to be present. The four named are the first four called (1:16-20) and Jesus' discourse will be exclusively addressed to them. They ask him when the destruction of the Temple will take place and

22. See Josephus, *Jewish Wars* 6.4.5.

what sign will announce that the end time has come. Although the secrecy and the esoteric audience are traditional elements of revelation in apocalyptic writing, the content of what Jesus says is aimed at a wider audience: 'let the reader understand' (13:14); 'And what I say to you I say to all' (13:37).

The beginning of the sufferings 13:5-13

[5]Then Jesus began to say to them, 'Beware that no one leads you astray. [6]Many will come in my name and say, "I am he!" and they will lead many astray. [7]When you hear of wars and rumours of wars, do not be alarmed; this must take place, but the end is still to come. [8]For nation will rise against nation, and kingdom against kingdom; there will be earthquakes in various places; there will be famines. This is but the beginning of the birthpangs.

[9] 'As for yourselves, beware; for they will hand you over to councils; and you will be beaten in synagogues; and you will stand before governors and kings because of me, as a testimony to them. [10]And the good news must first be proclaimed to all nations. [11]When they bring you to trial and hand you over, do not worry beforehand about what you are to say; but say whatever is given you at the time, for it is not you who speak, but the Holy Spirit. [12]Brother will betray brother to death, and a father his child, and children will rise against parents and have them put to death; [13]and you will be hated by all because of my name. But the one who endures to the end will be saved.

Jesus' reply ignores the disciples' question about the timing of the destruction of Jerusalem, and instead of answering their further question about a sign that would serve as an introduction to the end time, he lists confusing and chaotic events that should *not* be read as signs. In the discourse Mark as narrator is clearly concerned about his own time, characterised as it is by uncertainty and persecution. B. van Iersel comments:

> The difference in time between the utterances of Jesus, the writing of the book, and the reading of it, on the one hand, and the interpolation addressed to the reader in 13:14, on the other, gives us every reason to presume that the narrator wishes to warns the readers through this section of a situation that already exists or may arise at any moment.[23]

The first warning is about corruption within the Christian commu-

23. B. van Iersel, *Reading Mark* p. 162.

nity itself. In the absence of great leadership, impostors will try to fill the vacuum and lead the community astray. There will be some who will come in the name of Jesus, claiming *ego eimi* ('I am'). This might be a reference to messianic pretenders, although we have no evidence of such between the death of Jesus and the fall of Jerusalem. It may refer to people who make false claims to be representatives of Jesus, like Simon Magus in Acts 8:9.

Wars and rumours of war are not a sure signal that the end is nigh; however unsettling, they are to be understood as no more than inevitable events on the stage of human conflict. None of them is attributed to the vengeance of God, but to predictable human failings that should not be construed as having any cosmic significance.

The thought is similar to that expressed by Paul: 'As to the coming of our Lord Jesus Christ and our being gathered together with him, we beg you, brothers and sisters, not to be quickly shaken or alarmed ... Let no one deceive you in this way' (2 Thess 2:1-3). The thought moves from war between nations and kingdoms to earthquakes and famines: these have to be endured, for they mark but the beginning, not the end, of suffering. Again the thought is expressed that no matter how catastrophic events appear to be, interpreting them as sure signs of the end of the world is wholly mistaken; they are but the beginnings of suffering.

Turning from the confusion and upheaval in store for the world, the discourse turns to the fate awaiting the followers of Jesus, persecution by Jewish and Gentile authorities. As John the Baptist and Jesus were 'delivered up', the same fate will be experienced by the disciples. The suffering and death of Christians will be its own testimony in opening up the Gospel to the Gentiles, a truth witnessed in Acts 8. These persecutions, which lie in the future of Jesus as the speaker of the discourse, have already been suffered by Mark's community in the Neronian persecution.

These words, therefore, would be particularly reassuring for Mark's readers. The time of persecution is seen as a time for testimony. Hengel observes:

> This relation between persecution and confession becomes paradigmatically clear at the climax of the whole Gospel, i.e. at the death of Jesus. The centurion at the cross, the commander of

the execution squad, becomes the first "confessor" (Mark 15:39).[24]

In staying loyal to their own identity as confessors of Jesus, the disciples need not suffer anxiety about what words to employ, for the greater power of the Holy Spirit will speak through them. Since hate respects no ties, opposition to the disciples will know no bounds; even blood ties will not save them from betrayal by their own family. Traditionally, such unnatural strife was understood as a prelude to God's final intervention in history (see Mic 7:6). The paradox is that the disciples' enduring fidelity to the name of Jesus, not avoidance of suffering and pain, will gain them their lives.

The great tribulation   13:14-23

[14] 'But when you see the desolating sacrilege set up where it ought not to be (let the reader understand), then those in Judea must flee to the mountains; [15]the one on the housetop must not go down or enter the house to take anything away; [16]the one in the field must not turn back to get a coat. [17]Woe to those who are pregnant and to those who are nursing infants in those days! [18]Pray that it may not be in winter. [19]For in those days there will be suffering, such as has not been from the beginning of the creation that God created until now, no, and never will be. [20]And if the Lord had not cut short those days, no one would be saved; but for the sake of the elect, whom he chose, he has cut short those days. [21]And if anyone says to you at that time, "Look! Here is the Messiah!" or "Look! There he is!" – do not believe it. [22]False messiahs and false prophets will appear and produce signs and omens to lead astray, if possible, the elect. [23]But be alert; I have already told you everything.

As Jesus' warning takes on a more urgent tone, the meaning of the discourse becomes more opaque; this passage is among the most difficult to interpret in Mark. It speaks not of a supernatural event but of historical disaster and widespread suffering that will, presumably, take place in Judea. To avoid the disaster, the people in Judea should make flight to the mountains their singular goal. The signal for their flight is a highly mysterious sign, when they see 'the desolating sacrilege set up where it ought not to be'.

What is this desolating sacrilege or 'abomination of desolation' as it is sometimes translated? The expression is taken from the

24. M. Hengel, *Studies in the Gospel of Mark* p. 24.

apocalyptic tradition of Daniel (11:31; 12:11), a point underscored by Matthew 24:15, 'spoken of by the prophet Daniel'. The desolating sacrilege is identified in 1 Maccabees 1:54 as the altar to Zeus set up by Antiochus IV in the Temple at the time of the great persecution in 168 B.C. The pagan altar was built on top of the altar of burnt offering; there is no mention in the original account of an idol being erected. Although the Temple building was not destroyed, the sacrilegious act desecrated the sanctuary. In 164 B.C., inspired by the family of Judas Maccabeus, the Jews defeated the army of Antiochus and regained control of the Temple; this was cleansed of the abomination, an event that is still celebrated by the Jews in the feast of Hanukkah or Dedication.

The reference to the desolating sacrilege in Mark and Matthew 24:15 (Luke's parallel passage does not have the phrase) has been variously interpreted. It is worth noting that Mark first speaks of the abomination as neuter and then gives the participle *set up* a masculine form (*hestekota*), so the phrase should be translated: 'the desolating sacrilege set up where *he* ought not to be.'

Who is this evil individual? Some scholars link the reference to the crisis in Palestine in 40 A.D., when the emperor Caligula ordered his statue to be placed in the Temple – an order not carried out due to the fortuitous assassination of the proposer. Others have identified the abomination with the Zealots who in 68 A.D. profaned the Temple by turning it into a fortress or with the Roman standards advancing on Jerusalem. None of these seems to fit, since the abomination properly refers to a person, not a thing.

The meaning is obviously designed to be hidden from hostile outsiders, as the appeal 'let the reader understand' indicates. Some scholars prefer to interpret the abomination as the coming of the eschatological Antichrist, akin to the 'beast' of Revelation. While this would fit the category of an evil individual, it does not explain why his coming would endanger only the people of Judea.

Luke, who makes no reference to the abomination, refers to armies surrounding Jerusalem, to the people being killed and taken captive, while the Gentiles trample the city (Lk 21-20-24). Is Luke deliberately clarifying Mark's obscurity by drawing a parallel between the Maccabean experience under the tyrant Antiochus IV and the Jewish experience under Roman rule? Although not completely satisfactory, perhaps this is the most reasonable interpretation available. Whatever the precise identity of the abomination, it is a sign that disqualifies forever the Temple as the place of the parousia.

The emphasis on the magnitude of the distress – 'such as has not been from the beginning of creation' – is taken from Daniel 12:1: 'There shall be a time of anguish, such as has never occurred since nations first came in existence.' The notion of God's intervention through mercy for the elect is typical of apocalyptic writing (see Dan 12:7), and, in this case, probably refers to the Christian community.

The description of the end time leads to an appeal to the community living in the present. Verses 21-23 are a doublet of verses 2-6 and 9a. The earlier reference to the many who will come – confusing the community with their false claims to be Jesus – is repeated and clarified by this further reference to false messiahs and prophets. The new information is that they will be supported by miracles and signs, so the deception will be greater. The final appeal, to be on the alert, is given in the knowledge that the disciples have been told everything; they are not part of an ignorant multitude. This knowledge, while charging them to live in patient endurance through political and natural disasters, warns them that living in a state of permanent readiness is the best formation for a future of tribulation.

The coming of the Son of Man   13:24-27

²⁴ "But in those days, after that suffering,
    the sun will be darkened,
    and the moon will not give its light,
    ²⁵ and the stars will be falling from heaven,
    and the powers in the heavens will be shaken.
²⁶Then they will see "the Son of Man coming in clouds" with great power and glory. ²⁷Then he will send out the angels, and gather his elect from the four winds, from the ends of the earth to the ends of heaven.

After an undefined period of tribulation that includes the appearance of charlatans and wild rumours, political upheaval and natural calamities, persecution and betrayal, Mark makes a basic shift in the time frame as the apocalyptic drama unfolds. This celestial event is not associated with any historical event and cannot, therefore, be predicted. An upheaval on the celestial stage is now described, one that reverses the story of creation: the sun darkens, the moon gives no light, stars fall from their place in the firmament, and the powers of heaven are shaken.

The language of these four verses is taken from the Old Testament and woven into a tapestry that depicts the parousia. The disturbance of the heavenly bodies belongs to traditional apocalyptic imagery. For example, Isaiah writes: 'For the stars of the heavens and their constellations will not give their light; the sun will be dark at its rising, and the moon will not shed its light.' (13:10) The imagery refers not to the end time but to the destruction of Babylon by the Medes. Similar language is used in Ezekiel 32:7-8 for the judgement of Egypt, and in Amos 8:9 for the judgement of the northern kingdom. Paradoxically, there is no judgement in Mark's scene; neither is there any mention of the overthrow of the Antichrist. The language and imagery he borrows serve a new context, to illustrate the parousia of the Son of Man.

The Son of Man is seen coming in clouds with great power and glory (see Daniel 7:13). In Daniel a symbolic figure resembling a man is seen, whereas in Mark the description is of a superhuman person. If clouds are traditionally seen as the vehicle of God, this person is invested with divine authority and clothed in heavenly light. The Son of Man who is to suffer, be rejected, put to death and rise again (8:31; 9:31; 10:33-34) will finally be revealed in all his heavenly power. The vision of his final coming in glory is what enables the disciples to continue patiently in the midst of confusion, persecution and terror.

The four winds denote the four corners of the compass; the earth is pictured as a flat expanse overarched by the vault of heaven. The elect of God, scattered throughout the earth, are now gathered together by the angels (see Deut 30: 3-4; Is 11:11,16). This is not a gathering of the twelve tribes of Israel to the Temple in Jerusalem; the Temple is destroyed, and a new meeting place is fixed as the Son of Man gathers the elect to himself. There is no talk of annihilation of enemies or condemnation to eternal punishment. The imagery pictures a benevolent objective, that of the homecoming of the dispersed to fellowship with God. The coming of God in power and glory is what gives the community reason to endure and to hope.

Exhortation to vigilance   13:28-37

[28] 'From the fig tree learn its lesson: as soon as its branch becomes tender and puts forth its leaves, you know that summer is near. [29] So also, when you see these things taking place, you know that he is near, at the very gates. [30] Truly I tell you, this generation will not pass away until all these things have taken place. [31] Heaven and earth will pass away, but my words will not pass away.

[32] 'But about that day or hour no one knows, neither the angels in heaven, nor the Son, but only the Father. [33] Beware, keep alert; for you do not know when the time will come. [34] It is like a man going on a journey, when he leaves home and puts his slaves in charge, each with his work, and commands the doorkeeper to be on the watch. [35] Therefore, keep awake – for you do not know when the master of the house will come, in the evening, or at midnight, or at cockcrow, or at dawn, [36] or else he may find you asleep when he comes suddenly. [37] And what I say to you I say to all: Keep awake.'

The final section in this discourse is composed of two parables and three sayings, all linked together by catchwords and the general theme of watchfulness. The first parable, the lesson of the fig tree, appears to be an answer to the disciples' original question in 13:4: 'Tell us, when will this be, and what will be the sign that all these things are about to be accomplished?' During the winter the fig tree loses its leaves and, in a country where most trees are evergreen, appears to be dead. When the young branches that produce the leaves are softened by the sap flowing through them, this is a natural herald of the approaching summer. So, when the disciples 'see these things taking place, they know that he is very near, at the very gates.' The question about the time of the end is answered by describing the signs of the end: when all the signs occur, then the time of the end is at hand.

The time frame is made more precise in verse 30 where it states that the present generation will not have passed away until 'all these things have taken place.' This reflects the thought of 9:1: 'Truly I tell you, there are some standing here who will not taste death until they see that the kingdom of God has come with power.' The comprehensive phrase '*all* these things' in 13:30 comes after a catalogue of signs: it includes the signs leading up to the Son of

Man's coming, and the coming itself. This note on timing is then cancelled by the following verse, which states that no one knows about that time, not even the Son, but only the Father. Either the end is going to happen within a precise calendar, the lifetime of Jesus' generation (v. 30), or no one on earth knows when it will happen (v. 32). These two statements contradict one another. Which of the sayings goes back to the historical Jesus? The more difficult saying – that no one, not even the Son, knows when the end will be – is probably the authentic one. Meier notes:

> To deny its authenticity, one would have to suppose that some early Christian prophet went out of his way both to attribute ignorance of the Son of Man's coming to the Son of Man himself and to contradict various prophecies about the end already attributed to the Son of Man. The authenticity of 13:32 seems a much more likely hypothesis, but that in turn connotes the inauthenticity of 13:30.[25]

The corollary of this argument is that the early church adjusted Jesus' proclamation about the coming of the kingdom in the near future. Like John the Baptist before him, Jesus did not specify a time limit of the kingdom's arrival. Some early Christians, faced with a lengthy and hostile interval between the resurrection and the parousia, produced sayings that brought Jesus' undefined time into their own defined lifetime. While this would give encouragement to first-generation Christians, the thinking was not pure fiction attributed to the historical Jesus: the sayings presuppose the imminent but future eschatology of Jesus himself.

We know that the parousia did not happen within the generation of Mark's lifetime, and we know that it has not happened since then. The final parable only makes sense if no one knows the time of the end. In the parable a householder goes on a journey for an unspecified time. He hands over authority to his servants, specifying what service is expected of each of them, and leaves with the command that the doorkeeper remain on watch. What is *unsaid* in the parable is the point: the departing man does not say when he will return. The presumption is that, in the meantime, his servants will not be sitting idly behind the door waiting for his return; their attitude of watchful responsibility should not inhibit them from getting on with their work.

The point is then made to the disciples: 'Therefore, keep awake'. As the servants in the parable do not know the time of their master's return, neither do the *disciples* know the time of *their* master's return: he can return unannounced at any watch of the night. Their only protection in the face of uncertainty is to be mindful of the uncertainty, thus helping them to concentrate on their present duty. This exhortation to watchfulness is explicitly extended beyond the circle of the four disciples to the whole Christian community.

Throughout the discourse, the expectation is voiced that when the Son of Man comes, he will find the community engaged in responsible service, not paralysed by fear. The point is well illustrated by a story of how the state legislators in colonial New England reacted during the time of an eclipse. In their fright some moved to adjourn the meeting. But one of their number said: 'Mr Speaker, if it is not the end of the world and we adjourn, we shall appear to be fools. If it is the end of the world, I should choose to be found doing my duty. I move you, sir, that candles be brought.'

Mark's account of the ministry of Jesus comes to a close with the appeal, 'Watch. Keep awake.' This entreaty will be taken up again in the passion narrative, in the Garden of Gethsemane, where Mark places the inner circle of three disciples closer to Jesus than the eight other disciples. The evangelist will show how none of the disciples manage to stay awake even when Jesus is still present. All the more difficult, therefore, is the challenge for the whole community to stay awake during his absence.

7

The Passion and Resurrection

14:1-16:8

It has been argued in the Introduction that the Gospels developed backwards, that the earliest preaching about Jesus concerned his death and resurrection. A consequence of this is the likelihood that a basic account of the last days of Jesus was shaped relatively soon after the events happened. The manner of Jesus' death was the most publicly attested fact of his life: the earliest preaching had to account for the cross and the violent death of Jesus if was to make any redemptive sense of his mission. Since those who first preached Jesus addressed fellow Jews, they had to concentrate on making sense of the greatest stumbling block to understanding the work of Jesus, his execution as a common criminal. This concentration is reflected in each of the four Gospels, where the longest story about Jesus is his passion and death. It is the one part of the Gospels where there is most agreement among the evangelists. Scholars argue that they are the oldest part of the Gospels, the oldest stories about Jesus.

Narratives about Jesus' death were formed very quickly in the various Christian communities: the setting that formed them was probably the eucharistic celebration (see 1 Cor 11:23-26), the sacred memorial of Jesus' final days. Many Old Testament readings and prayers would have been integrated into the liturgical recitation of the final hours of Jesus. This puts the event of Jesus' death into the larger context of prophecy. The message is clear: what has happened was not a misadventure; it was meant to be; it was the result of God's saving will revealed in the Old Testament. Thus Old Testament prophecy is mined as a source of history for the passion of Jesus.

The earliest preaching of the Gospel includes notice of the essential role played by the Old Testament: 'For I handed on to you as of first importance what I in turn had received: that Christ died for our sins *in accordance with the scriptures*, and that he was buried, and that he was raised on the third day *in accordance with the scriptures*' (1 Cor 15:3-4). In its proclamation about Jesus, the early church had quickly come to understand how the saving deeds of Jesus brought the saving history of God's people to its designed fulfilment.

The details of the passion story have been bonded so closely with allusions to the Old Testament, that it is sometimes difficult to tell where the story finishes and the allusions begin. The evangelists are not just reporting history, but presenting their interpretation in the perspective of faith and prophecy. An apologetic slant is also evident: if the Son of God died a shameful death as a criminal, after a Roman trial, it is essential for the evangelists to present the case that he was innocent of the charges brought against him. Paradoxically, their principal spokesman for the innocence of Jesus is the judge of the trial, Pontius Pilate. Another fact that influenced the character of the passion narratives was exhortation: for example, the denial of Peter is included to give hope to other Christians who had failed by denying Jesus.

Most of the Gospel stories have no fixed time and place: they are oral traditions about Jesus that the evangelists have collected and reshaped into their major Gospel story. The passion narratives follow an in-built chronological sequence: the arrest; the appearance before the high priest; the trial before Pontius Pilate; the choice of Barabbas; the condemnation; the crucifixion; the death and burial. That continuity makes for a coherent and structured narrative, which is not true of the rest of the Gospel, composed of isolated passages or loosely connected collections of deeds and sayings in no particular sequence. All four evangelists reflect a continuity in agreement in the passion accounts unparalleled elsewhere in the Gospels. It is equally evident, however, that each evangelist exercises his own editorial control over his sources, giving his own perspective and interpretation to the passion and death of Jesus. They are not writing a history, but preaching a message about the meaning of Jesus' death.

The passion is written as a story that is larger than Jesus' story. Over half of the narratives concern other people and how they react to what happens in their midst. *Their* reactions are an integral part of the story: the responses of the disciples, especially Judas and Peter, the authorities, Caiaphas, the witnesses, Pilate, the crowd, the women, the soldiers, the centurion, are all noted. In that way we as the listeners/readers are drawn into the narrative, not least to wonder where we would stand in all this.

————————

At an early stage in Jesus' Galilean ministry, at the conclusion of a series of conflict stories, Mark noted that the Pharisees and the Herodians had conspired together to eliminate Jesus (3:6). After Jesus' opposition to the whole Temple system, the hostility to him intensified as the chief priests and the scribes looked for ways to kill him (11:18). Mark's passion narrative opens with the reminder that the chief priests and the scribes are still looking for ways to arrest and kill Jesus (14:1). The chief priests find an unusual ally in Judas Iscariot, who approaches them because he also is 'looking for a way' to betray his master (13:10-11).

Jesus is not a passive victim of cruel circumstances, for his suffering and death are told as the consequence of his own commitments. Throughout his account of the ministry Mark has demonstrated that what Jesus did and said provoked the opposition that would surely lead to his death. At various stages in his journey from Caesarea Philippi to Jerusalem, Jesus announced in his passion predictions what would happen to him. At the core of those predictions is the repeated truth: no one will understand who Jesus is until they understand his destiny. As that destiny is fulfilled only on the cross, so his identity is recognised only after he dies. The centurion is the first human being to give voice to the truth that introduced the Gospel, that Jesus is the Son of God. That individual seems to be the solitary supportive voice in Mark's passion narrative: everything else in his account seems to be depicted in terms of unrelieved gloom. While Jesus hangs on the cross, the only sympathy he receives seems to come from nature, when darkness covers the land. There is no voice from heaven, as there was at the baptism and transfiguration, and Mark's Jesus appears to die forsaken by God.

As the ministry told the story not only of Jesus but of the disciples, so Mark's passion narrative will interweave two stories, the passion of Jesus and the passion of his community. It is not only his story; it is also theirs. If the disciples' story during the ministry was told in terms of their attachment to Jesus, their story during the passion is told as one of separation and loss. Unlike the other evangelists, Mark underlines with brutal clarity the abandonment of Jesus by his chosen followers. Their separation and flight are softened only by the promise of new attachment in the resurrection: 'But after I am raised up, I will go before you to Galilee.' (14:28) However grim Mark's account appears to his audience, he closes his story not with the burial of Jesus and the separation of the disciples but with Jesus' resurrection and the assurance that his promise of new attachment will be honoured (16:7).

The conspiracy against Jesus 14:1-2

It was two days before the Passover and the festival of Unleavened Bread. The chief priests and the scribes were looking for a way to arrest Jesus by stealth and kill him; [2]for they said, 'Not during the festival, or there may be a riot among the people.'

Mark begins his account of the passion by indicating the time, two days before the Passover and the feast of Unleavened Bread. The Passover was the name of the feast celebrating the redemption of the Israelites from oppression in Egypt, although originally it was probably a *nomadic* festival celebrating the lambing season. In the afternoon of the 14th day of Nisan (usually April), the Passover lamb was sacrificed in the Temple precincts. With the Passover supper that evening, the 15th Nisan, the events of the exodus were retold in the family gathering and the lamb was eaten. The feast not only held holy the memory of past liberation but gave substance to a hope of similar vindication in the future.

The feast of Unleavened Bread was originally a distinct week-long festival that began on sunset of the 15th Nisan. During these seven days, the people were to avoid leaven and eat only unleavened bread: this probably originated in *settled* communities that celebrated a spring agricultural feast centring on the barley harvest. This festival was celebrated only after the Israelites had become settlers in the land of Canaan. By the first century, both festivals were celebrated together and referred to as one. Bokser observes:

Since the two festivals – the Passover and the Feast of Unleavened Bread – may have originated in different kinds of societies, they may represent alternative models of what each society viewed as most life-sustaining: the flock or the harvest. The experience and hopes of both groups would have been given new meaning in terms of the Exodus experience as a celebration of God's liberation of Israel.[1]

Jesus will celebrate the Passover with his disciples on Thursday evening (14:12) and he will die on the Passover – that is, Friday. On Wednesday, the day before he celebrates the Passover meal, the plot against his life gathers momentum. The chief priests and the scribes are anxious to make their final move against Jesus, but they remain apprehensive about the role of the crowd. As a pilgrimage feast, Passover would attract thousands of people into the city of Jerusalem. Prudence dictated that Jesus should not die 'during the festival' – in case there was a riot, especially by Galilean pilgrims. A mass gathering for a major festival and the death of a popular prophet would make for a dangerous coincidence.

With pilgrims already arriving for Passover, the priests probably planned to arrest Jesus after the feast, when everyone had returned home. Things turn out differently – perhaps because the offer of Judas precipitated their decision? Whatever the reason, Mark's point is clear: in spite of their clandestine plans, the Temple clergy are not in charge of the chronology of events: Jesus will die during the feast of great liberation.

The anointing at Bethany   14:3-9

[3] While he was at Bethany in the house of Simon the leper, as he sat at the table, a woman came with an alabaster jar of very costly ointment of nard, and she broke open the jar and poured the ointment on his head. [4]But some were there who said to one another in anger, 'Why was the ointment wasted in this way? [5]For this ointment could have been sold for more than three hundred denarii, and the money given to the poor.' And they scolded her. [6]But Jesus said, 'Let her alone; why do you trouble her? She has performed a good service for me. [7]For you always have the poor with you, and you can show kindness to them whenever you wish; but you will not always have me. [8]She has done what she could; she has anointed my body beforehand for its burial. [9]Truly I tell you, wherever the good news is proclaimed in the whole world, what she has done will be told in remembrance of her.'

The enemies of Jesus, named as the chief priests and the scribes, are

1. B. Bokser, 'Feast of Unleavened Bread and Passover,' *The Anchor Bible Dictionary* Vol. 6, p. 256.

plotting his death (14:1-2); a friend of Jesus, named as Judas, will soon make common alliance with them (14:10-11). Together this unlikely coalition will prepare for the death of Jesus. Sandwiched between these two stories of calculated hostility, Mark places his account of an unnamed woman who unwittingly prepares for Jesus' death by anointing him. The woman's public act of kindness to Jesus stands in dramatic contrast to the men's secretive planning to destroy him. Two different notes are sounded to introduce Mark's passion narrative, each one reinforcing the impact of the other: hostility and love. A variation of the story is found in all four Gospels (Mt 25:6-13; Lk 7:36-50; Jn 12:1-8). In the chart at the foot of this page I have attempted to outline the similarities and differences in the four accounts, which will avoid the need to refer to them in the commentary. Although the table is not comprehensive, it notes the principal points of the story.

Mark tells us that Jesus is staying in Bethany, which is a town located on the slopes of the Mount of Olives. It was about two miles from the city. Jesus appears to have made his headquarters in the house of Simon the leper during his final days in Jerusalem. Of Simon the leper we know nothing. Was he a leper or was his name

	Mark	**Matthew**	**Luke**	**John**
Place	Bethany	Bethany	Galilee	Bethany
Time	2 days before Passover	2 days before Passover	during Galilean ministry	6 days before Passover
House	Simon the Leper	Simon the Leper	Simon the Pharisee	Lazarus
Woman	unnamed	unnamed	unnamed sinner	Mary
Brings	alabaster jar of costly ointment	alabaster jar of costly ointment	alabaster jar of ointment	pound of costly perfume
Anoints	head of Jesus	head of Jesus	feet of Jesus	feet of Jesus
Objection	made openly by some there	made openly by disciples	made silently by Simon	made openly by Judas
Defence by Jesus	poor with you always; anointed body for burial.	poor with you always; anointed body for burial.	her many sins are forgiven her; she has shown great love.	always have the poor; she might keep it for burial.

remembered because Jesus cured him of his affliction? If the former, Jesus' association with him in a society where lepers were strictly segregated tells its own story.

While Jesus is at table, an unnamed woman comes into the dining room. It seems strange, in view of the final verse, that her name was not remembered, or that one was not supplied for her. She carries a small round jar, made from alabaster and used for carrying perfume. It contains 'ointment of nard' – an oil extracted from an aromatic Indian plant. She breaks the jar and pours the perfumed oil 'on the head of Jesus, thus marking him as *Christos* – the anointed one. It is a wonderful paradox: the Messiah is anointed not in the Temple by the chief priests but in the house of a leper by an unknown lay woman.

Others in the room are quick to express their anger at what they consider as waste. Mark, who habitually identifies Jesus' critics and highlights the disciples' obtuseness, does not identify this hostile group. Whoever these men are, they are good at calculating the cost of the woman's perfume without appreciating the value of her loving gesture. They suggest that the perfume could have been sold for three hundred denarii – the equivalent of a labourer's annual wage – and given to the poor. Not satisfied with making their objection known, they turn on the woman and berate her.

In his defence of the woman, Jesus rebukes her grouchy critics, telling them to leave her alone, for she has performed the only service within her power. The impassioned, extravagant gesture that was within her power is what Jesus wants. If the objectors are concerned about the poor, they have no need to worry: they will always have the poor around and they can exercise their own kindness to them whenever they please. Mark's focus is not on the constant presence of the poor, but on the temporary presence of Jesus. He will not always be around, not even in death. There will be no body to anoint, when the time comes for anointing his body (16:1-6). Jesus then interprets her act as an anointing of his body before its burial.

The final sentence reflects the missionary vocabulary of the Gentile Church and is probably a later addition that genuinely reflects Jesus' estimation of the woman's generosity. Although she left no name, she leaves behind a memory of incautious love that does not count the cost. It is a memorable gesture that is truly hers. That is why, wherever the Gospel is preached throughout the world, the story will be told not in memory of the anointed man but in memory of the loving woman.

The treachery of Judas   14:10-11

[10] Then Judas Iscariot, who was one of the twelve, went to the chief priests in order to betray him to them. [11]When they heard it, they were greatly pleased, and promised to give him money. So he began to look for an opportunity to betray him.

From a vivid account of a woman anointing the head of Jesus, Mark's narrative moves to a spare account of the treachery of Judas Iscariot. One of the most embarrassing memories in the early church was that Judas, one of the twelve disciples, betrayed Jesus. It is difficult, however, to uncover what exactly Judas betrayed. John 18:2 tells us that it was the place where Jesus often went at night with the disciples. If Jesus went regularly to a certain place, however, it does not seem beyond the wit of the authorities to discover its location without Judas. There is no suggestion in any of the accounts that Jesus was moving each night to different hide-outs, which would have required particular intelligence about his whereabouts. Nor is there any suggestion that the priests needed one of the disciples as a witness to substantiate a charge against Jesus: Judas does not appear as a witness at the trial, where everything depends on the testimony of the accused (14:61-64).

It is possible that Judas was sympathetic to the movement of the Zealots and hoped to force Jesus to take a public stance against the Roman authorities, but this is only conjecture.[2]

Mark emphasises Judas' objective in going to the chief priests, 'in order to betray him to them.' The Greek verb *paradidomi* literally means 'to hand over' or 'to deliver up' and is used of the death of John the Baptist (1:14) and the death of Jesus (3:19; 9:31; 10:33; 14:10,11,18,21,41,42,44; 15:1,10,15). Judas fulfils the prediction of 9:31 that the Son of Man would be handed over to men. But he is not alone in this. The Sanhedrin will hand Jesus over to Pilate; to placate the crowds, Pilate will hand him over to the

2. For a fictional exploration of this possibility, see D. McBride, 'Judas Iscariot,' in *Impressions of Jesus* (Alton: Redemptorist Publications, 1992) pp. 187-205.

soldiers, to be crucified. The whole passion narrative is the story of Jesus being handed over.

According to Mark, the promise of money is not made to Judas until after he declares his objective to the chief priests. The later Gospels try to explain the embarrassment of the disciple's treachery by postulating Satanic inspiration (Luke) or avarice (Matthew and John). Mark does not mention either of these, leaving open the possibility that Judas had reasons other than money to betray his Master. No sum is specified as payment to Judas, and we are not told if the money is ever paid. Confirmed by the delight of the chief priests, Judas begins to look for an opportune moment to betray Jesus.

Preparations for the Passover   14:12-16

¹² On the first day of Unleavened Bread, when the Passover lamb is sacrificed, his disciples said to him, 'Where do you want us to go and make the preparations for you to eat the Passover?' ¹³So he sent two of his disciples, saying to them, 'Go into the city, and a man carrying a jar of water will meet you; follow him, ¹⁴and wherever he enters, say to the owner of the house, "The Teacher asks, Where is my guest room where I may eat the Passover with my disciples?" ¹⁵He will show you a large room upstairs, furnished and ready. Make preparations for us there.' ¹⁶So the disciples set out and went to the city, and found everything as he had told them; and they prepared the Passover meal.

Mark, followed by Matthew and Luke, holds the view that the Last Supper was a Passover. In the opening verse, however, Mark's chronology is confusing. He refers to 'the first day of Unleavened Bread' – which was celebrated on 15th Nisan – as being the same time as 'when the Passover lamb is sacrificed', which was the afternoon of the 14th Nisan. Mark may have been using the Roman calculation for the day, or he may simply have been confused about the precise dating of Jewish feasts. The descriptive reference to the time when the Passover lambs were slaughtered in the Temple makes it clear that Mark was thinking of 14th Nisan, the late afternoon of Thursday. In the Jewish calculation, a day was reckoned from sunset to sunset. The Last Supper took place in the evening, after sunset, making it the new day of 15th Nisan. This day would finish on Friday at sunset, when the sabbath would begin, by which time Jesus would be already dead.

John puts the events of the passion twenty-fours earlier, dating the Last Supper on the night before the Passover (13:1; 18:28). By doing this, he deliberately has the crucifixion coincide with the killing of the paschal lambs in the Temple: thus, for John, the true Paschal Lamb dies unrecognised outside the gates of the city. This dating serves John's theological scheme, but the weight of tradition favours the chronology of the Synoptic tradition. After listing arguments to support the paschal character of the Last Supper, Jeremias adds:

> The report of the Synoptists that the Last Supper was a Passover does not agree with the rite of the early Church. The early Church did not celebrate the Eucharist according to the Passover ritual; nor yet only once a year, but daily on each Lord's day. Therefore, if the Synoptists nevertheless describe the Last Supper as a Passover, the reason is obviously that the recollection of the fact was so firmly established that it could not be removed even by the established ritual.[3]

The Passover, which was always eaten after sunset, was to be celebrated within the city of Jerusalem (Deut 16:5-7). This was no easy matter: with a population of about 30,000 people, the city had to host an influx of pilgrims estimated in the region of 100,000. To accommodate this press of people, the city limits were extended as far as Bethphage on the Mount of Olives. This extension excluded Bethany, where Jesus was staying, but included the Garden of Gethsemane.

The disciples ask Jesus where they are to make the preparations for the Passover meal. Jesus' instruction to two unnamed disciples is reminiscent of the arrangements made for the entry into the city earlier in the week (11:2-6). The two disciples will be met by a man carrying a water jar – an unusual sign, since men usually carried only wine, and then the wine was in skins, not jugs. The disciples are to follow this water carrier, apparently without saying anything. When he enters the house, they are to ask the owner about the guest room where the Teacher may eat the Passover. The householder will reply by showing the disciples a large upstairs room, which will be already furnished and made ready. The disciples do this and

---

3. J. Jeremias, *The Eucharistic Words of Jesus* (Oxford: Blackwell, 1955) p. 37.

find everything as Jesus commanded them. They make the final arrangements.

Although it is possible to argue that Jesus made prior arrangements with the unidentified householder, the more probable interpretation is that Mark is demonstrating Jesus' prophetic foreknowledge. This is not unlike the prophet Samuel's instructions to the newly anointed Saul (1 Sam 10:1-10). In this incident Saul is told where to go, whom he will meet, what they will be carrying ('another carrying a skin of wine'), what they will say. In presenting Jesus as the one who prepared his entrance into the city of Jerusalem (11:2-6) and now as carefully prepares for eating the Passover meal there, Mark is probably emphasising Jesus' freedom in choosing to do what is being asked of him by God. There is nothing haphazard about what lies ahead: it happens both by divine appointment and by conscious preparation.

Prophecy of betrayal   14:17-21

[17] When it was evening, he came with the twelve. [18]And when they had taken their places and were eating, Jesus said, 'Truly I tell you, one of you will betray me, one who is eating with me.' [19]They began to be distressed and to say to him one after another, 'Surely, not I?' [20]He said to them, 'It is one of the twelve, one who is dipping bread into the bowl with me. [21]For the Son of Man goes as it is written of him, but woe to that one by whom the Son of Man is betrayed! It would have been better for that one not to have been born.'

After reading about the mysterious preparations for the Passover meal, we might now expect Mark to tell us of the return of the two disciples and give us some details about the meal itself. It soon becomes clear in this passage, however, that Mark is not interested in making this link or in offering a narrative of the meal. His interest clearly lies in showing that Jesus had foreknowledge of his betrayal and that, in spite of that insight, he elected to continue on his appointed way.

Mark stresses the unity of the group that will share table fellowship: Jesus and the twelve make their final journey together into the city of Jerusalem, to celebrate the Passover. The Passover meal had to be shared by at least ten people, usually family members, as it was assumed that a year-old lamb would be sufficient food for that number. Mark tells us that Jesus and the twelve reclined (*anakeimai*) at table. Exodus 12:11 stipulated that people should eat the meal standing – 'your loins girded, your sandals on your feet, and your staff in your hand; and you shall it is hurriedly.' These rubrics were modified later, so that it became the custom to recline at table in a leisurely manner as a sign of freedom from slavery.

During the meal Jesus solemnly discloses to his disciples that one of them will betray him, one who is now eating with him. Their table fellowship is broken by the news and they become sorrowful as this tragic truth begins to dawn on them. Jesus' announcement is reminiscent of Psalm 149:9: 'Even my bosom friend in whom I trusted, who ate my bread, has lifted the heel against me.' In his account John quotes the verse and interprets this moment as a fulfilment of scripture (Jn 13:18).

Judas is not mentioned by name in the passage, and there is no suggestion that the disciples know the identity of the traitor. The reader, who has been told that Judas is the betrayer as early as the appointment of the twelve (3:19), is wiser than eleven of the disciples. By withholding the identification of the one who will hand Jesus over, Mark heightens the suspense in the room. A sentence has changed everything. From portraying a family of disciples celebrating the memory of freedom, the mood alters dramatically to one of hurt bewilderment: suddenly each disciple is under suspicion of betrayal. None of the disciples asks 'Who is it?' None of them accuses another. None excludes himself from consideration. Instead, one after another, each begins to wonder about his own capacity for betrayal as he asks Jesus, 'Surely, not I?' While the protest is evident, it is still framed as a question.

In his reply Jesus repeats the charge that it is one the disciples present, emphasising the break in fellowship by saying that the traitor is dipping bread into the same bowl. This does not have the effect of identifying Judas to the others, for the disciples are no wiser than before; it merely accentuates the point already made, that the treason will be committed by a table companion. As Mann comments:

All of this makes for more uncertainty in our attempts to unravel the mysterious character of Judas. For granted an insight of

Jesus into some flaw in the traitor, it is puzzling that apparently no one among the rest of the disciples had any inkling that Judas was potentially untrustworthy.[4]

The final verse emphasises the appointed destiny of the Son of Man and expresses anguish at the one who will betray him. Although Jesus' destiny is determined by God, that is not the only issue at stake. Jesus' destiny remains unfulfilled until he freely chooses and embraces it, a point that Mark will explore further when he describes Jesus' torment in Gethsemane.

Paradoxically, the betrayal by Judas advances the decreed plan of God: his handing Jesus over to the religious authorities is interpreted not as an unexpected act of madness but as a fulfilment of scripture. It is the nature of most tragic happenings that they appear inexplicable, 'Why did this happen?' They are made marginally more bearable by the protest, 'It was meant to be.' What first appeared as an arbitrary act ends up being interpreted as inevitable, and this way of making sense of tragedy is not something that is confined to the pages of scripture. That does not exonerate Judas, however, from responsibility for his own actions. Judas is neither God's designated victim nor Satan's hapless robot: he is accountable for his own deeds.

The Lord's Supper 14:22-25

[22] While they were eating, he took a loaf of bread, and after blessing it he broke it, gave it to them, and said, 'Take; this is my body.' [23]Then he took a cup, and after giving thanks he gave it to them, and all of them drank from it.

[24]He said to them, 'This is my blood of the covenant, which is poured out for many. [25]Truly I tell you, I will never again drink of the fruit of the vine until that day when I drink it new in the kingdom of God.'

Mark's account of the institution of the Eucharist is framed by emphasis on the disciples' failure. Before the account, we hear the prediction of a disciple's betrayal; immediately following, we hear Jesus' double prophecy of desertion by all the disciples and the denial by Peter. Taking only four verses, the account itself is brief and terse, perhaps favouring the view that it is a unit derived from primitive Christian liturgy – similar to the tradition quoted by Paul

4. C. Mann, *Mark* p. 567

in 1 Corinthians 11:23-26. Supporting this view, V. Taylor comments on Mark's passage: 'The purpose of 22-25 is not to describe all that happened, but to relate what Jesus did and said, in the interests of faith and worship.'[5] While that may be so, Mark's account does not stand unrelated to what went before in Jesus' ministry, to the way he used meals to extend table fellowship and forgiveness to outcasts and sinners, and particularly to his feeding of the two crowds.

Mark has related how Jesus, against the protests of his disciples, fed a multitude in Jewish territory (6:33-44) and another in Gentile territory (8:1-10). After the first feeding, Jesus tries to reveal himself to the disciples, but they react with a mixture of fright and incomprehension, 'for they did not understand about the loaves, but their hearts were hardened.' (6:52) After the second feeding story, the disciples are again in the boat and they refer to the one loaf they have; Jesus berates them for their obtuseness, 'Do you still not perceive or understand? Are your hearts hardened?' (8:17) Both accounts of the feeding are followed by stories depicting the failure of the disciples to understand the significance of what Jesus is doing.

After comparing the Greek that Mark uses for Jesus' action over the loaves in the feeding stories and his action over the loaf at the supper, Donald Senior comments:

> The meaning of the feeding stories as action summaries of Jesus' entire mission to Israel and to the nations is clearly in mind here ... The supper in 14:22-25 is, therefore, the third in a series of messianic meals in the Gospel. The ritualized action of Jesus over the loaves – blessing, breaking, distributing – is the same in each. In each, the disciples play major roles. Each, too, has some connection with the liberating exodus: the first two by their desert setting, the last by its connection to Passover. But the last meal brings an even greater depth to the loaves' significance. Not only are the loaves signs of Jesus' inclusive mission; now the loaf is *his body*, his very self.[6]

5. V. Taylor, *The Gospel according to St. Mark* p. 543.

6. D. Senior, *The Passion of Jesus in the Gospel of Mark* (Collegeville: Glazier, 1991) p. 58. See also his article, 'The Eucharist in Mark: Mission, Reconciliation, Hope,' *Biblical Theology Bulletin* 12 (1982) pp. 67-72.

Jesus takes a loaf of bread, and after the blessing gives the broken pieces to his disciples, saying, 'Take; this is my body.' Paul's formula, one that he 'received' from the Lord and 'delivered' to the church in Corinth, has the additional explanatory phrase, 'that is for you' with the command to repeat the action, 'Do this in remembrance of me.' (1 Cor 11:24) Jesus' invitation to take, and by implication eat, is the offer of self as a gift to the disciples. Before he is handed over to his enemies, Jesus hands himself over to his friends. Jesus' self-offering is in view of his approaching death; when the disciples take and eat what is offered, they are participating in his sacrificial mission. By partaking of the food/ body offered to God on their behalf, they share the blessings that come from that sacrifice.

The words over the cup are more explicitly sacrificial in tone, and the two sayings illuminate one another. Jesus takes the cup, says a prayer of thanksgiving, gives the cup to his disciples, and all of them drink from it. After this, he says: 'This is my blood of the covenant, which is poured out for many.' The use of the phrase 'blood poured out' is obviously a reference to the violent death of Jesus. In the Old Testament sacrificial system it was the blood of the sacrificial animal that made atonement. The blood of the covenant recalls the sacrifice of Exodus 24:8. After the animals are sacrificed, Moses takes half the blood and throws it against the altar (the symbol of God). After reading the Law, he throws the other half of the blood on the people, saying: 'See the blood of the covenant that the Lord has made with you in accordance with all these words.' Through sacrifice and the sprinkling of blood a common bond is forged between God and the people. The people now share in the blessings of the covenant made at Sinai. Immediately afterwards, the leaders of Israel 'beheld God, and they ate and drank.' (Ex 24:11)

In offering the disciples the cup, in telling them that the wine is his blood, Jesus declares that his life is poured out in sacrifice to forge a new bond of life, a new covenant between God and a new people. This new people is not limited to the people of Israel. The universality of Jesus' mission is emphasised in the phrase over the cup, 'poured out for many'. The word 'many' here is a semitism that does not mean 'many as opposed to all' but means 'all peoples'.

John's Gospel makes this even clearer when Jesus speaks of his flesh that will be given 'for the life of the world' (Jn 6:51).

What was implied in Jesus' feeding on Jewish and Gentile territory is now made explicit: what he does is done for all. What was mentioned earlier to the disciples as they journeyed up to Jerusalem, that the Son of Man came to serve and to give his life as a 'ransom for many' (10:45), is now made explicit: Jesus will pour out his life in a complete act of service for all. Thus the meaning of Jesus' whole ministry is gathered up in the Last Supper.

After the words of institution, Jesus concludes with a solemn affirmation that he will never again drink wine until the Messianic banquet in the kingdom of God. Jesus looks forward, beyond this meal and beyond his death, to complete fellowship in the fullness of the kingdom. For the disciples, and for all those who will come after them, sharing in the fellowship of the Lord's supper is an anticipation of that complete fellowship. Whenever the Eucharist is celebrated, the community is always invited to hold holy the memory of Jesus and look with confidence to the day of its completion in the eternal presence of the Lord. As Montague comments: 'Hereafter the Eucharist will celebrate the death of the Lord until he comes (1 Cor 11:26). Eucharist is therefore a celebration both of the Lord's presence and his absence; it is both feast and fast.'[7]

Finally, it is worth recalling what lies on either side of this account of the Last Supper. By the way he has framed the last meal of Jesus with predictions of the disciples' failure, abandonment and denial, Mark shows what kind of community is sharing table fellowship with Jesus. Moloney states:

> The meal that Jesus shared was not a meal for the worthy ones. It was a meal for those people who were closest to Jesus, but who, faced with the challenge to love him, even unto death, betrayed and abandoned their Lord.[8]

In spite of the fact that 'all of them drank' from the cup, another truth is told when 'all of them deserted him and fled.' (14:50) For

7. G. Montague, *Mark: Good News for Hard Times* (Ann Arbor: Servant, 1981) p. 165.

8. F. Moloney, *A Body Broken for a Broken People* (Quezon City: Claretians, 1990) p. 34.

all its special character, the Last Supper shares one fundamental characteristic with Jesus' other meals. Even in the solemn atmosphere of the upper room, even within the inner circle of the twelve, one can hear the echo of an older question: 'Why does he eat with tax collectors and sinners?'

Desertion, denial and beyond   14:26-31

²⁶ When they had sung the hymn, they went out to the Mount of Olives. ²⁷And Jesus said to them, 'You will all become deserters; for it is written,

"I will strike the shepherd,

and the sheep will be scattered."

²⁸But after I am raised up, I will go before you to Galilee.' ²⁹Peter said to him, 'Even though all become deserters, I will not.' ³⁰Jesus said to him, 'Truly I tell you, this day, this very night, before the cock crows twice, you will deny me three times.' ³¹But he said vehemently, 'Even though I must die with you, I will not deny you.' And all of them said the same.

Following the farewell meal, Mark has a transitional scene that moves the action from the upper room to Gethsemane, situated on the western slopes of the Mount of Olives. After Jesus and the disciples sing the second part of the *Hallel*, selections from Psalms 114-118 that traditionally ended the Passover meal, they leave the city. Nothing is said about Judas. The group would have to cross the Kidron, a narrow valley separating the walled city from the Mount of Olives. The name Kidron seems to mean 'dark' or 'unclear' – possibly a reference to the sediment stirred up by the winter stream that flowed there? At the time of Jesus, part of the valley was used as a graveyard. It is night, and the time of Passover would have meant a full moon. After the singing, the setting is suddenly sombre and strained: Jesus and his disciples walk through a graveyard and have an argument about how the disciples will conduct themselves during the impending crisis.

Jesus says to them, 'You will all become deserters' – a warning that literally speaks of their being scandalised at him. The sense of the Greek word *scandalizein* means 'to be an obstacle' or 'to cause offence'. Before the night is out, Jesus will become a scandal to his own community and they will lose faith in him. That sad truth is interpreted in terms of the prophecy of Zechariah 13:7: God will strike the shepherd and the sheep will be scattered. The prophecy of the disciples' abject failure is balanced by a promise that Jesus will not abandon his wayward community. After he is raised up, he will go before them to Galilee – a promise that is repeated by the young man in the tomb (16:7). This pledge looks beyond separation and flight to a time of new attachment with the Lord, to a place where the disciples were originally appointed to take up Jesus' proclamation of the kingdom of God.

Peter ignores the good news that the scattered flock will be gathered together again; instead, he objects to the negative prophecy that points to the defection of all the disciples. Peter grants Jesus the point that the other disciples could desert him, but he professes himself to be a notable exception: 'I will not.' Peter seems unable to imagine himself in the role of a defector. As if to aid his disciple's imagination, Jesus gives him details of when and in what form his defection will take place. Peter will not have to wait long: this very night, before the cock crows twice, Peter will deny his Master three times.

Peter protests vehemently at Jesus' detailed prophecy. He seems to believe in the real possibility that he might have to die with Jesus. In spite of that prospect, he confidently maintains that he will not deny Jesus. The vehemence of his protestation does not make it any more truthful, as events will show. The other disciples join Peter in a chorus that denies the reality of their moral frailty. Jesus' inner circle is united against him, sharing what Girard calls 'false eagerness for the Passion'.[9]

The disciples' genuine attachment to Jesus seems to make them unrealistic about their own capabilities. Jesus has attempted to introduce his own community to the reality of their fragility; they have responded with denial. His attempt to face what is ahead is characterised by both candour and compassion. Their abandonment of him will not be reciprocated by his abandonment of them. It is *this* community with whom he has shared the Last Supper; it is *this* community who will abandon him; it is *this* community he is pledged to lead after the resurrection.

---

9. R. Girard, *The Scapegoat* (Baltimore: John Hopkins University Press, 1986) p. 159.

Jesus' prayer in Gethsemane 14:32-42

[32] They went to a place called Gethsemane; and he said to his disciples, 'Sit here while I pray.' [33]He took with him Peter and James and John, and began to be distressed and agitated. [34]And he said to them, 'I am deeply grieved, even to death; remain here, and keep awake.' [35]And going a little farther, he threw himself on the ground and prayed that, if it were possible, the hour might pass from him. [36]He said, 'Abba, Father, for you all things are possible; remove this cup from me; yet, not what I want, but what you want.' [37]He came and found them sleeping; and he said to Peter, 'Simon, are you asleep? Could you not keep awake one hour? [38]Keep awake and pray that you may not come into the time of trial; the spirit indeed is willing, but the flesh is weak.' [39]And again he went away and prayed, saying the same words. [40]And once more he came and found them sleeping, for their eyes were very heavy; and they did not know what to say to him. [41]He came a third time and said to them, 'Are you still sleeping and taking your rest? Enough! The hour has come; the Son of Man is betrayed into the hands of sinners. [42]Get up, let us be going. See, my betrayer is at hand.'

Following the unresolved argument between Jesus and the disciples, the group now arrives at their destination on the Mount of Olives. The name Gethsemane derives from the Hebrew and Aramaic words for 'oil press'. Neither Luke nor John mentions Gethsemane by name; while Luke speaks of a place (*topos*) on the Mount of Olives, only John identifies it as a garden or enclosure (*kepos*). In all likelihood Gethsemane consisted of an olive grove and a press to crush the olives. According to Josephus, all the olive trees to the east of Jerusalem were cut down and used as tinder for burning the city in 70 A.D.[10] Since an olive grove is not the kind of place that would leave identifiable archaeological remains, the precise place cannot be determined, even if the general area can be securely known. About the year 380 the Byzantine Church of the Agony was built around a rock where it was thought Jesus prayed, which is where the modern Church of All Nations now stands.[11]

Mark develops the scene in Gethsemane with a dramatist's care as he graphically depicts the widening gap between Jesus and the disciples. This is the last time Jesus and the disciples are together in this Gospel. The scene begins as they all enter Gethsemane

10. Josephus, *War* 6.1.1.

11. For a summary of the earliest testimony about the location of Gethsemane, see C. Kopp, *The Holy Places in the Gospels* (New York: Herder & Herder, 1963) pp. 335-350.

together; it ends with Jesus and the disciples going their separate ways. Mark accounts for the ending by telling two stories: the story of the disciples' chronic failure to pay attention to Jesus' torment and the story of Jesus' gradual alienation from his own community as he struggles to discern and accept his Father's will.

Jesus says to the group of eleven disciples, 'Sit here while I pray.' He then separates Peter, James and John from the main group by taking them with him. These three disciples were the privileged witnesses at the raising of Jairus' daughter (5:37), the transfiguration (9:2), and, along with Andrew, sat on the Mount of Olives listening to Jesus' final discourse that ended with the appeal, 'Keep awake.' (13:37) Apart from this, the three disciples have sought to distinguish themselves from the others by their professions of confidence: James and John have assured Jesus that they are able to drink the cup that he is to drink (10:39), and Peter has just claimed his loyalty to be exceptional and unfailing.

While he is with the three disciples Jesus begins to show signs of being 'distressed and agitated.' Stanley comments:

> The first word (*ekthambeisthai*) is found only in this Gospel; it expresses surprise and something akin to fear (Mk 26:37), particularly when, as here, it occurs in tandem with a term signifying a state of disorientation (*ademonein*) almost equivalent to being in a state of shock ... The puzzling lack of any expression of sympathy, indeed of any reactions by the disciples, reminds us that, as the Suffering Servant of God, Jesus' vicarious Passion must be endured in total isolation.[12]

Mark's description moves to direct speech as Jesus shares with the three the intensity of his anguish: 'I am deeply grieved, even to death; remain here, and keep awake.' It is as if the reality of the approaching horror has made itself felt so keenly that it induces a state of mental torment. Jesus' grief is terminal. He tells the disciples to remain, this time charging them to stay awake.

The separation between Jesus and the disciples is further emphasised as Jesus goes a little farther and throws himself on the ground. Even though the physical distance that separates him from the others is small, the real distance appears to be a world away. As

12. D. Stanley, *Jesus in Gethsemane* (New York: Paulist, 1980) p. 132.

events will prove, Jesus is effectively disconnected from those he still hopes will befriend him in his acute distress.

By himself, Jesus becomes a beggar: prostrate on the ground, he pleads with God to change his mind. The opening request takes various forms:

Mark: 'Abba, Father, for you all things are possible ... '

Matthew: 'My Father, if it is possible ... '

Luke: 'Father, if you are willing ... '

John: Jesus is neither anxious nor pleading in John's garden scene, but the fourth evangelist has a form of both earlier in the ministry: 'Now my soul is troubled. And what shall I say – 'Father, save me from this hour'? No, it is for this reason I have come to this hour.' (Jn 12:27)

Hebrews: Jesus' prayer and anguish are described thus in the Epistle to the Hebrews: 'In the days of his flesh, Jesus offered up prayers and supplications, with loud cries and tears, to the one who was able to save him from death' (Heb 5:7). The 'loud cries and tears' even go beyond the inward anguish of Mark's account.

Jesus' request that the hour might pass him by and that the cup might be taken away from him probably refers not only to his approaching death but to the larger cosmic struggle against evil in establishing God's kingdom. Since Jesus has already declared in the three passion predictions that his destiny is by divine decree, it might seem scandalous to some that he should now plead with God to alter that course. But the pleading is a further illustration of the acute anxiety he underwent, and has the ring of observed truth about it: it is one thing to accept a fate that still lies in the future; it is another to accept it readily when it faces you. That recognition reminds Mark's persecuted community that even the most resolute may shrink before the horror of martyrdom. Besides, the request of Jesus submits to the overriding will of God: that pattern of asking God to change his mind while expressing an unconditional surrender to his will is one that has its own place in the Jewish tradition (see Exodus 32:10-14; 2 Kings 20:1-6; 2 Samuel 15:25-35).[13]

13. For a discussion of this as an established way of praying, see D. Daube, 'A Prayer Pattern in Judaism,' *Studia Evangelica* 1 (1959) pp. 539-545.

The threefold return of Jesus to the sleeping disciples has the effect of dramatising his isolation. On the first return Jesus treats Simon as the exception the disciple claimed to be, only to note in the question that Simon is no exception, but asleep like the others. He encourages the disciples to stay awake and pray that 'you may not come into the time of trial' – a petition contained in the Our Father, which is not found in Mark's Gospel. Jesus goes away and prays in the same words.

On his second return, he discovers the disciples still asleep. Nothing is said. Mark explains the disciples' silence by saying they did not know what to say to Jesus. As they cannot follow his command to stay awake, neither can they help him in his lonely vigil. They can no longer follow Jesus. On his third return, Jesus expresses a mixture of disappointment and surprise that they are sleeping. Ever hopeful, he says to them, 'Get up, let us be going. My betrayer is at hand.' This is Jesus' last request to his disciples, one that expresses the misplaced hope that they can still face the oncoming terror together. As for himself, Jesus is now resolved to continue on his appointed way.

Betrayal and arrest   14:43-52

⁴³ Immediately, while he was still speaking, Judas, one of the twelve, arrived; and with him there was a crowd with swords and clubs, from the chief priests, the scribes, and the elders. ⁴⁴Now the betrayer had given them a sign, saying, 'The one I will kiss is the man; arrest him and lead him away under guard.' ⁴⁵So when he came, he went up to him at once and said, 'Rabbi!' and kissed him. ⁴⁶Then they laid hands on him and arrested him. ⁴⁷But one of those who stood near drew his sword and struck the slave of the high priest, cutting off his ear. ⁴⁸Then Jesus said to them, 'Have you come out with swords and clubs to arrest me as though I were a bandit? ⁴⁹Day after day I was with you in the temple teaching, and you did not arrest me. But let the scriptures be fulfilled.' ⁵⁰All of them deserted him and fled.

⁵¹ A certain young man was following him, wearing nothing but a linen cloth. They caught hold of him, ⁵²but he left the linen cloth and ran off naked.

No sooner does Jesus announce that his betrayer is at hand than Judas arrives with the arresting party. By this immediacy, Mark illustrates how Jesus' declaration of the inevitable is confirmed; events will now move at a determined pace. Judas has openly allied himself with the adversaries of Jesus, indeed he appears to be the leader of the arresting party. The confrontation is dramatic: a now resolute Jesus, accompanied by indecisive disciples, is confronted by an unrepentant Judas, supported by a determined delegation. The repeated reference to Judas as one of the twelve accentuates the treachery of his deed. The arresting party is identified as a crowd with swords and clubs, rather than the Temple police (Lk 22:52) or the Roman soldiers (Jn 18:3,12). Although a crowd, they are not a rabble, for they come with the authority of the chief priests, scribes and elders. Representatives from these three groups make up the council of seventy, the Sanhedrin, headed by the high priest.

Using his role as omniscient narrator, Mark now tells us about instructions Judas gave earlier to the arresting party: 'The one I shall kiss is the man; arrest him and lead him away under guard.' Judas plays out the role he has assigned for himself, addressing Jesus as 'Rabbi' and kissing him. His chosen signal uses the traditional greeting between a disciple and rabbi and reverses the honour it usually implies. Jesus says nothing. The kiss, after all, is not for him but for his captors, who now carry out Judas' instructions by laying hands on Jesus and arresting him.

No protest is made by the disciples, but an unidentified by-stander wields his sword and cuts off the ear of the high priest's servant. The other three Gospels identify the impulsive assailant as a disciple, John going further by naming him as Peter and identifying the high priest's servant as Malchus. If Peter was the assailant, however, it is difficult to understand why he was not arrested. Only Luke has Jesus heal the afflicted man.

In Mark's account Jesus ignores this useless gesture of violence, choosing instead to protest about the manner of his arrest. It is as if he is a dangerous guerrilla bandit who has to be taken by surprise and force before being dragged away under heavy guard. Given Jesus' daily routine of being 'with you in the Temple' – which carries the suggestion that the arresting party could have easily identified him without Judas – the secrecy of this night-time arrest by an armed crowd looks not only unnecessary but absurd. This absurd piece of theatre, however, has a part to play in the overall design: it serves the fulfilment of scripture. Again the point is made that a particular event that seems purposeless or accidental furthers the saving design of God.

Not only is scripture being fulfilled but so also is Jesus' prophecy that all his disciples would become deserters and scatter (14:27). Their going is reported tersely and without comment: 'All of them deserted him and fled.' They can no longer follow Jesus because they cannot fulfil the requirement of discipleship: 'If any want to become my followers, let them deny themselves and take up their cross and follow me.' (8:34) The story of discipleship moves from one of attachment to Jesus to one of separation and abandonment.

The arrest scene concludes with a bizarre epilogue in the sudden appearance and equally sudden disappearance of a young man who is wearing nothing but a linen cloth. After all the disciples have fled, this young man tries to follow Jesus, but his brief attempt at discipleship is stopped short by the arresting party who try to seize him. The mystery surrounding this unknown figure has given licence to many writers to play detective and supply the missing identity.[14]

Guesses have included a neighbour who, aroused from sleep by the passing crowd, rose quickly and threw a sheet around himself; the evangelist himself; the unnamed disciple in John's Gospel who, together with Peter, follows Jesus into the high priest's palace (Jn 18:15); James, the brother of the Lord. Others argue that the young man (*neaniskos*) is a symbolic figure of disbelief that turns to faith, and is identical with the young man (*neaniskos*) in the tomb who is clothed in a white robe (16:5); a figure for Christian baptism; a repeat of the figure of Joseph, who escaped the clutches of Potiphar's wife by leaving his clothes in her hands (Gen 39:12). Smith thinks that the young man's presence and state of undress are a historical reminiscence of a secret initiatory rite that Jesus required of those who wanted to join his group.[15] The list goes on.

Perhaps Mark is doing something much simpler; maybe he is making a deliberate contrast between the generosity that character-

14. For a summary of views on the identity of the young man, see H. Fleddermann, 'The Flight of a Naked Young Man (Mark 14:51-52),' *The Catholic Biblical Quarterly* 41 (1979) pp. 412-417.

15. M. Smith, *Clement of Alexandria and a Secret Gospel of Mark* (Cambridge: Harvard University Press, 1973) pp. 167ff., and 'Clement of Alexandria and Secret Mark: The Score at the End of the First Decade,' *Harvard Theological Review* 75 (1982) pp. 449-461.

ised the beginning of the disciples' story and the desperation that characterises its conclusion. When Jesus called Simon and Andrew, they responded by immediately leaving their nets and following Jesus (1:18). When Jesus called James and John, they responded by immediately leaving their father and hired men to follow Jesus (1:20). When the twelve were appointed, Jesus called them 'to be with him' (3:14). Peter later summarised the generosity of the disciples' action when he reminded Jesus: 'Look, *we have left everything and followed you.*' (10:28) The young man in Gethsemane who wanted to follow Jesus ends up by following the disciples in their desperation to detach themselves from Jesus: he immediately *leaves everything so that he can get away from Jesus.* The flight of the disciples and the would-be disciple highlights the breakdown of discipleship, with the consequence that Jesus is left abandoned and alone. None of Jesus' disciples can follow him to the cross.

Jesus before the Sanhedrin   14:53-65

[53]They took Jesus to the high priest; and all the chief priests, the elders, and the scribes were assembled. [54]Peter had followed him at a distance, right into the courtyard of the high priest; and he was sitting with the guards, warming himself at the fire. [55]Now the chief priests and the whole council were looking for testimony against Jesus to put him to death; but they found none. [56]For many gave false testimony against him, and their testimony did not agree. [57]Some stood up and gave false testimony against him, saying, [58]'We heard him say, "I will destroy this temple that is made with hands, and in three days I will build another, not made with hands".' [59]But even on this point their testimony did not agree. [60]Then the high priest stood up before them and asked Jesus, 'Have you no answer? What is it that they testify against you?' [61] But he was silent and did not answer. Again the high priest asked him, 'Are you the Messiah, the Son of the Blessed One?'
[62]Jesus said, 'I am; and
"you will see the Son of Man seated at the right hand of the Power," and "coming with the clouds of heaven".'
[63]Then the high priest tore his clothes and said, 'Why do we still need witnesses? [64]You have heard his blasphemy! What is your decision?' All of them condemned him as deserving death. [65]Some began to spit on him, to blindfold him, and to strike him, saying to him, 'Prophesy!' The guards also took him over and beat him.

In the opening transition scene, Mark moves the action from

Gethsemane back to the city of Jerusalem as Jesus is taken to the high priest. Although Mark never mentions the high priest by name, we know that Joseph Caiaphas held that office from 18-36 A.D., the longest tenure held by any high priest in first century Jerusalem. It is not clear whether Mark locates the action in the house of the high priest, somewhere in the upper city, or in the meeting hall of the Sanhedrin, situated near the Temple. The text leans towards the former location. Only Mark has a full meeting of the Sanhedrin: 'all (*pantes*) the chief priests, the elders, and the scribes' are assembled.

Peter is the last disciple to follow Jesus. Unlike his journey with Jesus from the city to Gethsemane, his return journey is a model of cautious discipleship. He goes into the courtyard and keeps company with the high priest's guards/attendants, warming himself by the fire. Thus the stage is set for two trials: the trial of Jesus and the trial of Peter.

A library could be assembled on the subject of the trial of Jesus. Some scholars argue that there was no formal Jewish 'trial' by the Sanhedrin the night before Jesus died, only an interrogation by the high priest as a preliminary to handing Jesus over to the civil authorities – a view originating in John's account of what happened the night before Jesus' death (Jn 18:12-13,19-24). Going further, other scholars argue that a Jewish trial was created by the early church for apologetic purposes: it served to downplay Roman involvement by highlighting a Jewish condemnation of Jesus, thereby freeing Jesus from the embarrassing charge of sedition.[16]

The Mishnah – a second century compendium of legal regulations and beliefs that were foundational for rabbinic Judaism – has a special tract on the Sanhedrin. It forbids the trying of capital cases on the eve of the sabbath or the eve of a feast day; it states that capital cases must by tried by day and that there must be a lapse in time between the hearing of evidence and the judgement, which must be made during daytime (*Sanhedrin* 4:1). It is difficult to know if these rabbinic rules were in force at a very different time, prior to the destruction of the Temple, and we have no evidence to prove that they were. Moreover, the Mishnaic account of the

---

16. For a typical example of this approach, see S. Brandon, *The Trial of Jesus of Nazareth* (London: Paladin, 1968).

workings of the Sanhedrin, compiled at a time when this council had ceased to function as the supreme judicial court in Judaism, may itself be speculative and idealised.

The issue is made more complicated by the differences among the four Gospel accounts. After reviewing the different accounts and the Mishnaic laws, Brown comes to the conclusion:

> All the Gospels agree that a Sanhedrin session discussed Jesus' activities and decided that he should die. All the Gospels have Jesus interrogated by the high priest or priests during the last hours before the Romans executed him. John may well be more accurate in portraying these as two separate actions, with the Sanhedrin session a good number of days before Jesus was arrested; and Mark may have elided the once-distinct actions into one easily remembered final scene. In that case the only procedure on a feast day or the eve of a feast day would have consisted of questions posed to the accused – not a trial that might have infringed on the law protecting feasts.[17]

Mark says that the chief priests and the whole council are frustrated in their attempts to gather testimony against Jesus that would warrant their declared goal of a capital sentence. The trial seems irregular before it begins, since the verdict is predetermined. Although the witnesses are many, their testimony does not agree. According to Deuteronomy 19:15, two is the minimum number required for probative testimony. The description of all the witnesses as false echoes the language of an innocent sufferer, the just one (Pss. 27:12; 35:11; 109:2). It does appear strange, however, that witnesses suborned for the sole purpose of giving evidence against Jesus were not schooled into agreement.

The only concrete testimony mentioned is that some witnesses claim to have heard Jesus say that he would destroy the sanctuary (*naos*) 'made with hands' and in three days build another 'not made with hands.' This accusation will be made again when Jesus is on the cross (15:30). Already dismissed by Mark as 'false', this testimony might appear, however ironic, to be true to the reader. Mark has gone to some pains to describe Jesus' condemnation of the whole Temple system (11:15-17) – made all the more final by

17. R. Brown, *The Death of the Messiah* Vol. 1 (London: Chapman, 1994) p. 363.

its insertion into the story of the withered fig tree – a condemnation which leads the chief priests and scribes to look for ways to kill him (11:18). We have heard Jesus predict the destruction of the Temple (13:1-2) and the building of a new community of which he would be the cornerstone (12:10). As Christian readers we might interpret the phrase 'not built with hands' to refer to the Christian community, created through the death and resurrection of Jesus. Although Jesus never claimed to be the agent of the Temple's destruction – is this what makes for the witnesses' falsification? – the testimony sounds sufficiently close to what the Christian reader would consider true.

Since nothing can be made of the witnesses' testimony, the high priest intervenes to bring the process to its determined conclusion. He challenges Jesus to respond to the accusations made, inviting him to clarify the conflicting testimony of the witnesses. Jesus declines to say anything. Rather than consciously portraying Jesus in the language of Isaiah 53:7, perhaps Mark is simply showing Jesus' contempt for the testimony; or perhaps the silence of Jesus is a pragmatic recognition that nothing he says will make any discernible difference to the outcome.

The high priest asks: 'Are you the Messiah, the Son of the Blessed One?' The supposition that these titles go together and interpret one another is clearly a Christian observation. Sanders points out:

> The mere combination is suspicious, and the statement that the two titles, when combined constitute blasphemy also looks like Christian creativity. Some early Christians want to attribute his death to confessing the christology of the church.[18]

The Christian reader is not surprised when Jesus answers 'I am' (*ego emei*), since Jesus is affirming what Mark's Gospel was written to proclaim (1:1). It is another question to ask, as Brown does: 'Could a Jewish authority have asked Jesus whether he accepted such a title; and if Jesus said yes, what would he and the high priest have understood by this affirmed title?'[19] If Peter does not make the link between Messiah and Son of God in his partial

18. E. Sanders, *The Historical Figure of Jesus* p. 270.
19. R. Brown, *The Death of the Messiah* Vol. 1 p. 472.

confession at Caesarea Philippi, if the only voices that recognise Jesus as Son of God during the ministry are supernatural, if the first human being recognises Jesus as Son of God only after his death, it seems highly unlikely that a hostile high priest would have made the connection in his interrogation. Mark is clearly using the occasion of this trial to make Jesus into a Christian confessor, something that Matthew and Luke treat with reserve in their more nuanced accounts.

The confession of Jesus, using Psalm 110:1 and Daniel 7:13, now looks to a triumphant future in the exaltation of the Son of Man. The phrase 'you will see' is probably addressed more to the Christian community than to the members of the Sanhedrin.[20] Firstly, the Son of Man will be seated in the place of favour, at the right hand of Power, sharing God's rule – a reference to the time after the resurrection. Secondly, in a reference to the parousia, the Son of Man will return with the clouds of heaven. Both statements point to the truth that God will vindicate Jesus against his enemies by revealing Jesus to be the triumphant one.

As a sign of his passionate objection to Jesus' confession, the high priest tears his clothes. The tearing of clothes was traditionally regarded as the proper reaction to news of irrevocable loss (see 2 Samuel 1:11-12) or blasphemy (see 2 Kings 19:1). The high priest regards Jesus' confession as self-incriminating blasphemy: Jesus has insulted God by claiming for himself what properly belongs to God. When Caiaphas appeals to the Sanhedrin for their decision, they unanimously condemn Jesus as someone deserving death. It is left unexplained why, if Jesus was condemned for blasphemy, the authorities do not carry out the sentence prescribed by the Law and stone him to death (Lev 24:16). The trial ends with some members of the council showing their contempt for Jesus by spitting on him. After they cover his face and slap him, they invite him to play prophet as they challenge him to identify the assailant. The guards join in the game. Ironically, the mockery of Jesus fulfils the prophecy of Isaiah 50:6: 'I did not turn my face from insult and spitting.' In challenging Jesus to prophesy, they unwittingly fulfil prophecy. And, as we will presently discover, while Jesus is being

---

20. See N. Perrin, 'The High Priest's Question and Jesus' Answer,' in W. Kelber (ed.) *The Passion in Mark* (Philadelphia: Fortress, 1976) p. 92.

castigated for being a false prophet, his prophecy of Peter's denials is being fulfilled below in the courtyard.

The denial by Peter   14:66-72

[66] While Peter was below in the courtyard, one of the servant-girls of the high priest came by. [67] When she saw Peter warming himself, she stared at him and said, 'You also were with Jesus, the man from Nazareth.' [68] But he denied it, saying, 'I do not know or understand what you are talking about.' And he went out into the forecourt. Then the cock crowed. [69] And the servant-girl, on seeing him, began again to say to the bystanders, 'This man is one of them.' [70] But again he denied it. Then after a little while the bystanders again said to Peter, 'Certainly you are one of them; for you are a Galilean.' [71] But he began to curse, and he swore on oath, 'I do not know this man you are talking about.' [72] At that moment the cock crowed for the second time. Then Peter remembered that Jesus had said to him, 'Before the cock crows twice, you will deny me three times.' And he broke down and wept.

By his careful arrangement of the trial of Jesus before the Sanhedrin and the trial of Peter, Mark dramatises the difference between the two protagonists: while Jesus confesses who he is before the high priest and the highest court of the Jewish people, Peter denies who he is before the high priest's maidservant and attendants in the courtyard. Confession and denial are seen to run concurrently, one in an upper chamber, the other 'below' in the courtyard.

Mark connects his narrative to the earlier introduction (14:54) by repeating where Peter is and what he is doing: he is in the courtyard, warming himself by the fire. A maidservant comes by, stares at Peter in the light of the fire, and challenges him with the truth that he was with the Nazarene, Jesus. Being 'with' Jesus is a sign of membership of his group. It was, after all, what Jesus first appointed the twelve to do, 'to be with him' (3:14). The implication is that if Peter is with the accused, he has no right to be with the servants of the accusers. Whereas Jesus was silent before his accusers, Peter attempts to justify himself. He elects to play the role of the 'daft man', claiming that he has no idea what the woman is talking about. This is sharply observed, for, as Taylor notes, 'an evasion seems more psychologically probable than a lie at this stage in the story.'[21] Peter then retreats to the gateway, to escape

21. V. Taylor, *The Gospel according to St Mark* p. 574.

unwanted attention, although he does not make an exit.

Matthew, Luke, and John assign the second charge to a different speaker or speakers. In Mark's account the persistent maidservant, unimpressed by Peter's evasion, draws the bystanders' attention to her suspicions. She says to them: 'This man is one of them.' Although Peter is not being addressed directly, he feels obliged to defend himself publicly before such publicity. This time he does not feign ignorance but flatly denies that he is a disciple of Jesus.

After an interval, the bystanders take up the maidservant's challenge and add what they believe to be supporting evidence: 'Certainly you are one of them; for you are a Galilean.' The suggestion is that Galileans spoke Aramaic with a recognisable accent, probably regarded as uncouth by the citizens of Jerusalem. Although Peter's accent would indicate that he came from Galilee, it would hardly prove that he was a follower of Jesus. Rather than debate the logic of their assertion, Peter begins to curse and to swear an oath, as if this admixture of verbal violence and public avowal will guarantee his integrity. For Peter, Jesus is suddenly reduced to being 'this man you are talking about.' Scholars point out that since the Greek verb 'to curse' (*anathematizein*) is transitive, it needs an object: some argue that Jesus is the object, some that Peter himself is. If Jesus is the object of Peter's anathema, the principal disciple does what Christians were tempted to do elsewhere in order to avoid martyrdom. Pliny the Younger (*ca* 61-112 A.D.), writing as a pro-consul in Asia Minor, informs the Emperor Trajan that his method of handling Christians is to invite them three times to deny Christ and then confirm their sincerity by cursing his name.[22]

While Peter is speaking the cock crows for the second time, and Peter remembers the prophecy of Jesus (14:30). The realisation of what he has done reduces him to tears. However remorseful Peter feels, it does not lead him to change his mind and retract what he has said. The story finishes with his weeping. Notwithstanding that, if the denials of Peter have fulfilled Jesus' prophecy, there is another prophecy that still awaits its own time: 'But after I am raised up, I will go before you to Galilee.' (14:28)

In all four Gospels, it is not only Peter's faith but his failure that is offered to the reader as 'good news.' According to tradition,

22. See Pliny, *Epistles* 10.96-97.

Peter died a martyr's death in the Neronian persecution in Rome: he moved on from the punishing memory of denial, through reconciliation, to an unambiguous affirmation of loyalty to Christ. If Mark's Gospel is being written in Rome, the memory of Peter's denial and his martyrdom give hope to a community that if they have failed, their failure is not necessarily the last word. In a strange way, as Peter's denials fulfil Jesus' prophecy, so Peter's death will finally fulfil Peter's hope, 'Even though I must die with you, I will not deny you.' (14:31) Peter's last word is his martyrdom.

Jesus before Pilate   15:1-15

As soon as it was morning, the chief priests held a consultation with the elders and scribes and the whole council. They bound Jesus, led him away, and handed him over to Pilate. [2]Pilate asked him, 'Are you the King of the Jews?' He answered him, 'You say so.' [3]Then the chief priests accused him of many things. [4]Pilate asked him again, 'Have you no answer? See how many charges they bring against you.' [5]But Jesus made no further reply, so that Pilate was amazed.

[6] Now at the festival he used to release a prisoner for them, anyone for whom they asked. [7]Now a man called Barabbas was in prison with the rebels who had committed murder during the insurrection. [8]So the crowd came and began to ask Pilate to do for them according to his custom. [9]Then he answered them, 'Do you want me to release for you the King of the Jews?' [10]For he realized that it was out of jealousy that the chief priests had handed him over. [11]But the chief priests stirred up the crowd to have him release Barabbas for them instead. [12]Pilate spoke to them again, 'Then what do you wish me to do with the man you call the King of the Jews?' [13]They shouted back, 'Crucify him!' [14]Pilate asked them, 'Why, what evil has he done?' But they shouted all the more, 'Crucify him!' [15]So Pilate, wishing to satisfy the crowd, released Barabbas for them; and after flogging Jesus, he handed him over to be crucified.

Although it appears that Mark has a second meeting of the Sanhedrin in the morning, it seems more likely that he is summarising the meeting that concluded with the council's unanimous condemnation of Jesus (14:64). When Mark began the story of Peter's denials, he repeated information already given in 14:54, telling us where Peter was and what he was doing. Now, after the interruption of Peter's denials, Mark resumes Jesus' story by first summarising the earlier Sanhedrin session; he then moves the story on by telling us that Jesus is now bound, led away, and handed over to Pilate. The

Sanhedrin's condemnation and their handing Jesus over to Pilate fulfils Jesus' third passion prediction: 'the Son of Man will be handed over to the chief priests and the scribes, and they will condemn him to death; then they will hand him over to the Gentiles.' (10:33)

Pilate is mentioned without introduction, probably because his role was already well known to Mark's readers. Pontius Pilate was the fifth Roman governor/prefect in Judea and served from 26 A.D. until the spring of 37 A.D. when he was dismissed by his immediate superior, Vitellus, the imperial legate in Syria. Pilate's headquarters were situated at Caesarea on the Mediterranean coast, where in 1961 an inscribed tablet was discovered during an Israeli excavation: although part of the inscription is lost, it is easy to distinguish the original wording, 'Pontius Pilatus Praefectus Judaeae'. As governor of Judea, Pilate was responsible for the Roman administration of the region; he was head of the judicial system and was expected to guarantee the collection of tributes and taxes; he also had to forward to Rome the expected revenues and reports.

The troops that Pilate had at his disposal probably functioned more as a police force than a military one – the serious military presence in the region consisted of the four legions stationed in Syria. On major Jewish feasts Pilate would come to Jerusalem with auxiliary troops, to assert a visible Roman presence as a deterrent against Jewish rioting. It is uncertain where he established his praetorium in the city – either at the Antonia Fortress, which dominated the north-west corner of the Temple area, or, more probably, at the Herodian Palace in the upper city.

Mark's account of the interrogation by Pilate is brief, focusing on the charge that Jesus is the King of the Jews. In answer to the high priest's question before the Sanhedrin, Jesus confessed that he was the Messiah; the shift away from the high priest's terminology is significant. That religious title in the mouth of a non-Jew becomes 'King of the Jews'. The new title also heightens the political overtones, especially before the Roman governor. There were no longer any Jewish kings, only 'tetrarchs' who were vassals of Rome. To usurp the title of king amounted to high treason, punishable by death. Presumably the priests have already translated their charges to Pilate in such a way that Jesus can be charged with civil rebellion.

All four Gospels have Pilate's question, and all four have Jesus' qualified reply. Although this is the first time Mark uses the title 'King of the Jews' for Jesus, his regular use of it from this point onwards (15:9,12,18,26,32) focuses the reader's attention on the central issue of the passion story: the Roman governor, at the instigation and insistence of the Jewish leaders, condemns Jesus to die by crucifixion on the charge of being the King of the Jews. By his repetition of the title, Mark seems determined to show the Christian reader that Jesus is condemned to death *as the Messiah*. This is emphasised all the more by the fact that when the chief priests accuse Jesus of 'many things' and Pilate challenges him to respond, Jesus is silent. The unspecified charges and the silence of Jesus serve to focus on the only *specific* question: 'Are you the King of the Jews?'

Jesus' silence before the charges of the chief priests mirrors his silence before the false testimony of the earlier witnesses. Pilate is amazed that Jesus does not respond to the 'many charges' made by the chief priests. The number of the charges appears to occupy the governor more than the substance.

A possible solution presents itself in the custom of freeing a prisoner at the festival, which Mark says was Pilate's custom. Mann notes:

> There is abundant evidence for discretionary amnesty being granted by local Roman governors, and the term *abolitio* for the suspension of a charge was a well-known legal expression. There is therefore nothing inherently improbable in Pilate's action.[23]

Although there is no evidence for this custom outside the Gospels, the evangelists may have used some historical incident of amnesty to make a sub-plot for their own dramatic purposes.

The name of the prisoner, Barabbas, appears somewhat ironic to Christian readers of the Gospel. Barabbas is the Greek rendering of *bar abba* (son of the father). The irony is more pronounced in some early manuscripts of Matthew 27:16f which read the prisoner's name as 'Jesus Barabbas'. In that case the crowd have to choose

---

23. C. Mann, *Saint Mark* p. 637.

between Jesus the Messiah and Jesus Bar-abbas.[24]

Although Mark has the crowd appealing to Pilate to honour his custom of releasing a prisoner, Pilate phrases his question in favour of Jesus: 'Do you want me to release for you the King of the Jews?' Again playing the role of omniscient narrator, Mark tells us what Pilate is thinking: the governor knows the chief priests are moved by envy. Pilate is portrayed as an astute judge of character who is no stranger to religious ambiguity, whereas the Jewish leaders are presented as men driven by envy, shameless opportunists who incite the crowd to choose Barabbas and, therefore, reject Jesus. Pilate asks the crowd, as if they were a bench of trial judges skilled in the practice of sentencing, what they wish him to do with the King of the Jews. Whatever political adroitness he may possess, the governor does not have the priests' skill in manipulating the crowd: clearly, they are not his crowd. Given their growing restiveness and the danger of a riot, Pilate's behaviour seems a matter of ordinary political pragmatism rather than judicial propriety.

Paradoxically, the judgement specifying crucifixion is voiced from the crowd, not Pilate. When Pilate appeals for evidence to support such a judgement, the crowd responds with increased clamour, 'Crucify him!' Pilate can still use his discretionary power to release Jesus, but, under pressure from the crowd, he releases only the insurrectionist. Jesus is scourged, a standard punishment for provincial criminals condemned to death. For flogging, leather thongs were used with pieces of bone or metal attached; the victim's hands were tied to a low pillar, making the executioner's work easier. After this public torture, Pilate hands Jesus over to be crucified.

Throughout this trial narrative, Marks shows Pilate, the official representative of Rome, as someone who has no essential quarrel with Jesus. Luke and John take this further by having Pilate formally declare three times that Jesus is innocent. Although none of the evangelists presents Pilate in a favourable light, all of them seem to diminish the responsibility of the governor while enhancing the general guilt of the priests and the crowd. There is an obvious defensive reason for downplaying the role played by the

24. See S. Davies, 'Who Is Called Bar-Abbas?' *New Testament Studies* 27 (1981) pp. 260-263.

Roman authorities in the death of Jesus: if the representative of the imperial authority found, after due investigation, that there was no threat posed to the peace by Jesus, it could be assumed that the same judgement could be made about his followers.

It is worth noting that there is no Roman sentence of condemnation recorded by Mark: Pilate, after having failed to free Jesus through appealing for amnesty, submits to the wish of the priest-ridden crowd and hands Jesus over to be crucified. Thus Mark conceals what lies behind Jesus' death: a Roman governor sentenced Jesus of Nazareth to the Roman punishment of crucifixion.

The soldiers mock Jesus   15:16-20a

[16] Then the soldiers led him into the courtyard of the palace (that is, the governor's headquarters); and they called together the whole cohort. [17] And they clothed him in a purple cloak; and after twisting some thorns into a crown, they put in on him. [18] And they began saluting him, 'Hail, King of the Jews!' [19] They struck his head with a reed, spat upon him, and knelt down in homage to him. [20] After mocking him, they stripped him of the purple cloak and put his own clothes on him.

This brief episode fills the interval between the Roman sentence and the execution of Jesus; it also fulfils the first half of Jesus' passion prediction that refers to the Gentiles, 'they will mock him, and spit on him, and flog him, and kill him' (10:34). As the Jewish trial concluded with a scene where Jesus was mocked as a prophet and physically abused (14:65), the Roman trial concludes with the mockery of Jesus as the King of the Jews and the soldiers' physical abuse. Pilate hands Jesus over to the soldiers, who lead him into the open courtyard, and then call together the whole cohort (*speira*). A cohort consisted of anywhere between two hundred and six hundred troops, most of whom would have been non-Jews from Palestine and Syria. (Jews were exempted from military service in the Roman army.) The reference to the whole cohort probably means that those soldiers who were free joined the execution squad in the game of burlesque.

The soldiers' mockery of Jesus has an interesting parallel in the anti-Jewish rioters who greeted the King Herod Agrippa I in Alexandria in 38 A.D.[25] Agrippa had just been made King of Judea

25. See Philo, *Flaccus* 6.36-39.

by Caligula, and stopped off in Alexandria on his return journey from Rome. The rioters got hold of a half-witted Jew, who wandered naked around the streets of the city, crowned him with a paper crown, clothed him in a rug, and gave him a papyrus reed for a sceptre. After dressing up the mock king, the crowd then did homage to him as lord and pretended to consult him on matters of state. The victim was called Carabas, a name not unlike Barabbas, although there is no suggestion that the latter was mocked as a king by the Jerusalem crowd. However intriguing the parallel, Nineham's point is well made:

> St Mark was no doubt unaware of any such pagan parallels and they are therefore irrelevant to his understanding of the incident. For him it will have been one more piece of evidence – none the less cogent for being so back-handed – that it was as King of the Jews that Jesus suffered.[26]

The description of the mocking is specific to the charge against Jesus, that he claimed to be the Messiah or King of the Jews. It is unlikely that soldiers would have had ready access to a purple cloak, which was worn only by kings and emperors. Probably Matthew's reference to a scarlet cloak is more realistic (Mt 27:28), since the ordinary foot soldiers had a short red cape as part of their uniform. The soldiers plait some cuttings from a thorn bush into a crown, which they place on Jesus' head. The emphasis is on ridicule, not on physical torture.

The mock greeting, 'Hail, King of the Jews!' reflects the formal Latin salute made to the emperor, '*Ave, Caesar, victor, imperator*.' The ridicule moves to physical abuse as the soldiers strike Jesus and spit on him, concluding their game with mock worship as they kneel in homage before him. The game over, Jesus is stripped of his regal attire and dressed in his own clothes. The indignity of being stripped naked, a regular part of Roman punishment inflicted on criminals, will be held over until the crucifixion scene.

For the Christian reader, the whole macabre spectacle is deeply ironic: the soldiers' mock greeting is heard as true and their homage to Jesus as Messiah is warranted by the truth of who he is. However theatrical the regal insignia, its theological significance is correct

26. D. Nineham, *Saint Mark* p. 419.

and serves Mark's christology. The Roman victimisation of Jesus enshrines the truth so often emphasised by the evangelist: that Jesus' real identity is revealed only through his destiny of suffering, rejection, and death.

The crucifixion   15:20b-28

Then they led him out to crucify him.

[21] They compelled a passer-by, who was coming in from the country, to carry his cross; it was Simon of Cyrene, the father of Alexander and Rufus. [22]Then they brought Jesus to the place called Golgotha (which means the place of a skull). [23]And they offered him wine mixed with myrrh; but he did not take it. [24]And they crucified him, and divided his clothes among them, casting lots to decide what each should take.

[25] It was nine o'clock in the morning when they crucified him. [26] The inscription of the charge against him read, 'The King of the Jews'. [27]And with him they crucified two bandits, one on his right and one on his left.

Mark's account of the crucifixion is written not so much as a continual story but as a series of graphic scenes told almost wholly in the present tense. Nearly every sentence begins with 'And' (*kai*). The original text has the feel of an eyewitness's breathless account as details are crammed together to tell the story. The reader can catch a sense of Mark's immediacy from the way Matera sets out the original text:[27]

And they lead him out ...
And they compel a passer-by ...
And they bring him to a place called Golgotha ...
And they offered him wine ...
And they crucify him ...
And they divide his garments ...
And they crucified him ...
And the inscription of the charge against him read ...
And with him they crucify two robbers ...

Jesus is led out of the praetorium to the place of execution, outside the city walls. It was the normal Roman custom for the condemned criminal to carry the crossbeam (*patibulum*) across the

27. F. Matera, *Passion Narratives and Gospel Theologies* (New York: Paulist Press, 1986) p. 41.

back of his neck and shoulders like a yoke, with his hands fastened to the wood by ropes. The upright part of the cross was a permanent fixture at the site of execution. On arrival at the site, the victim was stripped, bound or nailed to the crossbeam, raised up, and seated on a small wooden peg on the vertical stake. His feet were then bound or nailed to the stake. Presumably Jesus has been so weakened by the flogging he has endured that the soldiers feel it necessary to compel a passer-by to carry the crossbeam. This is hardly compassion on their part, more likely their determination that Jesus should die from the decreed sentence of crucifixion.

We know nothing about Simon of Cyrene apart from the fact that he was pressed into service by the Romans as he was coming into the city from the countryside. John 19:17 says that Jesus carried the cross by himself, an affirmation that might be framed to counter the Gnostic charge that it was not Jesus who died on the cross but Simon.[28] Cyrene was the capital city of the Roman province of Cyrenaica (Libya) in North Africa, and Jews formed an important part of its population. Although we cannot be certain that Simon was a Jew, Acts 6:9 tells us of a synagogue in Jerusalem that was attended by Cyrenians and Alexandrians. Luke also tells us in Acts 11:20 that Hellenist converts from Cyrene and Cyprus were among the first to preach the Christian message to the Greeks in Antioch. The fact that Simon's name is preserved in the tradition might indicate that he became a Christian. That Mark introduces Simon not with reference to his father, which we might expect, but to his two sons, Alexander and Rufus, suggests that they were known to Mark's community.

It is worth noting that an ossuary was discovered in the Kidron valley in 1941, on which were found Greek and Hebrew inscriptions identifying the box as having been prepared for 'Alexander, son of Simon'. Additional evidence in the tomb suggests that its owners were a family from the Greek-speaking Jewish community of Cyrenaica.[29]

Mark preserves the Semitic name of the site of crucifixion, Golgotha, further explaining its meaning as the place of the skull. The traditional site is now found inside the present walls of the city,

28. See Ireneus, *Against Heresies* 1.24.4.

29. See N. Avigad, 'A Depository of Inscribed Ossuaries in the Kidron Valley,' *Israel Exploration Journal* 12 (1962) pp. 1-12.

in the crusader Church of the Holy Sepulchre, which was built over Constantine's fourth century Basilica of the Martyrion. It is unknown how Golgotha, which was outside the city walls at the time of Jesus, earned its name: some suggest that the shape of the mound looked like a human skull; others argue that it was so named from the legend that Adam's skull was buried there. Whatever the reason for the name, the place would have served as a brutal deterrent to passers-by: a public execution site near the city walls and beside a principal road, where everyone could see for themselves what fate befell those who opposed Rome's interests.

Mark says that before Jesus is crucified, they (presumably the soldiers) offer Jesus wine mixed with myrrh, a narcotic cocktail that was meant to dull the senses. In Proverbs 31:6-7 the advice is offered: 'Give strong drink to one who is perishing, and wine to those in bitter distress; let them drink and forget their poverty, and remember their misery no more.' Jesus' refusal to take the drink from his executioners is a signal that he will endure what is ahead with conscious conviction. That decision was made in Gethsemane, when Jesus decided to do the Father's will and drink the cup of suffering, not a cup of anaesthetic.

Like the other evangelists, Mark notes the actual crucifixion with remarkable restraint. No physical details are offered, no striving to capture the aching pain of it all, no appeal to the reader's sympathy. Perhaps the details surrounding this barbarous practice were too well known by those living under Roman authority to warrant any elaboration.[39] In Mark's account our attention is diverted from a naked crucified Jesus to what the soldiers are doing with his clothes. They use Jesus' clothes, now theirs by custom, as an opportunity for a game of dice. No doubt Mark has in mind Psalm 22:18: 'They divide my clothes among themselves, and for my clothing they cast lots.'

Mark punctuates the story of Jesus' death with three precise notes on time: Jesus is crucified at the third hour (9 a.m.); at the sixth hour (noon) darkness covers the earth (15:33); at the ninth hour (3 p.m.) Jesus cries out to God (15:34). This convenient division of time, which cannot be reconciled with John 19:14, was

30. See M. Hengel, *Crucifixion* (London: SCM, 1977); J. Fitzmyer, 'Crucifixion in Ancient Palestine, Qumran Literature, and the New Testament,' *Catholic Biblical Quarterly* 40 (1978) pp. 493-514.

probably made either to coincide with fixed hours of prayer in the Roman church or to facilitate easy remembrance of the progress of events.

When someone was sentenced to crucifixion, a tablet detailing the charge was made, probably as a warning to others. The tablet was sometimes hung around the neck of the convicted man, or paraded before him on the way to execution, then affixed to the cross. The four Gospels agree that the written charge against Jesus was 'King of the Jews' – although the wording is slightly different in each account. This appears to be the only thing written about Jesus in his lifetime, and it serves the evangelists' purpose in showing that it was as Messiah that Jesus was executed. This will be further emphasised in the mockery scene.

All four Gospels mention that there were two criminals crucified alongside Jesus; only Luke portrays one of the wrongdoers in a favourable light. In Mark's account of the arrest in Gethsemane, Jesus protested that he was being arrested as if he were a bandit (*lestes*); now he is shown to die between two bandits (*lestai*). In the language of Isaiah 53:12 Jesus 'was numbered with the transgressors' – a quotation that appears in some manuscripts of Mark.

The final mockery   15:29-32

29Those who passed by derided him, shaking their heads and saying, 'Aha! You who would destroy the temple and build it in three days, 30save yourself, and come down from the cross!' 31In the same way the chief priests, along with the scribes, were also mocking him among themselves and saying, 'He saved others; he cannot save himself. 32Let the Messiah, the King of Israel, come down from the cross now, so that we may see and believe.' Those who were crucified with him also taunted him.

Crucifixion was intended to be a public spectacle, humiliating the victim and warning others of the cruelty and finality of the Roman punishment. The focus now shifts from physical abuse to verbal abuse as three groups mock the crucified Jesus: the passers-by, the chief priests, and the two bandits. The mockery of Jesus, told through appropriate biblical imagery and language, serves to review the basic charges made against Jesus at the trial before the Sanhedrin.

Those who pass by shake their heads in derision, recalling the reaction of the wicked to the just one: 'All who see me mock at me; they make mouths at me, they shake their heads.' (Ps 22:7) The blasphemy of the passers-by summarises the charge against Jesus in the Jewish trial, that he is sanctuary-destroyer; they continue by taunting Jesus to save himself by coming down from the cross. Their call for Jesus to dissociate himself from the cross has been made earlier by Peter, after the first passion prediction (8:32). Jesus responded then by rebuking Peter and teaching the disciples and the crowd: 'For those who want to save their life will lose it, and those who lose their life for my sake, and for the sake of the gospel, will save it.' (8:35) Jesus' answer to the passers-by has already been eloquently made.

The second mockery, this time by the Sanhedrin authorities, recalls the Jewish charge that Jesus is the Messiah, the King of Israel. The chief priests and the scribes mock Jesus among themselves: they recall, correctly, that he saved others and then go on to deride him for failing to do the same for himself. Still talking among themselves, they challenge the Messiah to descend from the cross so that they may see and believe. The challenge of the chief priests voices a contrary wisdom to that of Jesus, who taught his disciples and the crowd not to avoid the cross, but to take it up and follow him (8:34). What the Jewish authorities cannot believe as they look on the crucified Jesus, a Gentile centurion will believe when he looks on the dead Jesus (15:39).

In the third mockery Mark returns to the two bandits crucified alongside Jesus. Jesus' fellow victims, who have no personal cause against him, join the passers-by and the Sanhedrin in reviling him. That even those who share Jesus' fate are eager to dissociate themselves from him and show their contempt highlights the complete isolation of Jesus. As the undeserving object of all this abuse, Jesus says nothing.

Not a whisper in support of Jesus is heard on Mark's Golgotha: it is as if Jesus' suffering makes him everyone's easy victim, leaving him completely abandoned during the last hours of his life. Mark, followed closely by Matthew, paints a picture of unrelieved wretchedness. Unlike Luke's account, there is no wrongdoer arguing Jesus' innocence, no talk of paradise, no crowd on the verge of beating their breasts, no mention of 'all his friends' standing at a distance. Unlike John's account, there is neither beloved disciple nor mother standing near the cross, there is no dying Jesus bringing them together in a new relationship. It is as if Mark illustrates on Golgotha the outcome of his own theological belief: that Jesus is seen most himself in suffering, rejection, and death.

The death of Jesus   15:33-39

[33] When it was noon, darkness came over the whole land until three in the afternoon. [34] At three o'clock Jesus cried out with a loud voice, 'Eloi, Eloi, lema sabachthani?' which means, 'My God, my God, why have you forsaken me?' [35] When some of the bystanders heard it, they said, 'Listen, he is calling for Elijah.' [36] And someone ran, filled a sponge with sour wine, put it on a stick, and gave it to him to drink, saying, 'Wait, let us see whether Elijah will come to take him down.' [37] Then Jesus gave a loud cry and breathed his last. [38] And the curtain of the temple was torn in two, from top to bottom. [39] Now when the centurion, who stood facing him, saw that in this way he breathed his last, he said, 'Truly this man was God's Son!'

[40] There were also some women looking on from a distance; among them were Mary Magdalene, and Mary the mother of James the younger and of Joses, and Salome. [41] These used to follow him and provided for him when he was in Galilee; and there were many other women who had come up with him to Jerusalem.

The death of Jesus is the climax towards which the whole of Mark's Gospel has been striving. For all its tragic atmosphere and mood of dereliction, the brief scene focuses intensely on the truth that the moment of Jesus' death marks the supreme moment of Jesus' revelation, the first time a human being identifies who Jesus is. A central point in Mark's christology is confirmed: only after his death can Jesus be recognised for truly who he is. Achtemeier observes:

> That is why the disciples were unable to recognise or acknowledge who Jesus was, simply because he could not be truly acknowledged as the king he is until he was enthroned – on the cross; he could not be confessed as king until he had been crowned – with death.[31]

31. P. Achtemeier, 'Gospel of Mark,' *The Anchor Bible Dictionary* Vol. 4 p. 553.

The supreme irony of Mark's Gospel is that when Jesus appears as only a king pretender, a dead impostor in the eyes of his persecutors, he is most truly the Messiah he was destined to be.

Mark opens the death scene with the dramatic image of darkness at noon. During the first three hours of Jesus' crucifixion, the persecutors have filled the time with uncontested mockery; no voice supporting Jesus has been heard. Now, it is as if nature itself intervenes to compensate for the absence of human sympathy; when no human voice grieves what is happening to Jesus, the realm of nature puts mourning on. The darkness covers the whole earth until 3 p.m. The words of Amos 8:9-10 speak of God making his protest felt through nature:

On that day, says the Lord God,
I will make the sun go down at noon,
and darken the earth in broad daylight ...
I will make it like the mourning for an only son,
and the end of it like a bitter day.

The image of darkness over the whole earth, not just darkness over Golgotha, serves to dramatise the belief that Jesus' death has cosmic significance. After three hours of darkness, we hear the voice of the crucified Jesus say something for the first and only time: 'My God, my God, why have you forsaken me?' (see Psalm 22:1) It is a cry coming from the depths of one whose suffering and desolation have led him to the extremities of loneliness, where he feels forsaken by God. Recalling the litany of punishment and rejection that *has happened to Jesus* in the passion story, the scream of dereliction comes as no surprise:

He is betrayed by one of the twelve;
    he is ignored by sleeping disciples.
He is arrested;
    he is abandoned by all his disciples.
He is led away to the high priest;
    he is interrogated.
He is accused falsely;
    he is condemned as deserving death.
He is spat on and struck;
    he is denied by Peter.

He is led away and handed over to Pilate;
  he is tried.
He is rejected in favour of Barabbas;
  he is flogged.
He is handed over to be crucified;
  he is mocked as king.
He is led away by the soldiers;
  he is helped by a stranger.
He is crucified;
  he is derided by passers-by.
He is mocked by the chief priests;
  he is taunted by the co-crucified.

According to Mark, the prayer that Jesus made in Gethsemane was addressed to *Abba* (Father). Mark retained the address in Aramaic, the native language of Jesus. The prayer on the cross is addressed more formally to 'My God' (*Eloi*). This time Mark retains the complete prayer in Aramaic – the only instance where Jesus addresses God as 'God'. Raymond Brown comments:

> Jesus is not questioning the existence of God or the power of God to do something about what is happening; he is questioning the silence of the one whom he calls 'My God' ... Feeling forsaken as if he were not being heard, he no longer presumes to speak intimately to the All-Powerful as 'Father' but employs the address common to all human beings, 'My God.' (The fact that Jesus is using psalm language – a fact to which Mark does not call our attention – does not make less noticeable the unusualness of such terminology on Jesus' lips.)[32]

It seems strange that those who hear Jesus' cry – and who speak the same mother tongue – hear it as an appeal for Elijah to come and rescue Jesus, since the cry is addressed to God and its content is accusation. The misunderstanding is sharpened all the more since we the readers have been told that Elijah's role in the Gospel is not as a deliverer from death but as a prophetic sign of Jesus' death: Elijah has already come and has suffered the same fate as Jesus (9:12-13). The drink of sour wine is offered to Jesus, apparently as

---

32. R. Brown, *The Death of the Messiah* Vol. 2 (London: Chapman, 1994) p. 1046.

a cruel joke (see Psalm 69:21), to keep him alive so that the onlookers can check the arrival/non-arrival of Elijah. But Jesus does not stay alive. After a loud, wordless cry, he breathes his last.

Rather than dwelling on the death of Jesus, Mark moves on to interpret the significance of Jesus' death for the Jewish world and for the Gentile world. All four Gospels speak of the tearing of the sanctuary veil. Before the assembled Sanhedrin, Jesus was accused of saying, 'I will destroy this sanctuary (*naos*) that is made with hands, and in three days I will build another, not made with hands.' (14:58) While hanging on the cross, Jesus was mocked as the one who would destroy the sanctuary (15:29). Now, immediately Jesus dies, he is vindicated by God who passes his own judgement. As the high priest tore his clothes and made his judgement when Jesus confessed to being the Son of the Blessed One, so God tears the sanctuary veil at the death of his Son. The veil, which protected the sacred character of the Holy of Holies from all that was profane, is now destroyed as it is rent 'in two, from top to bottom.' The earthly sanctuary, the one made by human hands, can no longer fulfil its function, for God is no longer present there.

A Gentile centurion, presumably in charge of the execution squad, is now introduced by Mark as someone who has been standing facing Jesus. He has witnessed everything that has happened, and he voices his reaction to the death of Jesus in the confession, 'Truly this man was God's Son.' What Mark announced in the first verse of the Gospel, what God said at the baptism of Jesus, what the Sanhedrin denied during the trial – the true identity of Jesus as God's Son – is now recognised for the first time by a human being.

Now that Jesus' *destiny* is fulfilled in his death, his *identity* is revealed: it is precisely the death of Jesus that leads this pagan soldier to recognise the truth of who Jesus is. The Gentile sees and believes what the hostile Jewish witnesses to Jesus' death did not see. It is particularly appropriate for Mark, writing in Rome, that the death of Jesus opens the door of faith to a Roman centurion and hence to the Gentile world.

By way of concluding this section and preparing for the two scenes at the tomb, Mark mentions for the first time the presence of the women on Golgotha. Up to the present they have been invisible in the Gospel narrative; now we are told they look on from a distance. Unlike the centurion who stood beside Jesus, the women do not become confessors: their role, a dramatic improvement on the disciples who abandoned Jesus, is to be there.

The women mentioned by name appear to be three in number. First there is Mary, who is from the town of Magdala on the northwest shore of the Sea of Galilee. Magdalene is described elsewhere as the woman from whom seven devils have been cast out (16:9; Lk 8:2). Second there is another Mary, identified through her sons as the mother of the younger James and Joses (not the brothers of Jesus).

It is impossible to identify the two brothers, but it is a fair presumption that their names have been retained, like those of Alexander and Rufus, because they were known to the community. The third woman, whom Mark names as Salome, is identified in Matthew 27:56 as the mother of the sons of Zebedee.

Mark further describes the three women in relation to Jesus as those who used 'to follow him' – the same phrase used to describe the response of Simon and Andrew, and also Levi, to the call of Jesus (1:18; 2:14). They also provided for Jesus when he was in Galilee, a service that was probably not limited to providing him with food and material support. Beyond the three, Mark mentions a wider group of many other women who were Jesus' travelling companions on the journey up to Jerusalem. Presumably all these women are Galileans.

Munro argues that as Peter, James and John formed an inner circle within the twelve, so these three named women form a corresponding inner circle within the larger group of women.[33] Whatever the precise relationship was between these three women and Jesus/the twelve during the ministry, their role will prove essential in a witnessing community: they are the only disciples who can 'cover' the complete narrative of Jesus' story. Only the inner circle of women can testify from their own experience to the unity of the Gospel as it is told by Mark: Jesus' ministry, his death, his burial in the tomb, and the first and only disclosure of his resurrection.

33. W. Munro, 'Women Disciples in Mark?' *Catholic Biblical Quarterly* 44 (1982) pp. 225-241.

The burial of Jesus

15:42-47

[42] When evening had come, and since it was the day of Preparation, that is, the day before the sabbath, [43]Joseph of Arimathea, a respected member of the council, who was also himself waiting expectantly for the kingdom of God, went boldly to Pilate and asked for the body of Jesus. [44]Then Pilate wondered if he were already dead; and summoning the centurion, he asked him whether he had been dead for some time. [45]When he learned from the centurion that he was dead, he granted the body to Joseph. [46]Then Joseph bought a linen cloth, and taking down the body, wrapped it in the linen cloth, and laid it in a tomb that had been hewn out of the rock. He then rolled a stone against the door of the tomb. [47]Mary Magdalene and Mary the mother of Joses saw where the body was laid.

The flow of events moves naturally from death on the cross to burial in the tomb, and Mark notes the transition by referring again to time. It is now late afternoon or early evening on Friday, which, as Mark explains to his non-Jewish readers, is the end of preparation day for the sabbath. This is the first time we learn that Jesus died on a Friday. According to Jewish Law, even the bodies of convicted criminals should be buried before sundown: 'When someone is convicted of a crime punishable by death and is executed, and you hang him on a tree, his corpse must not remain all night on the tree; you shall bury him that same day, for anyone hung on a tree is under God's curse.' (Deut 21:22-23)

Whereas the disciples of John the Baptist had stayed loyal to their master and buried his body in a tomb (6:29), Jesus' disciples have abandoned their master and are not present to honour his body with a proper burial. One of the embarrassing memories included in all four Gospels is that Jesus' body was buried by Joseph of Arimathea, a mysterious figure who appears for the first time in all four narratives after the death of Jesus. Joseph takes courage to do what all the disciples fail to do, publicly associate himself with the *crucified* Jesus.

If, according to Mark, all the members of the Sanhedrin found Jesus guilty and worthy of death (14:64) and handed him over to Pilate (15:1), why does Joseph, a respected member of that council, approach Pilate for permission to bury the body of Jesus? Since Mark tells us how the centurion responded to Jesus after his death, is he telling us that as a centurion could oversee the execution of

Jesus but then move to confess him as Son of God, so Joseph who cast his vote in favour of Jesus' execution could be moved by the crucified Jesus? Unlike Matthew and John, Mark does not say that Joseph is a disciple of Jesus, only that he is awaiting the kingdom of God – hence a pious Jew who lives in expectation of the fulfilment of Israel's messianic hopes. Perhaps Joseph simply wants to ensure the fulfilment of the Law by burying the body of Jesus, an interpretation supported by Acts 13:27-29, which states that the residents of Jerusalem and their leaders buried the body of Jesus.

Joseph of Arimathea goes boldly to Pilate for permission to arrange the burial. According to Mark, Jesus died after hanging on the cross for six hours. Crucifixion was intended as a lingering form of torture – some victims took days to die – and often the Romans would leave the bodies on the cross as a gruesome warning to others. What their practice was in provincial Judea we do not know; but they might have honoured Jewish religious sensibilities, particularly at the time of Passover. As Pilate was amazed at Jesus' silence during the trial, he is amazed that Jesus has already died. After checking the story of Jesus' death with the centurion, who confirms it, Pilate grants the corpse (*ptoma*) to Joseph, the word reflecting Mark's insistence on the reality of Jesus' death. Thus the Roman governor, the Roman centurion in charge of the execution squad, and a senior Jewish official concur that Jesus is truly dead.

After purchasing a linen cloth, Joseph, presumably aided by his servants, takes Jesus' body down from the cross, wraps it in the linen cloth, and lays it in a tomb. There is no mention of washing the body or anointing it; the burial is done, probably in haste, before sundown. The dead were buried outside the city walls, in natural caves or in large recesses cut out of the rock. Most of the cave-tombs surrounding Jerusalem were family vaults: bodies were laid on ledges inside the tomb until they had decomposed, when the bones would be gathered and placed in an urn. This would free the ledge for the laying out of the next body. Joseph seals the tomb by rolling a stone against the door. Although the two women take no part in the burial of Jesus, Mark notes their presence as observers at the scene. This is not so much to recall their perseverance to the end, which is true, but to prepare for their return to the same place on Sunday morning. The tomb where Jesus is laid to rest will be the site of the only Easter proclamation in Mark's Gospel.

The resurrection of Jesus   16:1-8

When the sabbath was over, Mary Magdalene, and Mary the mother of James, and Salome bought spices, so that they might go and anoint him. ²And very early on the first day of the week, when the sun had risen, they went to the tomb. ³They had been saying to one another, 'Who will roll away the stone for us from the entrance to the tomb?' ⁴When they looked up, they saw that the stone, which was very large, had already been rolled back. ⁵As they entered the tomb, they saw a young man, dressed in a white robe, sitting on the right side; and they were alarmed. ⁶But he said to them, 'Do not be alarmed; you are looking for Jesus of Nazareth, who was crucified. He has been raised; he is not here. Look, there is the place they laid him. ⁷But go, tell his disciples and Peter that he is going ahead of you to Galilee; there you will see him, just as he told you.' ⁸So they went out and fled from the tomb, for terror and amazement had seized them; and they said nothing to anyone, for they were afraid.

The Gospels proclaim the resurrection in different ways, but none of them attempts to describe its occurrence in narrative form. The accounts move from Jesus' burial in the tomb to a story of women finding the grave empty on Easter Sunday morning. There are no eye-witnesses to the resurrection, only witnesses to its truth. The fact that Jesus died and was raised from the dead stood firmly at the core of early Christian preaching (1 Cor 15:4-5; Rom 1:3-4). The manner and circumstances of the resurrection and the appearances were not described in the early preaching – the discovery of the empty tomb is never mentioned outside the Gospels – and so it comes as no surprise that the evangelists go their different ways in supplying a narrative form to the truth of the resurrection. This truth was unprecedented in the history of Israel: no one had ever been raised from the dead to eternal life and glory. For the early church, the truth that God raised the crucified Jesus from the dead became the ground for its proclamation.

Mark brought the events of the burial to a close on the eve of the sabbath (15:42) and he resumes his story after the interval of a day. The evangelist begins his story of the empty tomb by giving us three time indicators: 'when the Sabbath was over' (that is, after 6 p.m. on Saturday) the women buy spices; they go to the tomb 'very early on the first day of the week' (which suggests a time between 3 a.m. and 6 a.m.), but this is further specified by the phrase, 'when the sun had risen' (about 6 a.m.). The inner circle of three named women who followed Jesus in Galilee, who witnessed his death on Golgotha, two of whom are named as witnessing the burial of Jesus, are the link between Jesus' ministry, death, burial, and resurrection. In all four Gospels, the name of Mary Magdalene is the only one that appears in all the lists.

From Mark's text it is clear that the purpose of the women's visit to the tomb is to anoint the body of Jesus – though as readers we know that Jesus' body has already been anointed for burial by an unnamed woman (14:8). The women's purpose seems strange, as Taylor observes:

> It is hard to credit the women with the intention of going to anoint the body a day and two nights after death. Where the evidence is conflicting, no one will wish to speak with too much confidence. But, on the whole, it seems more probable that the women went to see the grave (Mt, Jn) rather than to anoint the body (Mk, Lk).[34]

On their way to the tomb they have a curious discussion about who will roll away the stone for them, as if helpful people usually hung around tombs in the early morning for that specific purpose. That curiosity aside, Mark is probably using the discussion for dramatic purposes: the women expect a sealed tomb enclosing a dead body. Their problem, however, is solved for them when they see that the very large stone has already been rolled back. Mark does not explain how this happened, nor does he record any reaction by the women to this unexpected event.

On entering the tomb, the women see a young man (*neaniskos*) sitting on the right side. Their reaction of amazement indicates that this is no ordinary young man who has strayed into the tomb, but an angel. His function as an interpreting angel (*angelus interpres*) is the same as the function of all such angels in the biblical texts: to announce what God has done and to make sense of what human witnesses cannot understand. The angel will interpret, for the women and the reader, the significance of the empty tomb.

34. V. Taylor, *The Gospel according to St. Mark* p. 604.

Angelophanies traditionally open with the counsel: 'Do not be afraid ... ' and this one is no different. The angel first tells the women something they already know, that they are looking for the Jesus of Nazareth who was crucified. This statement is a reminder that the Jesus who came from Nazareth and was crucified is the same Jesus who is the subject of the resurrection proclamation. The angel then announces to the women something that they do not know: 'He has been raised; he is not here.'

The order is worth noting: the resurrection is asserted first before the absence of the body is mentioned. The resurrection is not offered as a way of explaining the empty tomb; the empty tomb follows on what God has done in raising Jesus from the dead. The angel then directs the women's attention to the empty place where the body of Jesus was laid. That vacancy is now interpreted in the light of the Easter annunciation.

The angel does not command the women, 'Go and tell the disciples to come and see the empty tomb.' The community of disciples will not be re-founded around a vacant grave, but around the person of the risen Jesus. The women are bidden to leave the tomb with the message of resurrection, one that points them elsewhere: 'But go, tell his disciples and Peter that he is going ahead of you to Galilee; there you will see him, just as he told you.' The injunction takes up the earlier promise of Jesus, made on the way to Gethsemane (14:28), adding the new promise that the disciples will see the risen Jesus.

The women are overcome by terror and amazement, and they flee from the tomb. Mark ends his Gospel abruptly with the notice 'and they said nothing to anyone, for they were afraid.' The women's failure and flight compound the earlier failure of the disciples who fled at the beginning of the passion. Silence and fear seem a strange way to end the Gospel and we are left with a profound sense of incompleteness. By the second century, the so-called longer ending was added on to 16:8, to provide a suitable conclusion to Mark's story. No original lost ending has been discovered, and the challenge is to accept Mark's own ending, in spite of its manifest difficulties.[35]

---

35. See N. Petersen, 'When is the End Not the End? Literary Reflections on the Ending of Mark's Narrative,' *Interpretation* 34 (1980) pp. 151-166.

Its very incompleteness may be what recommends it. Its unfinished character appears as something that would win it favour
among much of modern literature, a perfect example of the theatre
of the absurd, worthy of Samuel Beckett's *Waiting for Godot*. That
aside, Mark has given the reader sufficient material in his text,
particularly in the promises of Jesus, to look beyond the women's
silence and fear. Kingsbury argues, 'As the reader projects the
fulfilment of Jesus' promise, the reader in effect projects the
resolution of Jesus' conflict with his disciples.'[36]

The disciples' reconciliation with the risen Jesus did take place;
otherwise there would be little point in Mark writing a story that
began, 'The beginning of the good news of Jesus Christ, the Son of
God.' (1:1) Even though the oldest manuscripts of the Gospel
contain no accounts of appearances by the risen Jesus, there can be
no doubt that Mark knew Jesus rose from the dead and appeared to
his disciples. The promises of Jesus, which Mark shows us are
reliable and sure, included the promise that he would go before his
followers to Galilee (14:28; 16:7). Each of the passion predictions
included a reference to the resurrection (8:31; 9:31; 10:34), and
after the transfiguration Jesus ordered the disciples 'to tell no one
about what they had seen, until after the Son of Man had risen from
the dead.' (9:9) In Chapter 13 Jesus delivered his apocalyptic
discourse to four disciples, focusing on events that would happen
between the resurrection and the parousia. All these passages,
based on the prophetic word of Jesus, clearly look forward to a
fulfilment and resolution beyond 16:8.

Mark's omission of appearance stories is in line with his strategy
for the whole Gospel. Achtemeier comments:

> It appears that one of Mark's theological goals with his gospel,
> therefore, was to move his readers from observers to partici-
> pants, and thus to move them to share in the gospel whose
> beginnings he had narrated in his account of Jesus of Nazareth.[37]

As Mark's readers we must provide the continuation of the
Gospel story; we are challenged to follow Jesus through pain and
bewilderment and disappointment to an outcome that only we

---

36. D. Kingsbury, *Conflict in Mark* (Minneapolis: Fortress, 1989) p. 113.

37. P. Achtemeier, 'Gospel of Mark,' *The Anchor Bible Dictionary* Vol. 4 p. 556.

ourselves can supply. Mark has kept his pledge to provide us, his readers, with what he called 'the beginning of the good news of Jesus' (1:1). The rest of the story is written by the participants.

8

Appendix: the endings of Mark's Gospel

While we cannot say for certain that Mark intended his Gospel to conclude with 16:8, there is a general consensus that the supplementary endings were not written by Mark.[1] Clearly the sense of incompleteness felt at the abrupt ending of Mark's Gospel moved others to provide a conclusion that would agree with the descendants of the Gospel – stories of appearances and a commission to preach in the name of Jesus.

The judgement that Mark is not the author of either ending is made on the basis of internal and external evidence. The internal evidence, based on a study of the subject-matter, vocabulary, and style, leads to the conclusion that they were not written by the hand of Mark. The shorter ending, which simply rounds off the Gospel text, is probably the earlier of the two additions, and there is only one surviving manuscript with this ending as the sole conclusion to Mark's Gospel. The shorter ending was either added to or replaced by the independent longer ending (16:9-20). The external evidence shows that the earliest manuscripts conclude the Gospel at 16:8, and we have the testimonies of Eusebius (320 A.D.) and Jerome (380 A.D.) that any supplementary ending is missing in almost all of the Greek manuscripts known to them. It is certainly absent from the extant codices B ('Vaticanus') and S ('Sinaiticus'), both dating around 325 A.D.

The shorter ending

> [And all that had been commanded them they told briefly to those around Peter. And afterward Jesus himself sent out through them, from east to west, the sacred and imperishable proclamation of eternal salvation.]

The unknown author makes no pretence to copy Mark's style or

---

1. See E. Gould, *The Gospel according to St. Mark* pp. 301-308; J. Elliott, 'The Text and Language of the Endings to Mark's Gospel,' *Theologische Zeitschrift* 27 (1981) pp. 255-262.

vocabulary, but simply provides what he believes to be a more edifying and satisfactory conclusion to Mark's sudden ending. The first sentence connects directly with 16:8: we are now to understand that the women's silence is not final, for they communicate the angel's message to those around Peter. The angel's command to the women is overtaken by Jesus' missionary command to the disciples. Although there is no distinctive story of a resurrection appearance, the appearance to the disciples in Galilee (16:7) is implied in the story of commission. The risen Jesus sends out the disciples on mission, to proclaim salvation 'from east to west'. This universal proclamation is regarded by the early church as the real fulfilment of Easter.

The longer ending   16:9-20

9 [Now after he rose early on the first day of the week, he appeared first to Mary Magdalen, from whom he had cast out seven demons. 10She went out and told those who had been with him, while they were mourning and weeping. 11But when they heard that he was alive and had been seen by her, they would not believe it.

12 After this he appeared in another form to two of them, as they were walking into the country. 13And they went back and told the rest, but they did not believe them.

14 Later he appeared to the eleven themselves as they were sitting at the table; and he upbraided them for their lack of faith and stubbornness, because they had not believed those who saw him after he had risen. 15And he said to them, 'Go into all the world and proclaim the good news to the whole creation. 16The one who believes and is baptized will be saved; but the one who does not believe will be condemned. 17And these signs will accompany those who believe: by using my name they will cast out demons; they will speak in new tongues; 18they will pick up snakes in their hands, and if they drink any deadly thing, it will not hurt them; they will lay their hands on the sick, and they will recover.'

19 So then the Lord Jesus, after he had spoken to them, was taken up into heaven and sat down at the right hand of God. 20And they went out and proclaimed the good news everywhere, while the Lord worked with them and confirmed the message by the signs that accompanied it.]

The longer ending established itself very quickly as the more popular conclusion to the Gospel, so that Irenaeus could quote it as part of Mark's Gospel before the end of the second century. This ending may have originated as a catechetical instruction summarising the post-resurrection events, one that was subsequently appended to Mark's Gospel as a suitable conclusion. It is a work of compilation that depends largely on Luke's writing.

Jesus appears to Mary Magdalene   *16:9-11*

Mary Magdalene is identified as if she has not appeared previously in the Gospel story, and this account appears to be derived from Luke 8:2 and John 20:11-18. Jesus appears first to Mary Magdalene, who tells her experience to the companions who are mourning and weeping. She is the first to testify to the truth that Jesus is alive, a truth validated by her own experience, but the disciples' reaction is one of disbelief and hence rejection.

Jesus appears to two disciples   *16:12-13*

This is a condensed variation of the Emmaus story in Luke 24:13-35. It is difficult to know what the author means when he speaks of Jesus' appearance 'in a different form'. Does this mean in the guise of a fellow pilgrim? Does it mean that he appears in a form different from that in which he appeared to Mary Magdalene? The conclusion to the appearance is different from that of the Emmaus story, for the disciples are disbelieved when they tell their story. Perhaps this is to emphasise what Luke also does in the conclusion of his story when he gives the prior testimony to the apostles. As I wrote elsewhere: 'The priority that Luke has given to the apostolic testimony ensures that the account of the two disciples is incorporated into that story, not vice-versa'.[2] In this passage, the disbelief of the eleven focuses on the fact that they will come to believe in the risen Jesus only through their own experience of him.

Jesus appears to the eleven and commissions them   *16:14-18*

The climax in this series of appearances focuses on the words of the risen Jesus. The author gives no setting or time. The risen Jesus appears to the eleven and his first action is to confront them about their stubborn disbelief; he then commissions them to proclaim the good news to all creation, assuring them that their mission will be

2. D. McBride, *Emmaus: the Gracious Visit of God according to Luke* (Dublin: Dominican Publications, 1991) p. 159.

confirmed by wonderful signs. This passage seems to rely on a combination of sources: Mt 28:16-20; Lk 24:44-49; Jn 20:19-23; Acts 1:6-8.

The commission, which follows abruptly on the reproach, situates the authority for the Gentile mission in the words of the risen Jesus. This seems strange in the light of Acts 11:1-18, where Peter defends his action of admitting Gentiles into the church not by appealing to the command of the risen Jesus, but by appealing to a new vision he had in Joppa. If the risen Jesus had commanded the eleven to preach to the Gentiles, why the controversy at the council of Jerusalem as reported in Acts 15? Furthermore, when Paul reflects on the outcome of the council, he states that the differences between Antioch and Jerusalem were resolved in terms of separation: James, Cephas and John are to go the circumcised, while Paul and Barnabas are to minister to the Gentiles (Gal 2:9). By the time the Gospels are written, however, the church's gradual commitment to the Gentile mission is given its original authorisation in the command of the risen Jesus.

In verse 16 the baptised believer is held up as the one who will be saved, while there is a dogmatic condemnation of those who do not believe. The emphasis on the believing community is stressed further in the next two verses: the charismatic gifts are given to all believers, not only to the commissioned preachers.

The ascension of Jesus   *16:19-20*

Still without any note about time or place, the longer ending concludes with a summary passage about Jesus' being taken up (Lk 24:50-53; Acts 1:2,11,22), his enthronement at the right hand of God, and the disciples' universal proclamation of the Gospel. The departure of the disciples is presumably from Jerusalem, which stands in contrast to the Galilean focus of Mark's own narrative in 16:1-8. The disciples do not work alone; the Lord co-operates with them by actively confirming their message through miraculous signs.

The Freer or Washington Logion

And they excused themselves saying, 'This age of lawlessness and unbelief is under Satan, who does not allow the truth and power of God to prevail over the unclean things of the spirits. Therefore reveal your righteousness now' – thus they spoke to Christ. And Christ replied to them, 'The term of years of Satan's power has been fulfilled, but other terrible things draw near. And for those who have sinned I was handed over to death, that they may return to the truth and sin no more, that they may inherit the spiritual and imperishable glory of righteousness which is in heaven.

Although not an ending, this passage is to be found incorporated in one extant Greek manuscript of the fifth century. The manuscript was discovered in Egypt in 1906 and is now preserved in the Freer Gallery in Washington. Parts of the passage are quoted by Jerome from a number of manuscripts known to him.

The passage is inserted between 16:14 and 16:15 as the disciples' response to Jesus' reprimand. It serves to soften the impact of Jesus' harsh rebuke, excusing the disciples' unbelief on the grounds that they live in an unbelieving age. The disciples argue that the present time is under the control of Satan, who is dedicated to the suppression of God's truth and power. In the light of this, they ask for an immediate parousia. While Christ's reply offers them the consoling truth that Satan has reached the limits of his power, it admits that outstanding difficulties still have to be faced. The speech concludes with the words of Christ exhorting his troubled disciples with the reminder that he has died for sinners so that they may stop sinning and return to the truth. This return will bring believers into their true inheritance, sharing in the glory of heaven.